Communicating in Intercultural Spaces

Communicating in Intercultural Spaces is a unique contribution to literature in intercultural communication from two authors who bring distinct socio-cultural voices to this work. Written for readers ranging from advanced undergraduate students to intercultural practitioners, this book offers a new conceptualisation for understanding intercultural communication. Eight propositions frame the concept of intercultural spaces.

Grounding the discussion on the framing of intercultural spaces, the authors engage with a range of topics such as perception, language, acculturation, and intercultural competence, couched in original personal narratives from 21 leading intercultural scholars. The narratives and vignettes add vibrant context to the scholars' works that are cited in this book. The book also delves into the origins of intercultural communication as a discipline and the dark side of communicating across differences. Each chapter ends with a brief dialogue between the authors, followed by questions for stimulating further reflection.

Readers should expect to walk away with an understanding of key theories and frameworks in intercultural communication and the tools with which to develop their own intercultural communication competence.

Lily A. Arasaratnam-Smith, PhD, is Deputy Vice President Faculty and Professor of Communication at Alphacrucis University College, Australia. Her expertise is in intercultural communication competence. Lily is a Fellow and President-Elect of the International Academy for Intercultural Research.

L. Ripley Smith, PhD, is Professor of Intercultural and Media Communication at Bethel University, St. Paul, MN, USA. His expertise includes intercultural adaptation, cultural identity, and the impact of social networks on intercultural relations. Ripley is a Fellow and three-term Board Secretary of the International Academy for Intercultural Research.

Communicating in Intercultural Spaces

**Lily A. Arasaratnam-Smith
and L. Ripley Smith**

Routledge
Taylor & Francis Group

LONDON AND NEW YORK

Designed cover image: © Getty Images

First published 2025
by Routledge
4 Park Square, Milton Park, Abingdon, Oxon OX14 4RN

and by Routledge
605 Third Avenue, New York, NY 10158

Routledge is an imprint of the Taylor & Francis Group, an informa business

British Library Cataloguing-in-Publication Data
A catalogue record for this book is available from the British Library

ISBN: 9781032331508 (hbk)
ISBN: 9781032331492 (pbk)
ISBN: 9781003318415 (ebk)

DOI: 10.4324/9781003318415

Typeset in Times New Roman
by Newgen Publishing UK

To the Prince of Peace, whose unconditional love for humanity inspires us to seek peace and relationship amidst intercultural spaces.

And to Clive and Barb, whose extravagant love transforms us to be better humans and scholars amidst every space.

Contents

Figures

Contributors

Narrative Contributors

Milton J. Bennett, PhD, is the Executive Director of the Intercultural Development Research Institute, Italy.

John W. Berry, PhD, is Professor Emeritus of Psychology at Queen's University, Canada.

Dharm Bhawuk, PhD, is a Professor of Psychology at University of Hawaii at Manoa, USA.

Jane Jackson, PhD, is Professor Emerita of Applied Linguistics at the Chinese University of Hong Kong.

Adam Komisarof, PhD, is Professor at Faculty of Letters, Keito University, Japan.

Jonas R. Kunst, PhD, is Professor of Psychology at University of Oslo, Norway.

Wendy Leeds-Hurwitz, PhD, is Director of the Center for Intercultural Dialogue and Professor Emerita of Communication at University of Wisconsin-Parkside, USA.

Young Yun Kim, PhD, is Professor Emerita of Communication at the University of Oklahoma, USA.

Chan-Hoong Leong, PhD, is Head of Policy Development, Evaluation, and Data Analytics at Kantar Public, Singapore.

Judith Martin, PhD, is Professor Emerita of Communication at Arizona State University, USA.

James W. Neuliep, PhD, is Professor Emeritus of Communication at Norbert College, USA.

John G. Oetzel, PhD, is Professor of Communication at University of Waikato, New Zealand.

Brent D. Ruben, PhD, is Distinguished Professor of Communication at Rutgers University, USA.

David L. Sam, PhD, is Professor of Cross-Cultural Psychology at University of Bergen, Norway.

Brian H. Spitzberg, PhD, is Professor Emeritus at San Diego State University, USA.

Karen I. Van der Zee, PhD, is Dean of Faculty at Vrije Universitiet Amsterdam, The Netherlands.

Jan Pieter Van Oudenhoven, PhD, is a retired Professor of Cross-Cultural Psychology from the University of Groningen, The Netherlands.

Colleen Ward, PhD, is Professor Emerita of Psychology at Victory University of Wellington, New Zealand.

Vignette Contributors

Kenneth Cushner, PhD, is Professor Emeritus of International and Intercultural Teacher Education at Kent State University, USA.

Darla K. Deardorff, PhD, is Executive Director of the Association of International Education Administrators, Duke University, USA.

Nan M. Sussman, PhD, is Professor and Dean Emerita of Humanities and Social Sciences at City University of New York, Staten Island, USA.

Introduction

This book project came together serendipitously through a number of encounters. In this introduction, each author offers their reflections on the inception of and objectives for this project as well as their personal relationships with the various contributors to narratives and vignettes shared in the chapters.

Lily

Decades ago, when I was an international student in the United States, I saw an advertisement for a teaching assistant role, and I strode into the office of the faculty member responsible for hiring. I had not met her or spoken to her before, but I knew who she was. As I hovered on the threshold, she glanced up from the papers on her desk. "Sorry honey," she said, "the position is only for English-speakers." She turned her attention back to her papers. I whirled around and walked away, not having uttered a single word in this exchange.

I have since reflected on this experience, wondering about the assumptions that undergirded that communication instance where my participation was entirely non-verbal. My intent in approaching the faculty person was to express my interest in the advertised position. However, when her words had implied that she assumed I did not speak English – or at least did not speak it with sufficient fluency, I did nothing to correct her assumption. I did not even introduce myself. I had simply walked away, feeling indignant and defeated in equal measure. I have since wondered whether the outcome would have been different had I spoken. I would have demonstrated that I did indeed speak English. However, would my "accented" English have been considered sufficient? Would my physical appearance, which led the faculty person to assume my lack of language skills in the first place, still have been a hindrance to me being considered suitable for the position? I would never know because I did not stay and participate in the conversation.

I contrast this experience with another experience several years later, in Australia. I was walking in a familiar neighbourhood when I was stopped by an older White couple. The man asked me, "Are you local?" I gave him a bright smile and confirmed I was. He proceeded to ask me directions for where he and his wife wanted to go, and I happily gave them the information they needed. As I walked

DOI: 10.4324/9781003318415-1

away, I reflected on this extraordinary incident in which I was (correctly) identified as a "local" to that neighbourhood, despite my physical appearance as a person of Sri Lankan heritage.

My own interest in intercultural communication arose from my desire to understand my personal experiences as an international student in the United States. Although I spoke fluent English, I found myself in countless situations where there was a clear gap in meaning between what I said and what the other person understood, based on the responses I received. My very appearance was often an obstacle to effective communication, as I stood out amongst a mostly homogenous group of classmates. At times, I found myself at a loss as to what to say or what to do in a situation, despite knowing the language and having socialised with relative ease in other contexts. When I started formally studying intercultural communication, I began to acquire the tools with which to not only understand my experiences, but also anticipate challenges I might encounter when communicating with persons from different cultural backgrounds. Although the world has become more integrated through new technologies since the time when I was an undergraduate student, cultural differences still influence the meaning-making processes in interpersonal communication.

A widely used framework of levels of competence (discussed further in Chapter 7) identifies the stages of unconscious incompetence, conscious incompetence, conscious competence, and unconscious competence. I have lived most of my life in a state of conscious incompetence, occasionally graduating to conscious competence when I have had sufficient opportunity to learn and understand my context. I lived in different countries from a young age, always being aware of my "foreignness" and often finding myself in situations where I was cognisant of my incompetence as a communicator. However, these extraordinary experiences gave me the opportunity to mindfully observe intercultural dynamics as I never would have, had I lived the majority of my life in my own culture. I say this to provide context for this book in which my research has been indelibly influenced by the way I have learned to see the world, both through my experiences as a "foreigner," as well as through my disciplinary training.

During the inception of this book project, I had the opportunity to converse with my colleague Ripley Smith in Switzerland, where we were both attendees of a conference. It soon became apparent that this project would be vastly enriched as a collaborative work rather than a solo-authored work. As I had already secured a publisher for my project at that point, I asked Ripley whether he would be amenable to combining our projects and, to my delight, he accepted. We have had rich and thought-provoking conversations in the months that have followed, as we've worked together to craft this book. What is now *our* book is exponentially better than what I had initially envisioned. The experience of collaborating with Ripley has been instructive, enriching, and rewarding.

The purpose of this book is threefold: namely, synthesis, contextualisation, and contribution. Firstly, the book is intended to synthesise what is known about intercultural communication drawing widely from research in communication, psychology, sociology, education, medical sciences, and anthropology. The relevance of intercultural communication (and especially intercultural competence) has sparked a plethora of research in different fields, sometimes causing confusion in nomenclature and conceptualisation. A synthesis is an essential part of progress in research. Secondly, intercultural communication is an embodied experience that needs to be understood contextually. Over the years, several scholars have contributed to the body of literature to which we now have access. Yet, apart from those who know these scholars personally, their embodied intercultural experiences that shaped their work are unknown to the generations of students who have benefited from their contribution to the field. We have endeavoured to contextualise theories and concepts by including narrative reflections from the relevant researchers, highlighting experiences in their own life that illustrate their understanding of their work. Our own first-person narratives are also used to illustrate concepts. Thirdly, this book is intended to be a contribution to existing literature in intercultural communication, learning from research in the past and offering insights for the future.

To elaborate on the part where the book contains personal narratives from significant scholars in the field, I wish to highlight my own relationship with some of these scholars to further humanise their contributions. Brent Ruben, for example, was one of the members of my doctoral dissertation committee. To say I was suitably intimidated by the presence of one of the founders of research in measuring intercultural communication competence in my dissertation committee is an understatement. But Brent was always gracious and encouraging, providing constructive feedback that boosted the confidence of a young scholar. He continues to be someone who encourages me in my work. I had read the works of Colleen Ward and Young Yun Kim extensively in my intercultural studies. When I had the opportunity to meet them at a conference, I was amazed by their approachability and warmth. I have since enjoyed their support and encouragement over the years. At the time of writing this book, I have been appointed as President-Elect of the International Academy for Intercultural Research (IAIR), a position previously held by Colleen, Young, and the next person I am about to introduce, Jan Pieter van Oudenhoven.

I "met" Jan Pieter in an embarrassing case of mistaken identity. I had read a book on intercultural research methodology by one of his colleagues, and written to Jan Pieter by mistake, thanking him for the excellent work in that book. Jan Pieter graciously responded, correcting my mistake and expressing his delight in making my acquaintance anyway. I since had the opportunity to meet him in person several times, being impressed by his genuine warmth and graciousness, not to mention his cheeky sense of humour. I was honoured when Jan Pieter and his wife Karen agreed to share their story for this project.

I have only met John Berry in person briefly, but I am impressed not only by his ability to remember people, but also the consistent way in which he encourages and lends support in the many times we have corresponded. In fact, it is John who initially suggested that Ripley and I should collaborate, because Ripley was working on a similar project involving personal narratives of intercultural scholars and he and I had both approached John about recording John's narrative. Ripley and I got the chance to talk about our projects in Switzerland, as I mentioned, and the rest, as they say, is history.

Similar to John, I have only met Jim Neuliep, Milton Bennett, Dharm Bhawuk, and David Sam in person a couple of times. But Jim's work in ethnocentrism has been an instrumental part of my own research, and he has been an encouraging colleague and mentor from afar. Milton's work on intercultural sensitivity is a significant part of intercultural competence literature with which I have engaged in my primary area of expertise. Dharm is one of the most overtly encouraging people one could meet, and David's genius is camouflaged by his unassuming manner and ready smile.

I have never had the opportunity to meet Brian Spitzberg, but I have been a fan of his work for many years. His early work in interpersonal communication competence significantly influenced my understanding of the nature of competence in communication between people of different cultures. When one of his co-authored works on intercultural competence was published some years ago, I wrote to thank him for his valuable contribution to the field and received a warm and gracious response. I am grateful to be able to include Brian's story in this book.

I got the opportunity to meet Wendy Leeds-Hurwitz, Darla Deardorff, and John Oetzel for the first time, on separate occasions, in Australia. All three of those meetings were meaningful and have led to easy collegiality over the years, and across the miles. Because of the similarities in our research interests, Darla and I have collaborated on several projects since that initial meeting.

There are two other past presidents of IAIR whose stories are featured in this book. I have had the opportunity to admire and appreciate the extent to which Nan Sussman and Ken Cushner invest in encouraging and championing the next generation of scholars. Their generosity of spirit is one which I hope all scholars can emulate.

Chan-Hoong Leong, Adam Komisarof (also a former president of IAIR), and Jonas Kunst are colleagues I have had the opportunity to get to know better in recent years. They represent a generation of highly skilled and highly productive scholars who are contributing to new knowledge in intercultural studies from different cultural perspectives.

Before I conclude my introduction, it is essential that I identify the parameters of what is meant by "intercultural" in the context of this book. Although a case could be made that cultural differences exist between various groups such as interest groups, socio-economic groups, identity groups, and so forth, the focus of this work is on cultural differences between national and ethnic groups. It must also be acknowledged that a significant portion of research in intercultural communication and related disciplines is from Westernised nations, arguably due to the opportunities and economic support present in those nations for intellectual pursuits. Although Ripley and I have endeavoured to include diverse perspectives, the influence of Westernised thinking in much of known research, including our own, must be noted.

Within these parameters and limitations, there is still much to discover about intercultural communication and developing our ability to communicate appropriately and effectively with people from diverse cultures in the diverse communities in which many of us live, study, and work. This book is one contribution to such discovery.

Ripley

As a result of events in my early childhood I became very adept at independent travel in the company of my siblings at a very young age. Whether it was getting onto a plane, traversing via Greyhound bus across multiple state lines, or eventually piling into a rental car or a 1963 dually farm truck and making our way across the country – boundaries, regional variations, and adaptability were coded into my system. I also had formed an early vision of the human potential for unity amidst diversity that sprung from my independent faith journey. The intersection of those two forces has resulted in my embrace of people from diverse backgrounds and love for new cultural experiences.

My intercultural engagement began during my youth in the context of the *beautiful game* and a friend group that challenged what I thought was *normal*. In college, the boundary-spanning included international teammates, multicultural student groups, and increasing familiarity with Native American cultures and relationships. Eventually, my father's international experiences, combined with my own trajectory, influenced my decision to seek a PhD in intercultural communication. At the same time, I had begun coaching soccer at the collegiate level with rosters that included first-generation Americans, international students, and missionary kids. It was also in the context of my coaching career that I was first introduced to a refugee community. I hired a recent immigrant from Bosnia, Voja Stojanovic, as an assistant coach in the mid-1990s. That friendship resulted in a life-altering journey alongside numerous displaced families and people groups, and an increasing appreciation for the beauty and resilience of the human spirit.

As a natural connector, I have always enjoyed the intersection of people and ideas for the fresh perspectives it can produce. My graduate programmes were quite interdisciplinary and I find that my research is most productive when merging concepts and methodologies from distinct fields. But, I employ the word *intersection* intentionally when discussing intercultural communication. Intersections imply things coming from different directions and meeting up. They hold the promise of bringing together, but also the possibility of collision. Norbert Wiener (1954), in his brilliant book *The Human Use of Human Beings*, framed the situation in terms of entropy: "As entropy increases, the universe and all closed systems in the universe, tend naturally to deteriorate and lose their distinctiveness" (p. 12). That is, according to the second law of thermodynamics things move from "a state of organization and differentiation in which distinctions and forms exist, to a state of chaos and sameness" (p. 12). The chaos of entropy produces the paradoxical effect of equilibrium. Wiener's point is that while there are isolated enclaves of order that will temporarily resist the natural tendency of entropy, left on its own for extended periods of time, all of life is gravitating towards instability. He observed that our human response to entropy is to establish "arbitrary enclaves of order and system" (p. xiii). I call that human response – culture. Our cultural systems are not self-sustaining in perpetuity. Left on their own, these communal systems would disintegrate into a fractious cacophony of individual bits (atoms). The fight is simply to exist, said Wiener, to preserve a future, and to embrace a memory of what has been; "to produce a temporary and local reversal of the normal direction of entropy" (p. 25). And once we create those cultural structures, they in turn shape us and mark our identities so strongly that we believe them to be innate and unalterable (at least by preference). The human instinct is to preserve our islands of decreasing entropy.

It is therefore an inescapable human reality to interact through barriers, amidst the unknown, the unfamiliar, as our islands of decreasing entropy intersect. As part of our interactional process, we have to take into account uncertainty and contingency because the nature of entropy is working against communal life. And communal life reflexively reinforces the barriers to intercultural communication. To summarise this point, each island of decreasing entropy has unique beauty and intrigue, the very things that draw us towards the intersections. But that beauty comes at the cost of symmetry and connection. No matter the context, communication is always subject to gravity, degradation, or disintegration as it is being performed, and therefore suffers the effects of meaningfulness.

The notion of working on a template for facilitating intercultural relations appealed to me. So, during a sabbatical in the spring of 2022 I began a book project to explore the idea of cultural intersections. One element I wanted to incorporate into the book was conversations with some of the leading interculturalists in the field that had shaped my thinking – I wanted readers to meet these scholars in a more personal way and learn about their motivations to explore intercultural relations. During my conversation with cross-cultural psychologist John Berry, he said, "You should really talk to Lily Arasaratnam-Smith, she asked me for a very similar contribution to a book she is working on." Lily and I were acquainted as colleagues within the International Academy for Intercultural Research (IAIR). We subsequently talked the following summer at IAIR's biennial meeting in Rapperswil, Switzerland and eventually decided to merge our projects. It is difficult to overstate how much my ideas have benefitted from the synergy and camaraderie this collaboration has provided. The clarity and creativity of Lily's thinking has sharpened, challenged, and extended my perspectives in every chapter. I have thoroughly enjoyed our many compositional conversations, pieces of which we have included as provocative end-of-chapter elements that we hope will serve as starting points for your own conversations.

One of the treasures in this book are the narratives from *scholar-mentor-friends*. I have chosen that label very intentionally. Each of the people I originally contacted for a conversation were first known to me through their scholarship. Some of them were giants in the field of intercultural communication and cross-cultural psychology. I had read many of their books and journal articles as a graduate student and young professor. They are literally celebrities in their respective disciplines – I kid you not. Then, in 1998 I submitted a paper to IAIR's inaugural meeting. Surprisingly, my paper was accepted, and I found myself presenting to a room packed with intercultural pioneers like Bill Gudykunst, Everett Rogers, Young Kim, Richard Bhouris (whom I roomed with at the conference, even though we had never met!), Milton Bennett, Rich Wiseman, and Stella Ting-Toomey. It was a nerve-wracking affair. However, the warmth, receptivity, and collegiality I found at IAIR quickly cemented its position as my academic home. Right after my presentation, one of my scholar-idols, Young Kim, invited me to coffee to talk about my research. I had cut my intercultural teeth reading her book with Bill Gudykunst titled, *Communicating with Strangers*. It has largely been in the context of IAIR that I have been directly or indirectly mentored by these scholars and have over time formed warm friendships.

One of the motivating factors for Lily and I to join forces in this project was because we had both independently landed on the idea of including narratives from key scholars in the field. It is important to me that readers understand why I reached out to these scholars to include their personal narratives in a project like this and what their insight and friendship has contributed to my own personal journey. As I mentioned, Young Kim has encouraged me personally and professionally for more than 20 years. She has also been instrumental in shaping my systems approach to the field. Our conversations over coffee, or serendipitously seated next to each other on planes to and from international conferences, were more meaningful to me than she probably imagined. Judith Martin was one of my first focus-area professors in my MA programme and set the bar for me in terms of thoroughness and sophistication in handling the literature of the field. She has been unfailingly encouraging over the years. I also had the pleasure of serving the academy for six years as secretary of the board, but it would not have happened without the encouragement of Nan Sussman. Nan's support and subsequent friendship is one of the things I most cherish about IAIR. Her research on cultural transition and re-entry has also guided my practice as I have taken students abroad and walked alongside resettling refugees over the years.

Milton Bennett is another one of those icons of the intercultural field. We both earned PhDs from the University of Minnesota, but Milton was an early trailblazer in that programme from whom those of us that came along later voraciously read books, chapters, and articles. The chance to share meals and spend informal time discussing constructivist implications with him has been surreal. John Berry and I interacted in conference sessions over the years, but it was a 2013 chance encounter in a Vietnamese restaurant where John invited me to join him over a bowl of Pho that we got to know each other on a more personal basis. That incident perfectly illustrates the relational ambiance of IAIR. John's scholarship, along with Kim's and Bennett's, has had an enormous influence on my approach. Similarly, Colleen Ward has provided me with a collegial simpatico relationship, as well as reliable instruments, that have helped me envision what meaningful scholarship can look like.

The mentor-friendship factor cannot be overstated in many of these relationships. Jan Pieter van Oudenhoven, Dharm Bhawuk, and I became fast friends during the 2004 post-conference trip around Taiwan that has led to becoming co-adventure-seekers, conference roommates and co-authors. And Adam Komisarof has truly become a brother from another mother, as we hold each other accountable in personal and professional endeavours. Involvement in IAIR leadership also blessed me with the opportunity to develop friendships with Executive Director Ken Cushner and past-President David Sam, both of whom influenced me with their graciousness, efficiency, and meaningful commitment to peacebuilding, both in their personal and professional lives. Ken has become a role model of a practicing scholar (and a musician) as I move forward in my career.

I have had less opportunity to interact personally with Darla Deardorff, Jane Jackson, Chan-Hoong Leong, and Jonas Kunst, largely on account of their impressive professional productivity I presume. But I hold them all in high esteem and have grown appreciably from having read their work. Darla, Chan-Hoong, and Jonas represent the future of the discipline and are blazing new trails and challenging entrenched ideas – as they should. Likewise, I know Jim Neuliep, Wendy Leeds-Hurwitz, Brent Ruben, and Brian Spitzberg only from across the room at large national conferences, but the pages of their books are well-worn on my shelves and their narratives contribute essential ideas to our project.

Intersecting cultures, ethnic groups, and races seems so simple and intuitive, as long as respect and cooperation are the rule. Yet the realities of our global village all too often reveal that our visions of the world are asymmetrical, which opens the door to demonisation, division, and disparity. As anti-apartheid revolutionary and the first democratically elected Black President of South Africa Nelson Mandela once observed, "No one is born hating another person because of the colour of his skin, or his background, or his religion. People must learn to hate, and if they can learn to hate, they can be taught to love, for love comes more naturally to the human heart than its opposite." Mandela's hopefulness epitomises my aspirations for this book – that it will help tip the scales towards those who live at peace with their neighbours from different backgrounds versus those who harbour suspicion, hate, and discrimination.

To that end, I have four primary objectives in writing this book: First, my hope is that we can move closer to the ideal of living peaceably with our neighbours, whoever they may be. Second, my desire is that you experience genuine growth in self-awareness. The starting place for understanding others more completely is a look inward to identify who we are and what unifies and differentiates us from others. Third, there is the opportunity to find courage and compassion in this journey. You will no doubt experience newfound appreciation and confidence in who you are and where you come from, but I hope you also recognise and reflect on the fact that no historical community or people group has gotten it all right. Power and oppression are a part of every communal story, and where our stories display some of that darkness, they open the door for compassion towards those who have borne the weight of that abuse. Finally, my sincere hope is that you will realise a sense of calling or purpose in this journey – whether you call it serendipity or providence, the ways in which our life trajectories overlap is not without meaning. It is coincidental in the true sense of the word. Your journey, with all your enculturation inputs, has equipped you in unique ways to engage others and bring value to those relationships. And as you meet others similarly equipped, amazing things can take place if we embrace the opportunity.

In the pages that follow you will learn about the forces that bind people together while paradoxically providing the foundation for setting one community against another. Intersections are paradoxical. A paradox is a seeming contradiction between two undeniably true premises. But it is precisely the paradox of the intersection that contains the core idea of an intercultural space. That is, two things can be true at the same time even though they appear to contradict each other. For example, the idea that less is more, or that people with remarkable potential fail more often than they succeed, or the more we invest in others, the richer we become, and close friendships are messy and taxing, but totally worth it. In a similar way, many of the things that we will encounter in this journey towards understanding the potential of intercultural spaces will seem paradoxical, but if we probe beyond the surface, we will be rewarded with a whole new perspective.

At the end of this journey you will realise that you have been handed a set of keys for unlocking attitudes, motivations, and skills that can improve the way you relate with others from different backgrounds, enable you to move more fluidly within diverse cultural settings, reduce your fear and uncertainty of the unfamiliar, and empower you to understand and confidently lead in increasingly diverse spheres of personal and professional life. You will be introduced to aspects of yourself that you may never have encountered before, and asked to confront biases and perspectives that may make you uncomfortable. Along the way you will meet courageous people motivated by trauma and injustice, but also perseverance and hope. My hope is that you begin to look forward to entering intercultural spaces that paradoxically bind and separate you from other people around the world, and realise that doing so enriches your life and creates new islands of reduced entropy.

Reference

Wiener, N. (1950). *The human use of human beings: Cybernetics and society.* The Riverside Press.

1 Communicating in Intercultural Spaces

There remains one other kind of practitioner, known as a "listener." This witch-doctor has the power to exorcise the devils that lodge in the heads of people who have been bewitched. The Nacirema believe that parents bewitch their own children… The patient simply tells the "listener" all his troubles and fears, beginning with the earliest difficulties he can remember. The memory displayed by the Nacirema in these exorcism sessions is truly remarkable. (Miner, 1956, p. 506)

One of the gifts of an intercultural experience or an interaction with someone from a different culture or different upbringing is the glimpse into our own normality from the perspective of an "outsider." While the practice of seeing a therapist on a regular basis may be par for the course in many Westernised cultures, seeing a witchdoctor to exorcise devils is a practice at which most people in the modern world would baulk. Horace Miner's clever retelling of everyday American practices (in case you missed it, Nacirema is "American" in reverse) illustrates the enlightening effect a different (cultural) perspective can have. The excerpt refers to the practice of visiting a psychologist or a counsellor to talk about your troubles, often (and supposedly inevitably) resulting in discussions of your childhood.

There is something instructive about seeing our own normality assessed or questioned through the eyes of someone whose normality is different to ours. When we communicate with someone from a different culture or background, we not only have the opportunity to understand another way of seeing the world, but also examine the assumptions on which we base our own worldview.

Interacting with people from other cultures also gives us the opportunity to see ourselves in a different light. Cooley (1922) suggested that our sense of self is informed by how we think others see us, what we think about how (we think) others see us, and how we respond to what we think about how we think others see us. This idea is known as the *looking-glass self*, or the self that we see reflected in others. Interacting with people from other cultures gives the opportunity to see a different type of self, reflected in them. For example, Lily grew up in a culture where beauty was associated with light skin, especially for women. The lighter the skin, the more beautiful the woman. Possessing a somewhat mocha skin tone,

DOI: 10.4324/9781003318415-2

she always assumed she was below average on the beauty scale. That sense of self was based on how she saw herself reflected in the eyes of people from her own culture. But when she interacted with people who grew up in the West, she saw a different picture because they said, "Wow, what lovely brown skin you've got!" The skin tone she always assumed was below average was suddenly relabelled as "lovely." She would not have had the opportunity to see this different looking-glass self if she had not had the opportunity to interact with people who saw things very differently.

The focus of this introductory chapter is on what happens when people from different cultures communicate with each other. Intercultural communication is commonly understood as interpersonal communication between persons of different cultures. In an increasingly diverse world, intercultural communication is a topic of relevance to most of us. For many of us, intercultural communication is part of our everyday reality, from interacting with people in our neighbourhood to working or studying with colleagues from different cultures. We will delve deeper into the need to understand intercultural communication in Chapter 2, but we begin by establishing what we mean by communication, culture, and intercultural communication in the context of this book.

Communication

Interpersonal communication is often characterised as a meaning-making process between two people, using verbal (language) and nonverbal codes (gestures, tone of voice, expressions, etc.), situated in a context, and sometimes mediated through technology. Examples of interpersonal communication are all around us, such as friends catching up over a coffee, co-workers discussing a project, siblings having an argument, or a salesperson phoning a potential customer.

Through the years, communication scholars have identified essential characteristics of all communication. Firstly, communication is a *process*, in that it is dynamic and ongoing. In other words, a single message is but a moment in time of a larger, more encompassing message. One of the earlier models of communication describes a linear process wherein a sender communicates a message through a channel, to a receiver (Shannon & Weaver, 1949). Others developed a more interactive view of communication, describing communication as a process that involves feedback to an initial message (Schramm, 1954). We propose that communication behaviour should always be seen as part of a continuous, historical process that is situated in a particular context.

Secondly, communication is *symbolic*. A symbol is something that represents something else, such as a red cross symbolising a hospital. As we communicate with language and nonverbal cues (more on this in Chapter 4), communication is inherently symbolic, although the nature of symbols varies depending on cultural and social contexts. Thirdly, and related to communication as a symbolic activity, communication is *contextual*. Human communication is about who says what, to whom, when, and with what effect. Meaning is dependent on context. It is precisely this nature of communication that makes conversing in another language so difficult. We often learn the vocabulary, but we are rarely taught the contexts in which to use the words and phrases. Examples of these context-dependent phrases abound in the form of idiomatic expressions such as "John is a chip off the old block," or "It's raining cats and dogs." Any second language speaker understands the challenge of navigating around idioms. Without the context to provide meaning, the interpretation of idiomatic expressions can be nonsensical. The contextual nature of communication also refers to the specificity introduced by the people involved in the communication and when the communication happened.

Fourthly, communication is *intentional*. This is a highly contested aspect of communication amongst scholars. A team of communication researchers (Watzlawick et al., 1967) studying the practical ways in which we send messages put forward the following statement that has resonated with many: one cannot not communicate. Watzlawick and colleagues pointed out that there were two aspects to every message, the content or task aspect and the meta-communication or relational aspect. Their statement about our inability to refrain from sending messages was aimed at that ongoing stream of relational signals we generate. The pragmatic perspective on communication includes all of those little relational messages we send that tell other people how we feel about them. Consequently, they believe we are unable to NOT communicate. The question is, are unintentional messages communication? If communication is what takes place *between* people in an effort to understand and share meaning, then does it also require an intentionality by the parties involved? Although the debate on intentionality of communication is by no means settled, our position is that there is an element of intentionality to communication because there are elements of selection and interpretation in the way we interact with an infinitely complex world using our finite ability to retain information (more on this in Chapter 3).

Fifthly, communication is *reflexive* in that it is a two-way, non-linear process in which the meaning-making between communicators happens. Sometimes this process follows a script in that it unfolds how you would expect it to unfold (e.g. someone holds the door open for you, you say, "Thank you," and she says, "You're welcome" or "No worries" or something to that effect), and at other times it doesn't. You thank someone for holding the door for you and she says, "I won't bother next time" – then the off-script conversation can get interesting! Such an unscripted, reflexive meeting is one in which the meaning of the event unfolds with every utterance.

In sum, communication is a contextual, reflexive, and symbolic process that is dependent on the communicators' intentionality. Now that we have examined communication, let's turn our attention to culture. When we think of intercultural communication as interpersonal communication between people from different cultures, how we define "culture" becomes important.

Culture

Culture can be an over-used and under-defined word because it is versatile and often intuitively understood without the need for clarification. If someone says, "I find it difficult to understand my neighbour because she's from a different culture," we may understand that sentence based on a lot of internal assumptions. We may assume the neighbour speaks a different language or perhaps the neighbour is from another country and has different customs or speaks with a strong accent. We may not normally interrogate this sentence by asking clarifying questions, such as "What do you mean when you say 'different culture?'" or "Is your neighbour from a different country, ethnicity, socio-economic background, religion…?"

Culture is a label often used to describe the shared values, norms, traditions, beliefs, and customs amongst a group of people such as a family, an organisation, an ethnic group, or a nation. The term was first used by anthropologist E. B. Tylor (1871) in his book *Primitive Culture* to describe "that complex whole which includes knowledge, belief, art, morals, law, customs, and any other capabilities and habits acquired by man [sic] as a member of society" (p. 1). There are individual variations within national or ethnic groups of course, such that not all members of a particular cultural group think the same way. As Gudykunst (2004) puts it, "No one individual knows all aspects of culture, and each person has a unique view of a culture. The theories that members of cultures share, however, overlap sufficiently so that they can coordinate their behavior in everyday life" (p. 42).

There are several aspects of culture that are worth noting. Firstly, culture is *shared.* In other words, the norms, traditions, and values that we associate with our "culture" are known to us because these were shared with us by others who are participants in our culture. Cultures are traditional in that sense in that "they are developed in the historical experience of social groups, and as a social heritage, they are acquired by social actors through various processes of social transmission" (Spiro, 1984, p. 323).

Secondly, culture is *learned.* An Australian isn't born knowing what it means to be an Australian. A Fijian infant doesn't know the "Fijian way" of doing things. Our cultural identity is formed over years of socialisation and enculturation, where we learn how to be a member of our cultural group by watching others, being taught by others, and being surrounded by cultural icons and artefacts (such as movies, festivals, and books, for example).

Thirdly, culture is *created* by people. An easy way to see the created nature of culture is to examine a new club or company. When the company is formed, one of the things that people who formed the company would consider is the mission (what we do), vision (what we aspire to be), and values (who we are) of the company. These in turn form what would become the "culture" of the company going forward. Because we are brought up in our ethnic or national cultures from a young age, we are often not cognisant of the fact that culture is something people jointly created. But it is important to remember the created nature of culture because it also reminds us of the changing nature of culture.

That is, culture is *dynamic,* or fluid. Although some festivals and traditions have stood the test of time, the dynamic or changing nature of culture is only too evident if you watch a movie from 30 or 40 years ago and compare it to a contemporary movie. From cultural artefacts such as fashion, music, and language patterns, to values, such as what is "appropriate" and "inappropriate" behaviour, has changed over time, demonstrating the dynamic nature of culture.

Among other things, culture is therefore shared, learned, created, and dynamic. We will delve further into "culture" later; but it is helpful to state that, within the context of this book, we largely focus on culture as it applies to ethnic and national groups and cultural identities as they relate to ethnic and/or national affiliations.

The study of intercultural communication examines how individuals' cultural values and worldview influence their meaning-making process when they interact with other people. Decades of research in intercultural communication has demonstrated that differences in cultures influence communication with potential for misunderstanding. Communication scholar Wendy Leeds-Hurwitz (2010) observes, "Intercultural communication occurs when individuals using different cultural symbols and meanings interact; thus intercultural communication often involves a mismatch of codes" (p. 21).

Lily's own awareness of intercultural communication came early in life. She grew up in a small town in the Tamil-speaking part of northern Sri Lanka which was ethnically homogenous but diverse in religious beliefs. The majority were Hindus, with a small minority of Muslims and Christians. Within the national context, Tamil people of all religions were the minority compared to Sinhalese people who were predominantly Buddhist, with some Muslims and Christians. Even as a small child, she was very aware of her place in the world as a "minority," both as a Tamil and as a Christian. She was aware that her beliefs and traditions were different from those of her classmates. For instance, the Hindus in her neighbourhood would share special festival foods with Lily's family. The Muslims did the same when they celebrated Eid, for example. It was Lily's family's turn to share food and treats at Christmastime. The celebration of a religious festival was neither cause for offense, nor cause to contemplate whether those not celebrating would feel "left out." It was simply understood that Hindus celebrated Deepavali, Muslims Eid, Christians Christmas, and, if you were on good terms with your neighbours, you got to enjoy a variety of treats throughout the year! But things were not always idyllic. Growing up in the midst of a civil war, Lily was acutely aware that Tamils were at odds with Sinhalese and that there were extremists in every ethnic and religious group who expressed their distrust of others through acts of varying degrees of violence, from throwing smoke bombs at churches during Christmas services to blowing up busloads of citizens who belonged to the "other" group. In this environment, the existence of cultural differences and the violence that could result from extreme discord based on those differences were part of her sense of normality. She never experienced homogeneity or a "politically correct" approach to diversity. Her world was one in which cultural differences simply existed on a continuum from neighbourly harmony to extreme violence.

When Lily's family migrated to the Maldives to escape the civil war, little did she know that that was the beginning of the rest of her life as a sojourner. She experienced first-hand the anxiety, frustrations, and curiosity of being a ten-year-old stranger in a land in which the language, religion, customs, lifestyle, and people were foreign to her in every sense of the word. Howell's (1982) model of levels of communication competence is one that has been widely adapted in different contexts. The model identifies unconscious incompetence, conscious incompetence, conscious competence, and unconscious competence as ascending stages of competence (more on this in Chapter 7). As a young immigrant, Lily found herself in a perpetual stage of conscious incompetence where she was acutely aware of her "foreignness" but not in possession of the tools to do much about it. This experience repeated itself at each of her major sojourn adventures, going from country to country and place to place where she remained a foreigner, or at the very least a "visible migrant," whose physicality is distinct from that of the majority population in that context. This reality is one of the factors that influenced her choice to study intercultural communication as an international student in the United States. Even after decades of study and reflection, the more she learns, the more she uncovers how much more there is to learn!

As Lily's journey exemplifies, many intercultural scholars come to study culture because of personal experiences, sometimes via circuitous routes. We will share the story of many intercultural scholars throughout this book. For example, Ken Cusher, a thought-leader especially in the area of international education, tells the story of how he came to be an intercultural scholar:

> I was in a crowd of students who were fired on, on May 4, 1970, at Kent State where I was a freshman. Hiding behind a car that had its windows shot out and that was kind of my wakeup call that there ought to be some alternative to violence when there's a difference of opinion. So, a year after that, rather than be on the campus that was pretty tense, a friend and I decided to do a backpacking trip to Europe. You know, so we put a pack on our back and got rail passes, and hitchhiked around and spent ten or twelve weeks around Europe and in Morocco. That was another wakeup call; there's this wide world out there, people do things differently, they speak differently, think differently, and act differently. And I was really intrigued by that... so when I came back I said well, there's a wonderful world out there. I'm not from a wealthy family, we don't have a family business that's going to go global. What can I do... and I think that's when I decided that maybe a teaching degree would enable me to get out in the world and do some things. I was able to do my student teaching in an American school in Zurich. And that was another eye opener for me, because then I saw a school that was doing education in a way that was really exciting and meaningful in a small community. (Cushner, personal communication, 19/05/2022)

Another story of how intercultural scholars become interested in studying culture is offered by Jonas Kunst, whose research focuses on experiences of acculturation. Similar to Lily's experiences of living in different cultures, Jonas too explains his exposure to diversity at an early age.

Acculturation as a Lifetime Project

Jonas R. Kunst

Although I reflected little on it as a child, I was raised into a family that consisted of many cultures. My grandparents on my father's side were from Lithuania and Silesia and met in the aftermath of the Second World War. My grandparents on my mother's side were from Norway. In the 80s, my parents then met each other as exchange students in Spain, which ultimately resulted in my birth.

I spent my first six years in two culturally diverse parts of Oslo, named "Grønland" and "Holmlia." Grønland has now become a hip, gentrified neigh-bourhood, whereas Holmlia is known for its challenges with crime and tense intercultural relations. During my early years, Pakistani samosas were my favourite food, and my friends had cultural backgrounds from many parts of the world. Nevertheless, I was little aware of intercultural relations and their complexities during the beginning of my childhood. This changed a lot when we moved to Germany.

I can still recall that I immediately noticed that people treated us differently and gave us strange looks because of our accents or when we talked Norwegian with each other. To be sure, the bias we experienced was subtle, and I can only imagine how moving to Germany must have been for children who belonged to groups that are devalued in society. Still, it was noticeable enough to make seven-year-old Jonas ask his mother whether they could try to speak German instead of Norwegian in public. However, my mother insisted on speaking her mother tongue, and this never changed. In retrospect, I consider her reaction as being in line with the rejection-identification model, where most minority-group members strengthen their ethnic identification in response to experiences of bias. However, in my opinion, my mother never rejected the German cul-ture. Likely our experiences as White immigrants were far from severe enough to make us distance ourselves from the majority society. However, I believe that these experiences made me aware early on of the processes of cultural rejection and exclusion, which nurtured a sympathy for the struggles of people less privileged than me.

From an acculturation perspective, I would say that I was a relatively integrated kid. However, I also realise that the classic two-fold model of accul-turation by John Berry that distinguishes between engagement in the national culture and one's heritage culture cannot fully describe my upbringing. There were virtually no other Norwegians in the city I lived in, so how could I have socialised with them? Thus, instead of spending time with other Norwegians, I built friendships with people who also had migration backgrounds. I believe that these experiences led to my later academic interest in majority-group acculturation, which focuses on how the cultures of minority-group members influence the culture of majority-group members. For instance, my best friend during adolescence was Lebanese, and his culture had a strong influence on me. I really liked and adopted his and his family's values of hospitality, loyalty, and humbleness, and their perspectives changed my views on many social and political issues.

Having friends from different religions, a question that preoccupied me as a teenager was why people from religious groups with an apparent theological overlap could act so hostile towards each other. I spent much time reading about the similarities between Judaism, Islam, and Christianity, and I thought of ways through which believers from different faiths could be united. This interest planted the seed for what later became my scholarly interest in what we have termed a "dual Abrahamic identity." Our general finding is that, when Jews, Muslims, and Christians acknowledge their shared Abrahamic heritage, they become more positive towards each other. Acknowledging this heritage does not mean that they must give up their own religious beliefs. Simply acknowledging similarities with others can be a powerful venue to improve intercultural relations by fostering unity.

After finishing secondary school in Germany, I moved back to Norway to study psychology. Re-immigrating to my country of birth was a strange experience. On the one hand, I felt a deep cultural connection to the country. On the other hand, a lot of this connection was built on childhood experiences and family visits. Luckily, my extended family helped me readjust to life in Oslo. One cannot underestimate the role of social support during migration, which I believe is a far more important predictor of adjustment than acculturation orientations or strategies. Moreover, I lived in a residence hall where about half the tenants were international students. The exposure to people from all parts of the world was such a rich experience and gave me a feeling of belonging to a world community. I believe that this experience led to my interest in the role of global identification. Many people who a classic acculturation framework may describe as marginalised because they do not identify much with either their heritage or national cultures may indeed primarily identify with a global community.

One experience that fundamentally changed me and the country I live in was the terror attack by right-wing extremist Anders Behring Breivik committed on July 22, 2011. I was walking the streets of Oslo with my mentee as the bomb went off. Right after the attack, we were harassed by a man who blamed Muslims for the attack and yelled at my mentee, a person of colour who was only about eight years old at that time. A few hours later, it became clear that the perpetrator was a White Norwegian man. Extremism of all kinds is a threat to culturally diverse societies. To prevent it, we need to understand it. As a result, I started researching the roots and consequences of Islamophobia and how conspiracy theories and perceptions of threat and relative deprivation can undermine the fundamentals of our societies by leading to violent extremism.

To sum up, acculturation and intercultural relations shaped who I was and who I became. Both continue to play important parts in my life. My partner is an immigrant from Poland. Our son now grows up triculturally, with family members living in Poland, Norway, and Germany. My goal is to help him constructively navigate the different cultural spheres and find his own place within them. Through this, he can become a constructive part of the culturally diverse world we live in.

Intercultural Spaces

A question that captured Lily's attention several years ago is, when does inter-personal communication become intercultural communication? In other words, if a Canadian and Indian communicate, is that inherently intercultural communica-tion? What if the Canadian is a second generation Indian and deeply familiar with the customs of her ancestors? What if the Indian was educated in Canada and has internalised many Canadian values? Is communication between these two individ-uals still intercultural communication merely based on their difference of nation-alities? She needed to understand the nature of instances when cultural differences influence communication in ways that would not have been relevant in the absence of those differences. As we alluded to earlier, we experience culture on varying levels, but it is also true that we engage at each level to varying degrees, making it unclear when we are actually having an intercultural interaction.

We are not alone in this particular quest. Others have attempted to understand how culture interacts with identity in a world where technological advances and opportunities for travel have made cultural boundaries more porous than ever before. For example, in proposing their multi-level model of culture, Erez and Gati (2004) observe, "Dynamic, rather than stable, models of culture should serve for understanding the changing work environment in response to globalisation" (p. 587). We need more complex and nuanced ways of understanding how multiple cultural identities influence the way we communicate with others whose own mul-tiple cultural identities interplay with ours. In other words, we need a more nuanced definition of intercultural communication that takes us beyond the starting point of "interpersonal communication between people from different cultures." In Lily's first attempt at such a definition, she suggested:

> Perhaps the determining factor is when cultural differences between relevant individuals affect the communication exchange in ways which would have been insignificant had those differences not existed. I see these particular com-munication interactions as occurring in *intercultural spaces*... In other words, intercultural communication occurs in intercultural spaces. An intercultural space is therefore a symbolic representation of an instance when communica-tion between individuals is affected by cultural differences in a way that would not have been noteworthy in the absence of these differences. (Arasaratnam, 2011, pp. vii–viii. Emphasis in original)

"Space" here isn't a physical location, but rather a metaphor to capture a situation where interpersonal communication becomes intercultural. Although metaphor-ical, intercultural spaces presumably have boundaries and other distinctives that set them apart from other "spaces." The nature of these boundaries and distinctives needs further elaboration. Additionally, a closer examination of Lily's initial attempt at defining intercultural communication revealed it to be somewhat cir-cular. She attempted to unpack the definition more in a later work (Arasaratnam, 2012), drawing from a framework in cognitive sociology.

Thought Communities

As a doctoral student, Lily had the opportunity to study the fundamentals of cognitive sociology under the tutelage of Eviatar Zerubavel. His work on social mindscapes (1997) captivated her, because it provided her with a way to understand shared worldviews between people from different ethnic or national cultures. She was particularly intrigued by the concept of thought communities. This concept of thought communities, or thought collective, was introduced by Fleck (1979; originally published in German in 1935) in his discussion of how what is already known affects cognition or what is perceived:

> the statement, "someone recognizes something," demands such a supplement as, "on the basis of a certain fund of knowledge," or better, "as a member of a certain cultural environment," and, best, "in a particular thought style, in a particular thought collective." (p. 39)

Fleck goes on to define thought collective as:

> a community of persons mutually exchanging ideas or maintaining intellectual interaction, we will find by implication that it also provides the special "carrier" for the historical development of any field of thought, as well as for the given stock of knowledge and level of culture. (p. 39)

In other words, the thinking of the collective to which we belong influences the way in which we perceive and process new information. For example, most of us have a group of friends who share similar values and ideas to us. We feel comfortable with them because they see the world like we do, at least for the most part. If this group of friends is the "collective" to which we feel a sense of belonging, then we can see how our friend's opinions and values influence our own thinking.

Ethnic or national culture is one such significant "thought collective" to which each one of us belongs. As children, we are taught the "right" and "wrong" ways of behaving; we are taught social decorum and the proper way of addressing another person. For example, when Lily was growing up, she was taught that she should never address an older person (even if that person was only one year older than her) by their first name alone. She was taught to tag the appropriate honorific to their name to show the respect owed to them as an older person. But these honorifics were relational ones, not formal ones. That is, she was taught to call older adults "uncle" or "aunty," not "Mr" or "Ms" The point is, such teaching is a deeply ingrained cultural value that age deserves respect, a value that Lily had to learn to navigate appropriately in Western cultures where permission to address someone by their first name is used as an invitation to closer relationship – "Please, call me Susan."

This kind of cultural teaching could be implicit or explicit. Parents or other adults in a child's life may teach her "good" behaviour by rewarding when she is "good" and reprimanding when she isn't. Children may also learn social norms by observing others, through media, or simply trial and error, discovering behaviour that they wish to emulate. As adults, these ingrained values often become reified (Berger & Luckmann, 1991). That is, they become so much part of our lives, so prevalent, that we forget that values are something we create together, not something that exists naturally (like trees or mountains). To reify something is to forget its social origin. We often forget the social origins of our culture to the point where we use the values of our culture (thought community) as the benchmarks with which to evaluate the merit of those who do not belong to our culture. That is, we often use our culture as the "normal" or "right" way of seeing the world such that other cultures may look "strange," "exotic," or even "wrong" compared to how we do things.

In his classic work *Ideology and Utopia*, Mannheim (1936) elaborates on this idea of how the collective influences the individual's thinking:

> Only in a quite limited sense does the individual create out of himself the mode of speech and thought we attribute to him. He speaks the language of his group; he thinks in the manner in which his group thinks. He finds at his disposal only certain words and their meanings. These not only determine to a large extent the avenues of approach to the surrounding world, but also they show at the same time from which angle and in which context of activity objects hitherto been perceptible and accessible to the group or the individual. (p. 2)

The social groups or thought communities to which we belong therefore indelibly influence how we see the world. Zerubavel (1997) says, "what goes on in our heads is... affected by the particular thought communities to which we belong. Such communities – churches, professions, political movements, generations, nations – are clearly larger than the individual yet considerably smaller than the entire human race" (p. 9). In other words, our ethnic or national culture is only one of many thought communities to which we belong. Just as a person is Ugandan, he is also Christian, a nurse, an environmentalist, and a parent. Each of these thought communities influences the way he sees the world and processes information because thought communities subject him to a process of optical socialisation that is particular to that community. According to Zerubavel:

> "Optical" socialization typically takes place within particular thought communities (a particular profession, a particular religion, a particular generation), which is how we come to perceive things not only as individuals but also as engineers, as Catholics, or as baby boomers. Each of these *"optical" communities* has its own distinctive *"optical" tradition*, and membership in it entails learning to "see" the world through its particular lenses. (p. 9. Emphasis in original)

Zerubavel goes on to explain that a person not only belongs to multiple thought communities, but also is influenced by a particular thought community at a particular time – more so than the other thought communities to which he belongs. For example, if someone is at a professional conference, the prominent thought community which influences her thinking in that context might be that of her discipline or profession. Our optical socialisation is such that we are trained to see the world in specific ways that may not be obvious to those who have not been subjected to the same optical socialisation. For instance, an American might glance at a woman's "ring" finger on her left hand to ascertain whether she is married, whereas an Indian might glance at a woman's neck for the presence of *thaali*, a wedding necklace, to gain the same information. In other words, ethnic culture is one type of thought community to which we belong.

Factors That "Create" Intercultural Spaces

There are conditions under which we perceive the same stimulus differently compared to when those conditions are absent (more on this in Chapter 3). For example, we notice "for rent" signs everywhere when we are looking for a place to rent, whereas we may have walked past many such signs without noticing them at other times. Each person, through their interpretations and communication, is performing a cultural identity by attributing meaning to events, behaviour, and messages. These performed identities are created and reinforced in specific social situations and vary by context. They are expressions of learned group behaviour and interpretations. We propose that there are certain conditions or factors whose presence creates intercultural spaces, noting that ours is not an exhaustive list. We present these factors in the form of propositions based on what we know from research so far, and with the intent of facilitating future research.

We therefore propose:

Proposition 1: Intercultural spaces exist when differences in ethnic or cultural thought community are salient within a communicative context.

To restate Proposition 1 in other words, cultural differences affect or interfere with the process of mutual understanding, in intercultural spaces. Mutual understanding is a hallmark of communication. Habermas (1979) describes communication competence as "a speaker's capacity to introduce a correctly formulated sentence that is in accordance with reality and with the latter's orientation towards mutual understanding" (p. 29). In intercultural spaces, the social reality of each person is likely to be different, because of the differences in their culture which in turn influences the way they see things, as we discussed earlier.

Proposition 1 accounts for instances when two people from different cultures could have a conversation that is as utterly "interpersonal" as a conversation from two people from the same culture and for other instances when the conversation suddenly veers into an intercultural space.

Several years ago, Lily was hanging out with an American friend one afternoon and she suggested they should watch one of the Indian films from Lily's collection to spend the time. They shared snacks and chatted amiably as the film progressed, sharing interpersonal communication as any friends would do, regardless of cultural differences. Partway through the film, a scene unfolded in which an unmarried girl from a rural village was having a shower behind closed doors when a handyman who had come to repair the shower inadvertently walked in on her. She screams, and he averts his eyes and dashes out quickly, yelling profuse apologies in his wake. The girls' mother and sisters hear the scream and rush into the bathroom to find the girl in great distress, as she haltingly explains what had happened, between heaving sobs. The mother and sisters gasp in horror, and soon their own wailing joins the girl's cries.

As they watched, Lily's friend's expression became increasingly puzzled. "What's going on?" she asked. To which Lily replied, "The girl's family is distressed because she's unmarried and she has been seen unclothed by a man."

"So?" her friend asked, as she studied the crying girl appraisingly. "What's the problem? She has a nice figure. Why's she embarrassed that some guy saw her? It was just an accident!"

Lily's instinct was to feel taken aback by her friend's insensitivity to the gravity of the situation. Once Lily got over her initial reaction, however, she realised that her friend and her were watching the film with different cultural lenses. To Lily, it made perfect sense that an unmarried young woman in a rural Indian village would be deeply distressed by what had happened – as would her family. What had happened was akin to her virtue being assaulted; they would see her as "spoilt goods" that no man (other than the one who saw her disrobed) could marry. Lily implicitly understood these deep cultural values at play, whereas to her friend, the reaction of the girl and her family was way over the top. Lily paused the film to explain her understanding of the scene to her friend, and the two of them discussed whether the family's response to the incident was appropriately calibrated or not. This was an instance where Lily's American friend and her had ventured into an intercultural space when cultural differences in the way they understood the world became salient.

Research shows that ethnic or cultural thought community becomes salient under certain conditions. For example, Yip and Fuligni (2002) note that ethnic identity salience fluctuates based on different conditions such as ethnic behaviours (eating ethnic food, speaking ethnic language) or situational variables such as being at the receiving end of a racist comment. In Lily's example, the engagement with an ethnic artefact (an Indian film which was a common cultural artefact in her childhood) arguably brought to forefront her identity as someone from the Indian subcontinent, regardless of the fact that she not only understood but also had internalised many American values during her time in the United States, and was perfectly capable of "seeing" the film as her friend did.

The incident also highlights several important characteristics of intercultural spaces. First, these spaces have a dual nature – both an interior and an exterior dimension. In the shared exterior space, Lily and her friend were enjoying a film in a room that reflected culture-specific architecture, conversing in a common language, and perhaps eating something that was characteristic to their location; while in their respective interior spaces, they were interpreting the meaning of that film in distinct ways. This duality of culture is well established in sociolinguistic and intercultural studies, and specifically interiority has come to represent the inner, subjective thoughts and feelings that both define and distinguish individuality of experience (Campe & Weber, 2014).[1] Anthropologist Edward T. Hall observed early on in his studies of cultural communication that interiorised space is where we most often encounter out-of-awareness aspects of culture: "people from different cultures not only speak different languages but, what is possibly more important, *inhabit different sensory worlds*" (Hall, 1966, p. 2, emphasis in original; see also Hall, 1959).

That asymmetry in sensory experience points up a second important feature of these spaces; occupying a space implies both positionality and boundary. As we have seen, Lily's interaction with her friend from a different cultural background involved both an internal, subjective boundary and an external, "topological" or material boundary involving language, nonverbal behaviours, and other visible cues, all of which served to position them to interpret the film scene in particular ways (Klyukanov, 2005, p. 143). At first glance, our interiority of positions and boundaries can appear to isolate us from those that occupy other positions across a boundary. But the philosopher Heidegger reminds us that spaces also have horizons where the known and the unknown intersect. We will explore those horizons in future chapters as opportunities to create intersubjective meaning (Heidegger, 1977; Triandis, 1972).

Cultural Mosaic

Although the concept of thought communities is helpful in understanding differences in a more nuanced way beyond nationalities or ethnicities, those differences aren't entirely cognitive. Chao and Moon (2005) present an identity-based framework that is helpful for further understanding the nature of intercultural spaces. They propose a mosaic model of culture which approaches culture as an individual-level construct rather than a national-level construct.

An example of approaching culture as a national-level construct is Hofstede's Dimensions of Culture (Hofstede, 2003; Hofstede & Bond, 1984) which identify broad continuums within which national cultural values are situated. For instance, individualism versus collectivism, where individualistic cultures value independence, autonomy, and individual agency, while collectivistic cultures value cohesion, harmony, and interdependence (more of this in Chapter 3). Chao and Moon propose that each of us is a composite of multiple cultural identities which interplay with one another in predictable and unpredictable ways. The authors distinguish between geographic identities (e.g., Italian) and other group affiliations (e.g., left handed people) by noting that, "cultures do not spontaneously generate from nominal groups with minimal interaction among group members" (2005, p. 1131), and therefore cultural identities are linked to shared values (see Figure 1.1). The authors argue that each of our cultural mosaics which consists of various identity "tiles" combine to form various patterns, at the core of each of which are three primary categories, namely, demographic (age, gender, other physical traits inherited from parents), geographic (climate, landscape, other geographical features), and associative (religion, profession, and other groups with which you choose to associate). According to Chao and Moon, a person's cultural mosaic is a complex system where some tiles dominate, other tiles consolidate, and other tiles behave independently, manifesting themselves in "unpredictable ways" (2005, p. 1134).

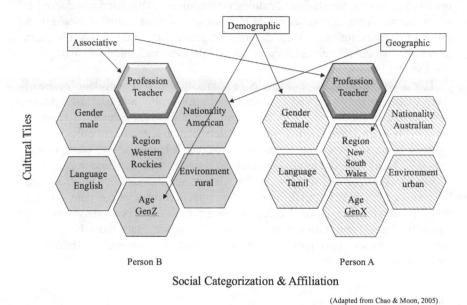

Person B   Person A

Social Categorization & Affiliation

(Adapted from Chao & Moon, 2005)

Figure 1.1 Cultural Mosaic Model, adapted from Chao and Moon (2005).

Chao and Moon further propose that shared cultural identities facilitate inter-personal interactions and that people who share cultural identity "tiles" with people of other groups are best placed to "bridge structural holes between these groups" (2005, p. 1136). Examining how this principle might apply to the concept of thought communities discussed earlier, an example could be communication between an Italian physicist and an Indian physicist where each may have multiple differences between their national and ethnic identities, but their shared profes-sional identity where they both belong to the thought community of "physicists" would be a common ground on which to base their meaning-making process.

According to Chao and Moon, "Interpersonal interactions are facilitated by shared cultural identities. Shared cultural identities are localized structures in an interpersonal network, providing common frames of reference, values and behav-ioral expectations between people" (2005, p. 1135). As such,

Proposition 2: Shared thought communities or cultural identities facilitate com-munication in intercultural spaces.

Conversely,

Proposition 3: The lack of shared thought communities or cultural identities debilitate communication in intercultural spaces.

To be clear, it is possible for people to belong to different thought communities in terms of "culture," while belonging to the same thought community in terms of shared interest or shared life experiences, for example. In other words, a Black American and a White South African may belong to different cultural thought communities, but if they are both structural engineers, then they belong to the same disciplinary thought community.

To illustrate, sitting across the table to negotiate peace talks between hostile nations could be a man who is a father of young children, a diplomat, a Buddhist, and a patriot who is committed to the peace process. On the other side is a Hindu, an economist, and a mother of young children who wants a secure future for her children regardless of the means to obtain it. Although they may not have much in common, they both understand the burden of responsibility for the future of their children and the desire to give their children a better experience than the present. This shared "parent" identity could be a foundation on which they could understand each other. In this scenario, it is easy to see those negotiators with some commonality have a better chance of communicating effectively across their differences than negotiators with no commonalities and no way of truly relating to one another.

This principle of effective communication based on common ground is well-established in other research. For example, Allport's (1954) work on Intergroup Contact Hypothesis theorises that positive outcomes from intergroup contact (or intercultural communication) are predicated on conditions of perceived equal status, shared goals, cooperation, relational intimacy, and support/acceptance by systems or authority. Although Allport's hypothesis does not refer to shared identities or thought communities, the notion of common ground is evident in this early work. In a meta-analysis of intergroup contact theory, Pettigrew et al. (2011) found that positive intergroup contact not only resulted in reduction of prejudice but also reduced anxiety, facilitated empathy and perspective-taking, and fostered trust. Another study on intergroup contact theory demonstrated that members of a minority group that were typically subjected to prejudice were successful in engaging in meaningful and positive interactions with majority group members by starting with their shared common identity as law-abiding fellow-citizens (Yilmaz et al., 2021).

We mentioned earlier that intercultural spaces are where cultural differences become salient such as to influence the meaning-making process in noteworthy ways. The Cultural Mosaic framework is a helpful one with which to further understand intercultural spaces. For instance, one of Chao and Moon's propositions is, "Behaviors influenced by concordant cultural identities are likely to be more predictable than behaviors influenced by discordant cultural identities" (2005, p. 1133). In the earlier illustration of the conversation between Lily and her American friend when they were watching the Indian film, had Lily been watching the film with her "American" lenses, her friend and Lily may never have ventured into an intercultural space. However, the stimulus of a cultural artefact from Lily's childhood prompted her "Asian" identity to be dominant in that moment in discordance with her Westernised identity which would have responded to the film exactly as her American friend did.

Based on this, we surmise that cultural identities are discordant in intercultural spaces because the transition from interpersonal communication to intercultural communication is often unpredictable.

Proposition 4: When in an intercultural space, there is usually discordance in one's internal cultural identities.

While Proposition 4 is helpful for understanding situations like the one illustrated in the example of Lily and her American friend, it is not descriptive of all instances of communication in intercultural spaces. The word "usually" is an important word in Proposition 4. But in our quest to understand intercultural spaces, we believe Proposition 4 is still helpful because it accounts for the experiences of people who are cultural hybrids or who switch from one cultural identity to another, depending on context, because they have internalised multiple cultural identities based on heritage or past experiences.

So far, we have discussed that intercultural communication occurs in intercultural spaces where cultural differences become salient in the meaning-making process. We have further proposed that there is usually a discordance in one's internal cultural identities in intercultural spaces, and that shared identities facilitate communication in intercultural spaces whereas the lack of shared identities debilitates intercultural communication. These propositions are based largely on Chao and Moon's Mosaic framework in which various (cultural) identities form a composite mosaic of a person's multi-faceted identity in which different identity tiles interact with one another or dominate others depending on contextual variables. It is necessary to also account for situations where people may venture in and out of an intercultural space without being aware of it, or only becoming aware of it in hindsight. Often, new knowledge and experience, as well as the practice of self-reflection, enable us to gain new insight from past experiences. It is conceivable therefore that, upon reflecting on a past experience, a person could see in hindsight that she was in an intercultural space without realising it. Proposition 5 accounts for this scenario.

Proposition 5: An intercultural space can exist regardless of the participants' awareness of the salience of cultural differences.

Mindfulness

Referring back to Arasaratnam's (2011) original definition of intercultural spaces, if intercultural communication occurs in intercultural spaces, how do we know when we are in such a space? Drawing on Gudykunst (1993, 1995), Arasaratnam (2012) says, "intercultural spaces necessitate the participants to exercise a measure of mindfulness" (p. 137).

In his work on Anxiety/Uncertainty Management (AUM) Theory, Gudykunst proposes that intercultural communication involves a process of management of the anxiety that results from the inherent uncertainty involved in communicating with a "stranger" or someone from a different culture. Gudykunst identifies mindfulness as a necessary tool for effective and appropriate intercultural communication. Mindfulness is a state of awareness in which a person is open to new information, conscious of the fact that there is more than one point of view present in the conversation, and also ready to use new information to form new mental categories to suit the new information. We will discuss categorisation and other social cognitive processes in further detail in Chapter 3. For the purposes of the present discussion, a mindful person is not only alert to new information, but also willing and able to change their pre-existing mental categories to accommodate this new information.

For example, assume that Mike, who was born and raised in Australia, believes that immigrants from Thailand don't speak English very well. This belief is based on his past experiences of meeting Thai immigrants who weren't very proficient in English. One day, Mike meets a co-worker from Thailand and notices his co-worker speaks fluent English. The fact that Mike notices the anomaly between his pre-existing belief and his present experience itself attests to Mike's mindfulness of new information. If Mike then wonders why this particular co-worker speaks fluent English, finds out that this co-worker had a particular type of schooling, and wonders whether Thai immigrants who have had a particular type of schooling speak fluent English, this thinking process demonstrates Mike's openness to challenge and alter his pre-existing mental category in which he put all Thai immigrants.

Gudykunst's AUM Theory identifies mindfulness as a mediating variable between anxiety/uncertainty management and effective (intercultural) communication. This premise of AUM has been empirically validated in several studies (e.g., Khukhlaev et al., 2022; Nadeem & Koschmann, 2021). Mindfulness is arguably necessary for recognising when an interpersonal communication becomes intercultural – or when we step into an intercultural space. When we are mindful, we are not only alert to the fact that the other person has a point of view that is distinct from ours, but also alert to any shift in conversation that provides us with new information. How do we know when we are in an intercultural space? The answer lies with mindfulness.

Proposition 6: Mindfulness is necessary for perceiving an intercultural space.

Navigating Intercultural Spaces

We have presented the premise that interpersonal communication becomes intercultural when cultural differences influence the meaning-making process in ways that would not be noteworthy in the absence of those differences. We have used the metaphor of intercultural spaces to characterise the instances when interpersonal communication becomes intercultural. Lesenciuc and Codreanu (2012) characterise intercultural communication as "an instantiation of interpersonal communication" (p. 127). We claim this instantiation happens in intercultural spaces. Communicators may venture in and out of intercultural spaces in the same conversation.

Although intercultural spaces are conceptual rather than geographical spaces, there are times when a person's presence in an intercultural space is conceptual as well as geographical. An example of such an instance is when you travel to a different country or to a part of your own country that is populated by people who are different from you in appearance, culture, language, or a combination thereof. The geographical cues that signal "difference" makes it easier for us to be cognisant of our presence in an intercultural space in such situations, compared to situations where those cues are absent. Sojourners and immigrants who travel from one culture to another, for example, are aware of their presence in intercultural spaces because of the geographic displacement inherent in sojourn. We will discuss migration and acculturation further in Chapter 6. For now, it is helpful to acknowledge that intercultural spaces are, at times, literal.

> **Proposition 7**: In situations where a person ventures into a different cultural context, that person exists in an intercultural space that is both conceptual and literal.

While Proposition 7 might seem obvious, identifying situations where intercultural spaces may seem literal is helpful because it provides us with an understanding of how the concept of intercultural spaces is relevant to the individual. In other words, if Ripley travels to Sydney to visit Lily, he knows he is venturing into a geographical space that embodies a cultural context that is different to his own. While in Australia, he may have a combination of interpersonal and intercultural communication exchanges with Lily, all the while being aware of the larger contextual intercultural space within which they are conversing. Lily, on the other hand, being at "home" in Sydney, would not consider herself as being in a (literal) intercultural space – while, arguably, venturing in and out of (conceptual) intercultural spaces in our conversations where the cultural differences between them become salient (as noted in Proposition 1). When Ripley returns home to the United States, he leaves the geographical awareness of having been in an intercultural space behind, while the possibility of finding himself in conceptual intercultural spaces remains.

Successfully navigating intercultural spaces (both conceptual and literal) requires one to develop a number of attitudes and skills that will be discussed further in Chapter 7 in which we will discuss the concept of intercultural competence or intercultural communication competence (ICC), which is often understood as effective and appropriate intercultural communication. Consistent with research in ICC, we propose that successful navigation through an intercultural space involves coming out on the other side with the relationship between the communicators intact (appropriate) and the communicators having achieved the objectives of the communication (effective). As such, the variables that contribute to ICC also contribute to successful navigation of intercultural spaces.

> **Proposition 8**: The variables that contribute to ICC also contribute to successful navigation of intercultural spaces.

An Invitation

We invite you on a quest of self-reflection and discovery that we hope will facilitate life-affirming intercultural dialogues and relationships in your communities. This quest will require both courage and humility. Along the way, your core assumptions may be challenged, and your very worldview may be questioned. While confronting some assumptions and views on the one hand, this quest may also reward you with allies in places you least expected and offer transformative insights. In this book, we offer you an opportunity and a challenge: an opportunity for discovery, and a challenge to do something about what you discover. If we are successful, our hope is that you will return to your spheres of influence as beacons who guide others through intercultural spaces.

The concept of intercultural spaces takes a while to process, and we think that process is going to be ongoing, as you experience intercultural spaces in your own interactions and reflect and learn from those spaces. Below is an excerpt from one of our conversations, as we too grappled with what we mean by intercultural spaces. We hope this gives you insight into our thinking as we shaped this chapter.

In Conversation: Intercultural Spaces

Ripley: Let me get that scenario, because I think that might be interesting. So, the example I include in Chapter 5 of me co-teaching a class with a Japanese grad student...

Lily: Yes, I think that's a great example of how in hindsight you looked at that situation... I was just thinking of another example. Another example would be, this is a Sri Lankan going to the UK for the first time and staying with an English family and he was hungry from the travel and it was lunchtime or whatever and the host said, you must be hungry, do you want a sandwich, and he said, oh no, don't trouble yourself and she said okay that's fine.

Ripley: Even though he was hungry?

Lily: He was very hungry. And she said that's fine, and that was it. The offer was withdrawn, and he went hungry. And in his mind the expectation was that she would say, no, no, it's no trouble at all, let me fix you a sandwich and he says no, truly I'm okay; (and she says) no, I insist, it will make *me* feel better if I feed you, let me fix it; (and he says) okay... and that's the interaction!

Ripley: That's what he wanted.

Lily: That's what he wanted; that's what he was used to. But... he went with the first no, and she said okay, that's fine, and she let it go.
   [Both laugh]

Ripley: No more offers forthcoming.

Lily: Yes. So, I thought that's a good example of intercultural spaces where one person was aware of it. In your case your colleague was aware of it while she was in that space; you weren't. And in this other example

Ripley:

Lily:

the guy was aware of it and the host wasn't... oh actually, I wonder whether he was aware of it. He might've not been...

Ripley: They both could've been unaware of it.

Lily: Yes, exactly. But clearly culture had played a role in that miscommunication, misalignment of meaning – to me that's an intercultural space.

Ripley: So, intercultural spaces... it's almost like a wormhole in space... they exist, people just aren't there yet or aware of them, right?

Lily: No.

[Both laugh]

(Note: If you're interested in reading Ripley and Lily's whole conversation about intercultural spaces, see Appendix A).

Questions for Reflection

The following questions are meant to stimulate further thinking. Use them for self-reflection or to engage in conversation with someone else.

1. When was the last time you were in an intercultural space? Did you realise you were in one at that time?
2. How would you explain an intercultural space to someone else?
3. What do you think Proposition 4 means? Have you experienced something like that?

Note

1 Of course, this understanding of interiority as opposed to exteriority dates at least as far back as Descartes' *Passions of the Soul* where he made the well-known observation that "*res cogitans, res extensa*" [I think, therefore I am] (Campe & Weber, 2014).

References

Allport, G. W. (1954). *The nature of prejudice*. Addison-Wesley.

Arasaratnam, L. A. (2011). *Perception and communication in intercultural spaces*. University Press of America.

Arasaratnam, L. A. (2012). Intercultural spaces and communication within: An explication. *Australian Journal of Communication, 39*(3), 135–141.

Berger, P. L., & Luckmann, T. (1991). *The social construction of reality*. Penguin Books.

Campe, R., & Weber, J. (2014). Rethinking emotion: Moving beyond interiority. In R. Campe & J. Weber (Eds.), *Rethinking emotion: Interiority and exteriority in premodern, modern, and contemporary thought* (pp. 1–18). De Gruyter. http://ebookcentral.proquest. com/lib/betheluniversity-ebooks/detail.action?docID=1121620

Chao, G. T., & Moon, H. (2005). The cultural mosaic: A metatheory for understanding the complexity of culture. *Journal of Applied Psychology, 90*(6), 1128–1140.

Cooley, C. H. (1922). *Human nature and the social order*. Scribner.

Erez, M., & Gati, E. (2004). A dynamic, multi-level model of culture: From the micro level of the individual to the macro level of the global culture. *Applied Psychology: An International Review*, *53*(4), 583–598.

Fleck, L. (1979). Epistemological conclusions from the established history of a concept. In T. J. Trenn and R. K. Merton (Eds.), *Genesis and development of a scientific fact* (pp. 20–51). The University of Chicago Press.

Gudykunst, W. B. (1993). Toward a theory of effective interpersonal and intergroup communication: An anxiety/uncertainty management (AUM) perspective. In R. L. Wiseman & J. Koester (Eds.), *Intercultural communication competence* (pp. 33–71). Sage.

Gudykunst, W. B. (1995). Anxiety/Uncertainty Management (AUM) Theory: Current status. In R. L. Wiseman (Ed.), *Intercultural communication theory* (pp. 8–58). Sage.

Gudykunst, W. B. (2004). *Bridging differences: Effective integroup communication* (4th ed.). Sage.

Habermas, J. (1979). *Communication and the evolution of society*. Beacon Press.

Hall, E. T. (1959). *The silent language*. Doubleday & Company.

Hall, E. T. (1966). *The hidden dimension*. Doubleday & Company.

Heidegger, M. (1977). Letter on humanism. In D. F. Krell (Ed.), *Basic writings* (pp. 193–214). Harper & Row.

Hofstede, G. (2003). Cultural dimensions. https://geerthofstede.com/culture-geert-hofstede-gert-jan-hofstede/6d-model-of-national-culture/

Hofstede, G., & Bond, M. H. (1984). Hofstede's culture dimensions: An independent validation using Rokeach's value survey. *Journal of Cross-Cultural Psychology*, *15*(4), 417–433.

Howell, W. S. (1982). *The empathic communicator*. Waveland Press.

Khukhlaev, O., Novikova, I., & Chernaya, A. (2022). Interpersonal mindfulness, intergroup anxiety, and intercultural communication effectiveness among international students studying in Russia. *Frontiers in Psychology*, *13*, 841361. doi:10.3389/fpsyg.2022.841361.

Klyukanov, I. E. (2005). *Principles of intercultural communication*. Pearson Education.

Leeds-Hurwitz, W. (2010). Writing the intellectual history of intercultural communication. In R. T. Halualani & T. K. Nakayama (Eds.), *Blackwell handbook of critical intercultural communication* (pp. 21–33). Blackwell.

Lesenciuc, A., & Codreanu, A. (2012). Interpersonal communication competence: Cultural underpinnings. *Journal of Defense Resources Management*, *3*(1), 127.

Mannheim, K. (1936). *Ideology and utopia*. Routledge.

Miner, H. (1956). Body ritual among the Nacirema. *American Anthropologist*, *58*(3), 503–507.

Nadeem, M. U., & Koschmann, M. A. (2021). Does mindfulness moderate the relationship between anxiety, uncertainty, and intercultural communication effectiveness of the students in Pakistan? *Current Psychology*. https://doi.org/10.1007/s12144-021-01429-9

Pettigrew, T. F., Tropp, L. R., Wagner, U., & Christ, O. (2011). Recent advances in intergroup contact theory. *International Journal of Intercultural Relations*, *35*(3), 271–280.

Schramm, W. L. (1954). *The process and effects of mass communication*. University of Illinois Press.

Shannon, C., & Weaver, W. (1949). *The mathematical theory of communication*. University of Illinois Press.

Spiro, M. (1984). Some reflections on cultural determinism and relativism with special reference to emotion and reason. In R. A. Shweder & R. A. LeVine (Eds.), *Culture theory: Essays on mind, self, and emotion* (1st ed., pp. 323–346). Cambridge University Press.

Triandis, H. C. (1972). *The analysis of subjective culture*. Wiley.

Tylor, E. B. (1871). *Primitive culture: Researches into the development of mythology, philosophy, religion, language, art, and custom* (1st ed.). John Murray.

Watzlawick, P., Beavin, J., & Jackson, D. (1967). *Pragmatics of human communication: A study of interactional patterns, pathologies & paradoxes*. Norton.

Yilmaz, I., Bliuc, A. M., Mansouri, F., & Bashirov, G. (2021). Young Muslim Australians' experiences of intergroup contact and its implications for intercultural relations. *Ethnic and Racial Studies*, *44*(15), 2772–2793.

Yip, T., & Fuligni, A. J. (2002). Daily variation in ethnic identity, ethnic behaviors, and psychological well-being among American adolescents of Chinese descent. *Child Development*, *73*(5), 1557–1572.

Zerubavel, E. (1997). *Social mindscapes: An invitation to cognitive sociology*. Harvard University Press.

2 Origins of Intercultural Communication

What Is Intercultural Communication and Why Study It?

Ripley was walking through a shanty village on the outskirts of a large city in the western state of Sonora, Mexico in December, 1985. It was his first extended exposure to an international, second language environment, a culture that he had mostly read about and seen depicted in movies, and an area within a developing country with abject poverty on a scale he had never experienced. At night, when he was done with his work for the day, he would wander down the dirt avenues near his hosting church building, noticing the shops and restaurants filled with products, people, and entrees that he didn't recognise. The speech was unfamiliar, the pattern of the day was unfamiliar, the architecture was unfamiliar, the logic was unfamiliar, even the use of silence was unfamiliar. The streets were laid out differently too. They all seemed to reach out from the centre of town beckoning pedestrians to walk towards a common intersection where meeting up was a geometric certainty. Ripley was having difficulty wrapping his head around it, as a naïve 21-year-old.

We mentioned in Chapter 1 that culture could be illustrated using the metaphor of a mosaic. Mosaics are composed of small diverse pieces fitted together in micro patterns that when viewed as a whole reveal a larger, cohesive image. The distinct pieces are meaningful in themselves, but as parts within a mosaic, they assume a complex interdependence with other parts that make up the whole. As with any complex system, understanding requires a multi-level analysis. We can study the characteristics of the individual pieces, or we can zoom out and reference the adjacent tiles to examine interrelationships and effects. In either case, the nature of the subject requires that while investigating one piece of the mosaic, we keep in mind all of the surrounding interlocking pieces and their holistic meaning. That leads us to questions of how and why people form cultures. Keeping in mind the interlocking pieces of the mosaic that encompasses cultural identity also helps us to see and experience the asymmetry of culture. That is exactly what Ripley was beginning to realise during his sojourn in Sonora, that the people, who were similar to him in many universal, biological, and even spiritual ways, were also very different in often subtle or subconscious aspects (Hofstede, 1984).

One afternoon when Ripley was out in the surrounding community, he was welcomed into a strangers' home for conversation and a *refresco* when it became

DOI: 10.4324/9781003318415-3

even more clear that he was an outsider. A *gringo* that did not understand the hidden meanings of expressions and behaviours in this setting. The parents and children seated across from Ripley on a worn sofa shared about the things that were important to them, evidenced by the emblems on the wall and meagre possessions in their ramshackle residence. Ripley's three years of K-12 Spanish seemed pathetically inadequate in the moment. But the humbling hospitality and authentic joy needed no translation and seemed incommensurate with the external living conditions. The entire experience intrigued and challenged Ripley as it tugged against his sensibilities. He wondered, could we be so different, yet share so many things in common? What accounted for the disparities in living conditions he was observing? What was the glue that held these families and communities together? What gave them hope or caused despair? Was it different from the bonds and motivations that Ripley was familiar with in his own community? And what would it take for Ripley and that family to understand and connect with one another in a way that maximised respect, appreciation, and cooperation? Whether Ripley knew it or not, he was navigating the boundaries of language, culture, social class, and authenticity.

It wasn't that Ripley was unfamiliar with different geographic regions growing up. His family moved a lot when he was young, exposing him to a diverse cross-section of US American society from Buffalo, New York to Seattle, Washington to Denver, Colorado. Ripley was born in Hot Springs County, Wyoming just north of the Wind River Reservation. The reservation is home to both the Eastern Shoshone and the Northern Arapaho tribes and is the third largest reservation in the US at 2.2 million acres. The Shoshone had migrated out of Nevada in the 1600s, and the Arapahoe migrated from Minnesota around the same time. Why they chose to migrate at that time is a subject relevant to this book, but must be held for another time. His father's first veterinary practice with his freshly minted DVM brought Ripley's family to the sleepy town on the edge of the hot springs that gave the county its name. It was a symbolic beginning for someone that would be drawn to cultural boundaries and the complexities of interconnecting networks for the rest of his life.

However, Ripley spent most of his formative years in Colorado, a state at the time with only a 4.1% non-White population, mainly comprised of Latino, African American, and Native tribes. As such, during most of Ripley's upbringing he was a member of the majority population, operating in his first language, and unknowingly speaking from the dominant ethnic and cultural perspective. But that did not mean that Ripley was completely ignorant of the diversity that comprised his somewhat homogeneous hometown. Because Ripley came from a large family with a modest income, he was given the option of taking piano lessons or playing an affordable sport. As a young fourth grader he chose to play soccer. And it was a choice that shaped his friendship network for the rest of his life. The "beautiful game" exposed him to the beautiful world of languages, cultures, and worldviews. His diverse set of friends with more recent immigrant experiences and multilingual homes showed Ripley that boundaries did not have to be threatening, and in fact, could be really interesting and rewarding.

Unfortunately, cultural boundaries have had a less positive interpretation throughout most of human history…

A Warrant for Intercultural Understanding

One of the earliest preserved written records of intercultural interaction is captured in Homer's epic 8th century BCE poem, the *Odyssey*. It tells of the ten-year perilous journey Odysseus, king of Ithaca, endured on his way home from the Trojan War. While most scholars believe the story is a mix of fact and fiction, there is enough corresponding astronomical and archaeological evidence to substantiate at least partial historical validity of the tale (Borderwich, 2006). What the poem represents, though, in both myth and reality. is the way in which unfamiliar lands and peoples are often thought of and portrayed in the minds and narratives of those who encounter them. Unfortunately, the *Odyssey's* depiction of interaction with those who were considered foreign, or the "other," is all too common in the earliest records of historical narratives, journals of bygone explorers and trade expeditions, and even in some past anthropological writings. Unfamiliar people groups and cultures have been characterised as strange, threatening, inferior, or backward (uncivilised). It is no wonder, then, that from the beginning of recorded history, in civilisations around the world, the annals of intergroup interaction are marked by suspicion, misunderstanding, colonialism, and conflict.

Unfortunately, one of the reasons we need a book like this is that rather than recognising the dignity of fellow humanity and the value of diversity, the human race has a long history of oppressing and annihilating "foreign" people groups while seeking land, accolades, and riches.[1] This pattern of fear and inhumane behaviour operates on macro and micro levels, with fault lines involving ethnicity, race, religion, land, and language. Even today, it breeds a kind of hostility that affects national borders, corporate boardrooms, and local beer halls. One of the questions that must be asked is, why is the history of intercultural interaction filled with more conquest than collaboration and co-existence?

Isolation Is Not an Option

At the time when this book is being written, the International Organization for Migration (IOM) estimates that there are 281 million people currently living outside the country of their birth; this figure does not include the estimated 48 million internally displaced people around the world. That is roughly 3.6% of the entire global population (UNHCR, 2022). And the trend is increasing, having grown by 45% since 1990 (IOM, 2022). If the significant religious diaspora of the 20th century is factored in, the number of migrants increases to 12.5% of the world's population, or 859 million people from 327 different ethnic groups (Johnson & Bellofatto, 2012).

Globally, workplaces and neighbourhoods are increasingly multilingual, multifaith, and multicultural. In Ripley's immediate neighbourhood, there are eight Euro-American families, two multi-generational families that immigrated from India, a multi-generational Lao family, a Hmong family, and a family that immigrated from Lebanon. That means Ripley's suburban neighbourhood in a large metropolitan city reflects 38% people of foreign birth or recent immigrant heritage, compared to the average of 8% in the suburban neighbourhood of his youth.

The reasons for migration are varied, but recent data show that 164 million of the current migrants are motivated by seeking work outside their country of origin and 35.3 million people are refugees that have been forcibly displaced. Over the past 20 years, migration has increased by 74% in Asia (approximately 37 million people), and 52.3% in Europe. In North America migration has surged by 45.2%, or about 18.3 million people (UNHCR, 2022). Of course, things like population density and migration only tell part of the story. People move about because they can, and sometimes, because they have to.

One explanation for the surge in migration is the development of sophisticated transportation systems. Moving about the globe has become easier, safer, and relatively less expensive over time. Within the last 20 years, airline passenger traffic has experienced 2.3 times growth (Burgueño Salas, 2022). Compare the ease of international travel today with that of the 18th century. Immediately after the US colonies won the war of independence from Great Britain, Benjamin Franklin, who had just turned 70, was appointed ambassador to France and tasked with negotiating a formal alliance with the government that secretly supported the US during the war. Unfortunately for Franklin, depending on the weather conditions, the trip from Philadelphia to Paris took between six and eight weeks. Today, a direct flight from Philadelphia to Paris takes six to eight hours.

Mobility is not confined to transportation these days – when the iPhone debuted in 2007, "mobile" took on a whole new level of connection and "distance" evaporated into digital proximity. In the short 15+ years since that time the proliferation of apps that provide global interconnectivity is astonishing. A quick survey of communication channels that pave the way for international friendships and conversation includes WhatsApp, WeChat, Facebook, Snapchat, Instagram, TikTok, Messenger, Youtube, Twitter, LinkedIn, Sina Weibo (China), Renren (China's answer to Facebook), Qzone (Tencent QQ), Vkontakte (Russia), Orkut (Brazil), Taringa! (Latin America), Netlog (Europe), hi5 (Southeast Asia), mixi (Japan), Ibibo (India), and Cyworld (South Korea). Add to these mobile devices in-text translation, downloadable maps, direction assistance, digital payments, and transportation ticketing, and it equals the removal of a great deal of uncertainty in international excursions.

On top of all of those features, or better, underlying all of those features, is the decentralisation that digital interfaces introduce. They help us to bridge geographic barriers in order to capitalise on shared interests, redefining proximity in the process. Digital technologies enable any-to-any contact and promise a more direct, less formal platform for meeting people where relationships can develop very quickly around a narrow subject area, resulting in restricted intimacies. But while mobile devices and the internet have ushered in McLuhan's (1962) *Global Village*, they have also exposed existing racial, social class, and cultural disparities via phenomena like digital divides (Quan-Haase, 2020).

A final, and some might argue primary, cause of a more interconnected world is globalisation. Economic trade has long been a motivation to preserve harmony between nations and people groups. Take a moment and check the labels and tags on the products you are using and wearing right now. The tags will say something like "made in" or "hecho en." Chances are, the material world around you reflects a constellation of products manufactured around the world, and none of that would be possible without globalisation. Most of us are blind to the degree to which we are connected to, and dependent upon, goods and services that originate from other parts of the world. As technology and transportation have made markets more accessible, trade interdependencies have expanded to include an entire network of goods, services, and personnel, foreign direct investment, tourism, political treaties and trade agreements, and access to media channels. The entire process "erodes national boundaries, integrates national economies, cultures, technologies and governance, and produces complex relations of mutual interdependence" (Gygli et al., 2019, p. 546).

But despite there being solid evidence in support of globalisation, certain geopolitical trends disrupt these kinds of partnerships. During the US Trump administration, protectionist policies were put in place that jeopardised longstanding trade relationships and fuelled tariff wars. Likewise, the United Kingdom's "Brexit" from the European Union suggests an era of globalisation with isolationist implications (Gygli et al., 2019).

In the waning years of the 20th century, one that witnessed two global wars, two significant multinational wars in Southeast Asia, and countless inter-state and intra-state conflicts, there had been a short-lived period of relative peace and stability. There was a tacit international agreement around hegemonic regions and a resigned submission to a unipolar world with one remaining global superpower (Kupchan, 2003). Amidst that brief pause in global hostilities, a theory emerged that idealised the advantages of economic integration. As related by author Thomas Friedman (2000), the argument held that if nations became so economically entangled, they wouldn't be willing to risk the fallout of war on their GDP bottom lines. The thesis acquired a metaphor to the effect of "No two countries that both have a McDonald's have ever fought a war against each other" (Musgrave, 2020). The thesis would obviously have to be revised given the 2022 Ukraine war. But even if Friedman didn't get it exactly right, economic integration is undoubtedly a disincentive to international disputes. Hence, movements towards isolationism are taking us in the wrong direction.

For reasons that will become clear in these pages, we often fail to appreciate and leverage the advantages human diversity has to offer. The process of understanding others is often resisted by something deep in our psycho-social system (Hanvey, 1979). Instead, a human tendency observed over millennia is *xenophobia*, or a fear of people who are different from ourselves. The word "xénos" is a Greek term that refers to someone that is foreign or alien, and it is typically applied to people that are from a different country than one's own. And of course, the word "phobia" derives from the Greek word for "fear." Together, the word betrays a condition that is hidden deep in our human nature that is often difficult to confront, but it also serves as a motivation for the important work we do in the field of intercultural communication.

The critical issue confronting the world today is not how to prevent nuclear war, or how to address migration crises from catastrophic events or conflict. Neither is it how to restructure debt-ridden and failing economies, or even how to slow global warming before coastal cities are flooded and prime cropland is ruined by desertification. No, all of these admittedly dire problems are secondary to, if not dependent upon, solving an even more pressing need. The singular crisis of our times, from local communities to global entities, is how to communicate effectively and appropriately across cultural differences. With each crisis, each conflict, each passing year of elusive peace, the urgency of this task is heightened. Never before has there been such a need. By the same token, never before has there been such an opportunity for intercultural understanding, cooperation, and collective action. The key to solving the previously mentioned problems is finding a way to build trust, respect, and empathy so that we can create cooperative relationships across local, regional, ethnic, cultural, political, and ideological borders.

History of the Discipline

Tracing the origins of any idea or field of study is never straightforward. Ideas, like people, are derived from long histories of family lineages that combine and evolve over time to become what we encounter them as today. As Leeds-Hurwitz (personal communication) points out, "Documenting the history of a research tradition is the way to stop and examine why we study the topics we do, and in the ways we take for granted." In other words, we recall historical origins to understand our motivations and the assumptions we bring to the table. One assumption we should address at the outset is the existence of this thing we're calling culture.

Human beings are not unique in that we live in community, but we *are* distinctly society-builders. French sociologist Émile Durkheim (1961) argued that society is that which makes a person:

> That which makes a man is the totality of the intellectual property which constitutes civilization, and civilization is the work of society… from the moment when it is recognized that above the individual there is society, and that this is not a nominal being created by reason, but a system of active forces, a new manner of explaining men becomes possible. (pp. 465, 495)

This understanding that society precedes the individual goes at least as far back as Aristotle, who observed, "Anyone who either cannot lead the common life or is so self-sufficient as not to need to, and therefore does not partake of society, is either a beast or a god" (Aristotle, 1998, bk.1, 1253a 27–29). We think it can be safely concluded that since we are by nature social creatures, when we agree to live in community, we adopt a common moral matrix, which we call culture (Haidt, 2012).[2]

To set the stage for our historical journey, imagine a time before mechanised transportation and electronic communication. Prior to the inventions of steam powered locomotion in 1804, the steamboat in 1807, automobiles in 1886, and motorised human flight in 1903, travelling to another place in the world was a labour- and time-intensive process, dependent on walking or beasts of burden. Likewise, communication between communities was tied to those slow, laborious forms of transportation prior to the invention of the telegraph (1753/1837[3]), known as the first technology that made communication independent of transportation. Pause for a moment and reflect on the relatively brief period in which it has become "easy" to travel and/ communicate with distant peoples and lands.

In contrast, humankind spent millennia dealing with barriers to communication and difficult boundaries between distinct people groups. What that meant for the people living during the barriers and boundaries age in our earlier story about Odysseus is that much of what we knew about people outside of our own community was based on the observations and interactions of a very limited number of people who brought those experiences and stories back home. Often these were early explorers, military personnel, trade merchants, missionaries, and later academic anthropologists, linguists, novelists, etc. Put in scientific terms, what we knew about people outside of our own communities had been constructed based upon a very small sample size, for millennia!

Setting aside the sample size issue for the time being, consider also the human proclivity for sensationalism. We love a good story. We are also prone to social categorisation and in-group/out-group biases (more on both of those subjects later). When added together, limited sample size, in-group bias, and exaggeration creates the perfect storm for stereotypes, prejudice, and discrimination. The field of intercultural communication's work in offsetting millennia of xenophobia build-up has a shorter history, one which we will explore next.

Lead Up to Intercultural Communication

Less than 40 years after its war for independence, the United States had to once again rebuff British intrusions upon US sovereignty resulting in the war of 1812. Ongoing European involvements in North, Central, and South America were also forcing the nascent republic to increasingly assert its authority and "jurisdictional sovereignty" in its relative sphere of influence in order to "preserve peace and security." Those socio-political and economic environmental factors eventually triggered then President James Monroe's famous international relations doctrine on December 2, 1823 that bears his name. In what became known as the "Monroe Doctrine," the United States officially asserted itself as a global power with hegemony over the Western Hemisphere.

That move from colonial picayune to international hegemony was a result of gradual territorial expansion, economic and political engagement, and growing military influence. It is a familiar pattern that global empires have traced for centuries (Chua, 2007). In the case of the US, the Monroe Doctrine is indicative of the nation's hesitancy to become entangled in international disputes that did not directly impact the country and led to years of pseudo isolationism. That international introversion is also not uncommon, and one of the consequences was a national norm of ethnocentrism, xenophobia, and cultural ignorance despite nearly two centuries of unrestricted immigration from 1621 to 1864 when the US Immigration Bureau was established (Smith, 2016).

Within that era of growing US international relations, it became clear that the US needed a system that trained career diplomats (Melosi, 1971). The US Department of State (DOS) sought to professionalise the training of foreign diplomats, forming an institute originally called the Wilson Diplomatic School (1909). The Wilson Diplomatic School eventually morphed into The Foreign Service School in 1924, then, The Foreign Service Officer's Training School in 1931, followed by The Division of Training Services in 1945. But despite the fairly long history of diplomatic training schools, DOS personnel were still woefully ignorant and lacking when it came to geography, international political systems, macroeconomics, and most glaringly, proficiency in a second language. This quickly became apparent after the Second World War when the United States gained even more influence in global politics. It was only then, following the passage of the Foreign Service Act in 1946, that the current US Foreign Service Institute (FSI) was established in 1947 (Honley, 2017; Leeds-Hurwitz, 1990). The FSI was tasked with preparing DOS employees for service in international settings, complete with foreign language proficiency and cultural competence.

Here is the point of this lengthy historical backdrop. One of the early trainers at the FSI was an anthropologist named Edward T. Hall. It was Hall's experience training international diplomats and foreign service employees that led to the publication of his 1959 book titled *The Silent Language*, in which he articulated a theory of culture that treated it "in its entirety as a form of communication" (p. 28). Hall's approach "to understand the 'out-of-awareness' aspects of communication" (p. 29) birthed the field of intercultural communication (Leeds-Hurwitz, 1990). What he represented was a fusion of academic training in human observation and culture, multicultural life experience, and a desire to solve real-world problems; and he became the first of many to call themselves *interculturalists* (see "Born Intercultural," Professor Wendy Leeds-Hurwitz's story, and "The Mystery and Hopefulness of Intercultural Relations," Professor Dharm Bhawuk's story, later in this chapter).

Disciplinary Contributors

Many academic disciplines have taken up the mission of explaining how and why cultures differ from one another, and, in fact, why humankind has cultures at all. Anthropology, sociolinguistics, communication studies, sociology, migration studies, and cross-cultural psychology all offer unique methodological and theoretical approaches to explaining the causes and consequences of socio-cultural shifts and divides. What each of those disciplines share in common is a curiosity about how humans live in, and across, communities. Where they differ is in the kinds of questions they ask and the vantage point from which they ask them.

Each of the aforementioned disciplines also approaches the study of culture and intercultural relations from a distinct set of methodological and theoretical assumptions. To understand those assumptions, we need to be clear that there is a difference between a person with lived experience of something (a particular cultural upbringing for example), a person who has learned something, and a person who is an expert in that same something. The person with lived experience has an authentic, but experientially limited perspective. The one who has acquired knowledge apart from lived experience might have a theoretical grasp, but is missing the nuances of how actual practice diverges from theoretical concepts. And the expert's perspective will differ from both the lived and learned perspectives in that it analyses structures, systems, and patterns that form a grammar of abstractions that relate particulars to universals across communities. What follows is a short introduction to the various disciplines that have emerged over time to investigate intercultural relations from these various perspectives, and in turn, informed our study of intercultural communication.

Anthropology

One of the oldest disciplines to investigate different cultures is anthropology. This is the discipline that first authored our foundational assumptions by viewing the active creation of civilisation and cultures as distinctively human. Cultural anthropologists traditionally enter into a community as a multi-year resident to gain an *emic* understanding in order to identify the significant features of that culture.[4] Then, through analysis they reduce the complexity of the culture into underlying forms and systems, in a sense exposing the hidden patterns that operate and may offer points of comparison to other regional or even global cultures. Anthropologists are interested in the meaning of social behaviour from the perspective of the local community.

An argument can be made that anthropologists didn't fully embrace the concept of culture as "separability of societies" until Ruth Benedict's 1934 *Patterns of Culture*. Anthropology's connection to the origins of intercultural communication lay in the relationship of Benedict to her mentor, and that mentor's relationship to Edward T. Hall, whom we mentioned earlier. Benedict was a protégé of American anthropologist Franz Boas, who embraced a distinct methodology, and whom Hall (1966) credited with laying "the foundation of the view which I hold that communication constitutes the core of culture and indeed of life itself" (p. 1). One of the ideas Hall gleaned from Boas was the notion that cultures should be understood in their own terms, or *emic-ally*. Part of Hall's innovation was that an assisting *etic* category should be juxtaposed to help bridge our understanding of dissimilar values and behaviours. Certainly, any attempt to understand another culture using an imposed framework was considered *ethnocentric*. But looking for patterns among cultures was not the same as assuming there was a universal hierarchy of traits and features on which cultures could be ranked as early anthropologists believed. This insight dramatically affected the field of intercultural communication as it embraced *cultural relativism* as an approach to learning about distinct cultures (Bennett, 2010).

Several underlying assumptions adhered to in intercultural communication can be traced back to the field of anthropology. One is that symbolic reality exists on two levels, the instrumental and the expressive. Cultural values and behaviour are enacted both in order to achieve results (cause) and to simply "say" something. In other words, there is a reality to which people simply respond and with which they have a somewhat objective relationship. But there is also a reality of ritual which is purely expressive. For example, take the simple act of recycling plastics. If you are committed to a sustainable environment, when you finish a bottle of water, you would probably dispose of the bottle in a distinct recycling bin as opposed to just throwing it away where it will end up in a landfill somewhere. That act of recycling is both instrumental (functional) in its end result *and* you are saying something through your ritual, that you are committed to a sustainable environment, or what Smith (1992) called *life consciousness*. There is both a social consequence to the action and an intrinsic meaning that cannot be measured or examined for effectiveness in the same way.

A second assumption related to anthropology that has informed intercultural communication is the asymmetry between cultures. This means that culture A and culture B have worldviews that are incommensurate on various levels, whether linguistically, ontologically, epistemologically, and certainly axiologically. What this means in practice is that a given culture must be understood in its own terms, not through the cultural filter of an outside perspective. It prioritises indigenous, emic understanding. This perspective complicates our goal of growing in intercultural competence once it is understood that even members of a culture themselves often practise behaviours that have latent, or out-of-awareness meanings. In other words, how are we to understand a culture that may or may not even understand itself entirely! As we shall explore later, in order to merge mental models with another culture, one has to move beyond empathy and approach a level of *transpection* wherein you can feel *with* a culture as an active participant (Hanvey, 1979).

Linguistics

Early approaches to culture training at the FSI were developed by anthropologists alongside trained linguists, who were themselves innovating a new language learning curriculum seen as the cornerstone of engaging myriad cultural systems. In the early 1940s the field of linguistics was viewed as one of the more scientifically rigorous social sciences (Leeds-Hurwitz, 1990). Specifically, as it relates to the field of intercultural communication, when we talk about linguistics, we're really referring to the field of *sociolinguistics*, or the sociology of language (Penalosa, 1981). If culture is the bond we share with a community via beliefs, values, and customs (behavioural norms), then we do the sharing part through communication. And when you drill down to the mechanics of communication as it relates to meaning-making and culture, then functionally we are forced to discuss how language operates in that process.

Linguists' central focus is the process of human meaning-making. Language, while the object of linguists' study, is first and foremost the system whereby humans engage one another. But it is not merely a vehicle for relationship, it *is* the relationship. Because language is embedded in every aspect of life, both thought and behaviour, at least on the social plane it constitutes our lived socio-cultural reality (Trudgill, 1974). The historical scientific study of languages operates on several key assumptions about culture's relationship to language that the field of intercultural communication has adopted. Particularly:

- Humans are unique language users in that we can communicate abstract ideas and hypothesise about situations outside of our actual conditions or experience.
- Language is a rule-governed system.
- Language makes a difference. It is an instrument for both expression and action in tangible contexts (and it reflects culture within those settings).
- Language varies according to community boundaries, and groups within a culture emphasise their unity via a common language (solidarity function).
- Language creates social reality (constructivist perspective). Daily interactions create an intersubjective reality to which a group of people more or less subscribe.

These assumptions reflect the idea that "every language is… a special way of looking at the world and interpreting experience. Concealed in the structure of each different language are a whole set of unconscious assumptions about the world and life in it" (Kluckhohn, 1972, p. 109).

Sociolinguistics, then, looks at the interrelationship between language and its socio-cultural context. One rendering of this field is known as the *ethnography of communication*, and a prominent scholar in that stream, Donal Carbaugh (1990), frames sociolinguistic concerns nicely with these observations:

> That communication is everywhere "contested," locally designed, situationally managed, and individually applied; that cultural identity, at some times, on some occasions, has something to do with the nature of this patterning; that the meaningfulness of such patterns to participants is something always in need of discovery… (p. xvi)

It is not surprising that sociolinguistic and anthropological traditions share a common approach to investigating culture. A number of early anthropologists like Franz Boas (1911), Edward Sapir (1949), Margaret Mead (1930), Bronislaw Maliknowski (1956), and Gregory Bateson (1936) endorsed both a pragmatic view of language and a belief that a full description and understanding of culture without the study of language was not possible. Keep in mind that when these folks were studying a particular culture group, they were embedded in that culture for years at a time. During the era they were conducting their research, there were not clear-cut lines drawn around disciplinary subjects. So, if a given anthropologist was intrigued by language questions, she would dive into the situated data set and attempt to frame how that particular people group used language to create and maintain their society. They were laying the foundation for the investigation of meaning-making, with culture as a lens through which to view language (Bateson, 1972).

Cross-Cultural Psychology

While the fields of anthropology and sociolinguistics had the most direct influence on the formation of intercultural communication as a discipline, it is perhaps the field of cross-cultural psychology that has the strongest contemporary connection. At least in terms of the kinds of questions under investigation and theoretical perspectives employed.

A claim can be made that the first cross-cultural studies to appear in the psychological literature were in the early 1900s with the work of W. H. R. Rivers in England and Wilhelm Wundt in Germany (Berry, 1980). However, embracing culture fully as a variable of concern came relatively late to the field of psychology compared to the fields of anthropology or linguistics. It didn't really catch on until the early 1970s as evidenced by the flurry of attempts to define the field (Berry & Lonner, 1975; Brislin et al., 1973; Eckensberger, 1972; Triandis et al., 1971). And even then, recognition of culture's role in shaping human behaviour has been an evolving journey and a topic that has received more than a few calls for action from key scholars (Berry, 2013).

One of the rationales given for the emerging field was that, "if we are to understand the determinants of behaviour, we need to understand how culture influences it" (Triandis et al., 1971, p. 205). That critique was echoed years later, noting that "human behaviour is meaningful *only* when viewed in the sociocultural context in which it occurs" (Segall et al., 1998, p. 1101). Both statements were aimed at one of psychology's foremost goals, identifying universal human attributes.

Cross-cultural psychology challenged the long-held assumption of social psychology that the processes under investigation were universal, invariant across space, time, and cultures (Triandis et al., 1973). By testing psychological theories, propositions and hypotheses using cross-cultural methodologies, we could know with more certainty whether those theories were indeed universally valid statements about systematic relationships among variables (Berry, 1980, p. 5). The importance of striving for "pan-human validity" as a core goal of the field was echoed years later by Berry (Segall et al., 1998). It was perhaps that dual concern for explaining diversity (or variability) across samples alongside its attempt to find universals, or common denominators in human behaviour, that led the field to consider culture. In other words, to what extent is human behaviour and our understanding of it culture-bound? And, through what processes are we able to become more culturally aware and interculturally sensitive (Bhawuk & Brislin, 1992, 2000)?

That question reveals a distinctive feature of cross-cultural psychology in that it approaches culture as the context, or an antecedent variable, of individual behaviour (Segall et al., 1998). Lonner (2015) put it this way: "All sentient human behaviour is bounded by two powerful and towering masters: biology and culture; they are, at their highest level of abstraction and at all times, universal" (p. 808).

One implication of this perspective is the distinction between the internal versus the external. Whereas psychology's focus is on what goes on inside of interactants, communication observes what transpires *between* people. That difference alone sparks a world of distinct questions. Instead of investigating collectives like cultures and societies, the cross-cultural psychologist has traditionally trained her attention on the participants themselves (Beattie, 1984). Past distinctions, however, may not be as valid today since almost every intercultural scholar seeks to understand the interdependencies between participants and environment, the thinker within the context of social thought. Most intercultural researchers see "belief and action, values and social institutions [as] inextricably bound up with one another" (Beattie, 2004, p. 74).

Several other defining characteristics of cross-cultural psychology are its emphasis on the comparative method and its use of non-manipulative/non-intrusive (naturalistic) research designs. Berry (1980) highlighted the fact that while "most areas of psychological enquiry are defined by their *content*... cross-cultural psychology is defined primarily by its *method*" (p. 1). Those who were studying psychological variables across cultures were attempting to identify cause and effect relationships (or covariation) between independent variables (culture) and dependent (behavioural) variables.

But just like the debates that divided American and British social and cultural anthropologists regarding naturalistic, positivist comparative methodology versus a more humanistic, interpretive set of tools, an argument about what could be included in the definition of comparative studies, particularly comparative studies across cultures, separated close friends in psychology. As Berry (1980) pointed out, if it weren't for the fact that the word *comparative* had been restricted to the relatively narrow meaning of "phylogenetic comparison" (contrasting evolutionary diversification within a species) there might not be a field called *cross-cultural* psychology today. Instead, comparisons using culture as an independent variable would be just another subject within psychology writ large. Similarly, cross-cultural psychology also embraced a level of pragmatism that was not reflected in the broader discipline at the time (Segall et al., 1998).

The Mystery and Hopefulness of Intercultural Relations

Dharm Bhawuk

If you have some faith in the mysterious working of the universe you will actually love this story. Imagine you applied to the University of Minnesota, but you got accepted at the University of Wisconsin. You'd be like, but I didn't apply to Wisconsin. How on earth did an acceptance letter come to me? Well, for some unknown reason, the processing agency thought you were a better fit for an opportunity you didn't even apply for. And, what if serendipity knows that you will fit somewhere else, not where you thought you would fit. That's what happened to me.

I am from Nepal, and after completing a degree in mechanical engineering from the Indian Institute of Technology in Kharagpur, India (IIT), I had worked for the Royal Nepal Airlines Corporation (RNAC) training mechanics and pilots on aircraft systems, flight controls, hydraulic systems, etc. After a number of years in my career I began applying for Fulbright scholarships to continue my

studies in California, USA. I was interested in studying in California because
I had a brother living there. After submitting Fulbright applications for several
years in a row, I was completely surprised in 1987 to learn that I was selected
for the East-West Center scholarship at the University of Hawaii – a completely
separate programme from the Fulbright award. In fact, I learned about it when
the announcement was published in the local paper! When I spoke to the local
US Education Foundation director in Kathmandu, I said "I didn't apply to the
East-West Center; I want to study on the mainland where I have family." She
replied, "we thought you had a better shot at competing for the international
fellowship position in Hawaii, so we chose that for you." I ended up going
to Hawaii, although not without more than a little frustration. I did not know
anyone there really, except for a friend from engineering school, but I hadn't
seen him for ten years. That was only the first move serendipity would make.

While on the plane to Hawaii, I was sitting there reading the package from
the East-West Center and looking at the faculty list attached to the Culture
Learning Institute, perusing their biographies and areas of interest. And there,
in a brief announcement with a small picture, was something about Professor
Richard Brislin, who had a research interest in preparing managers for international assignments. Given my work at the RNAC I thought, "it would be
interesting for our airline since we send our managers abroad and interact
with people from other countries quite frequently." Upon arrival I learned
that I was pre-assigned to another advisor, Professor Gregory Trifonovitch.
Unfortunately, or serendipitously, he was not in town when I arrived. After
seeking permission to change advisors, I knocked on Brislin's door and said
"I'd like to work with you." He was very happy and immediately gave me a
copy of Geert Hofstede's book *Cultures Consequences* which had only been
out for a few years. I actually did end up developing a close relationship with
Trifonovitch as well, but Brislin's research programme set the course for my
academic career.

What struck me early on was how management practices in Nepal were
aberrations from the Western practices I had studied in my coursework at IIT.
My initial assessment was that we had lousy managers in Nepal who just didn't
do things right. But learning about culture provided me with a fresh perspective that management practices emerge in a cultural context, and often things
are not working because of culturally incongruent practices. Once I had that
insight, I did not look back; that was the transformational moment that I began
to solve problems from an ecological perspective. You have to find a culturally
appropriate way to manage in different ecological settings. It does not have to
be the Western way of doing things. So this was my motivation. I saw the relevance of cultural awareness and the consequences of culture.

One of the most wonderful things about working with Brislin during my
years at the East-West Center was the weekly seminar; we had a brown-bag
lunch seminar every Wednesday where we gathered to talk about culture. The
room was usually packed, 40 people or more. That fellowship to the East-
West Center and the serendipitous relationship with Richard Brislin led to my

30+ year career as a professor of management, culture, and community psychology. It resulted in our collaboration on the Individualism–Collectivism scale for measuring intercultural sensitivity, my work on leadership across culture groups, and cross-cultural training, and numerous books, chapters, and articles.

Sociology

As a field centred on social institutions, it is understandable that culture figured into the equation earlier in sociology than in some of the other disciplines we have discussed. Sociology is interested in social relations within society, but exclusively as it relates to social structures and how people organise themselves. Because its focus tends to be on the macro level, it examines larger institutions in contemporary and technologically advanced societies and the global effects of variables on those societies (like poverty, education, urbanisation, etc.). Culture is still comprised of the shared beliefs, values, and practices of people who constitute a society, but it is understood as something that is shaped by those larger structures and systems.

An important assumption in sociology is that societies are more than an aggregation of individuals; they are systems of interrelated parts, tiles in the mosaic, with certain distinguishing features and specific relationships (Beattie, 2004). From a sociological perspective, "actors and their actions are viewed as interdependent rather than independent, autonomous units" (Galaskiewicz & Wasserman, 1994, p. xiii). To understand them, we need to examine the form, function, and expression of the institutions within societies holistically, and as understood by the members themselves (again, this discipline endorses an emic understanding). Why focus on institutional features? Because culture is not something that an individual possesses in and of themselves. It is a product of community, groups of people that coalesce around a set of beliefs, values, and behavioural norms that eventually express themselves in institutions. Thus, culture will manifest itself in the formation of agreements that get "institutionalised" and therefore perpetuate the culture.

Prominent intercultural scholars like Bill Gudykunst and Young Y. Kim were influenced by important sociological thinkers like Georg Simmel and Daniel Lerner who emphasised the importance of form and context in human behaviour. These and other scholars from this tradition believe strongly that "well controlled thought and action are dependent on further structures, beyond the range of the actors' explicit knowledge and attention... the structures of the institutions and other social orders within which we must live and which are the creations of language, culture, and history" (Harre et al., 1985, p. 65). To fully explain an event or behaviour, then, requires an account of the way the components fit together, or are structured.

Communication Studies

Cohen (1994) refers to communication studies as a *derivative* discipline. That pretty well sums it up. If you look up the word "derivative," you will find synonyms including unoriginal, uninspired, and not innovative. But there is more to the story than just grifting off of concepts and theories from other disciplines. In order to understand the nuance of derivative status, it is helpful to understand its mathematical application. In the world of mathematics, a derivative is something that helps you predict and understand something else. For instance, if you wanted to know the position of a rocket at a given *time* in its flight path, you would figure it out using its derivative, *velocity*. A derivative in this sense is its own function which helps you predict something else. In its modern form, the discipline of communication has absorbed theories and concepts from many other fields of study, but it has done so by becoming its own function that is reciprocally used by those disciplines to predict and explain other variables.[5] In a series of articles, founding scholars in speech communication debated whether the discipline had a "distinctive mark which differentiates it from other disciplines," and even insisted that "the strength of the new discipline was based on its general nature... [it] could not be confined to a particular subject" (Cohen, 1994, p. 55). We bring this up because the origin and tradition of intercultural communication bears the hallmarks of its parent discipline.

As mentioned earlier, the genesis of *intercultural communication* is often attributed to anthropologist Edward T. Hall, beginning with his 1959 book *The Silent Language*. It was in that book that Hall first began to put forward his theory of cultural context and the notion that communication and culture are inseparable. Remember, the comparative method was in vogue in his discipline of anthropology at the time, but he noticed that his students at the FSI did not find those kinds of comparisons useful. So instead, he turned the focus to actual interactions between people of different backgrounds. The result was *intercultural* communication (Leeds-Hurwitz, 1990).

The redesign of Hall's FSI training material focused on what he called microcultural phenomena, like situational nonverbal behaviours and interaction styles, with the purpose of preparing students for cultural sensitisation and/or immersion. It set the tone for the kinds of research, analysis, and applications that are common in the field today (Leeds-Hurwitz, 1990). A sampling of common questions investigated includes the following: How do people adjust to new cultural environments? What attitudes and aptitudes are necessary to successfully bridge cultural differences during interaction? What conditions are necessary in order to promote satisfying intergroup contact? And what are the complexities of a multilingual, mixed heritage person's identity?

In the United States, intercultural communication as a discipline emerged from the Speech Communication Association (SCA), which broke off from the National Council of Teachers of English in 1914. The early voices of speech and rhetoric left an imprint on the discipline similar to Hall's anthropological roots. Speech was a "practical" skill, or *techne*, in Aristotle's terms. That genesis only added to the applied orientation of the field begun by Hall and his FSI colleagues. In the early 1970s the SCA approved a Commission on International and Intercultural Speech Communication at the request of a group of scholars that were cooperating with foreign universities and interested in exploring the effects of culture as it related to intergroup communication. From there, a flurry of books, graduate programmes, and research ensued. Many of the pioneers in intercultural relations were motivated by their own stories of migration, encounters with stereotypes and prejudice, or immersion in the benefits of multilingual, multicultural communities. In this book, we have attempted to share some of those stories with you by weaving their first-person narratives throughout the book. Together, those scholars forged a discipline that views understanding intercultural communication as a multi-step process (Gudykunst & Mody, 2002).

The first in the process is understanding that cross-cultural communication is a prerequisite to understanding intercultural communication. That means we must first understand cultural communication, which is the "role of communication in the creation and negotiation of shared identities" (Gudykunst, 2003, p. vii). Investigating cultural communication is most influenced by anthropology's emic approach as it seeks to understand communication practices from the insider's perspective. Then we must understand communication that originates within a particular culture in comparison to distinct cultural communication practices of other cultures. Again, this is the comparative step and clearly borrows from sister disciplines of anthropology and psychology. Finally, and this is what makes intercultural communication unique, the focus is placed on what takes place *between* people during an interaction. Those steps provide a methodological pathway towards intercultural understanding.

Two unifying elements present themselves in that multi-step process of intercultural understanding. First, symbolic exchange is at the core of communicative and cultural interaction. That is the insight that made Hall believe there was an implicit link between culture and communication. It originated from the symbolic nature of communication. All communication relies upon imbuing symbols with meaning through an encoding process. It is that symbolic element that is common to both communication and culture. It is not just that culture is perpetuated via communicative channels. Cultural features are *themselves* symbolic, meaning infused, ideas and actions. Most behaviour is both instrumental and expressive and can be understood as accomplishing something, or having consequences, as well as saying something (Beattie, 2004).

A second unifying element is that distinct symbolic systems are asymmetrical. All of the disciplines mentioned have in common the goal of explaining the tensions that result from cultural asymmetry and finding the pathways to mutual understanding. Because of its eclectic heritage, intercultural communication has been able to approach communication and culture from both a quantitative-reductionist-analytical paradigm (cross-cultural psychology, sociology, linguistics) and a qualitative-holistic-interpretive paradigm (anthropology). Hall (1959) concluded that "The idea of looking at culture as communication has been profitable in that it has raised problems which had not been thought of before and provided solutions which might not otherwise have been possible" (p. 102). He wasn't wrong. The fusion of disciplines ignited a hopeful pursuit of solutions to cultural misunderstanding, misattribution, maladaptation, and xenophobia.

Born Intercultural

Wendy Leeds-Hurwitz

The question here is: how did I choose to study intercultural communication? The short answer is that, really, the subject chose me. The questions of why I studied an aspect no one else was studying at that time and why I later focused on intercultural dialogue will become clear as my narrative unfolds.

I grew up in a multilingual, multicultural home. My mother was German, my father had Romanian parents, but was born in the USA; both sides of the family were Jewish, always a minority religion in the USA. My mother was fluent in German, Spanish, and English, and competent in French. My father's first language was English; he learned some Yiddish at home and was sent to Hebrew school; he learned French and German in college, and Italian and Russian while in the US army. I was seven before my mother noticed that I was not learning a second language in school, so she arranged private lessons. French was the language of culture for her, and so the obvious choice, and she knew that dialect mattered, thus a Parisian tutor. She saw little need for me to learn German, though I eventually took a course in college, learning enough to pass the mandatory language exams in both French and German in graduate school. I did attend Hebrew school for several years, where the focus was on reading, rather than speaking.

My father mostly used his languages to read widely, as his reading skills were far better than his speaking. During the Second World War, he translated documents from French, German, Italian, and Russian into English. I was born and raised in Indiana, where my mother made a few friends with whom she spoke German or Spanish. She was fluent enough that she didn't even notice when she code-switched. She once answered a question a stranger had asked someone else in Spanish, much to their astonishment, and said later she hadn't realised it wasn't English. My father was the director of what was then called a "home for the aged" sponsored by the Jewish community, where he led services for residents in Hebrew. At home, he would often introduce Yiddish into a conversation.

We moved to a suburb of Washington, DC when I was 9, the land of foreign embassies, so my parents' group of friends expanded to include embassy staff, as well as international visitors to the capitol. My experience of world cultures grew considerably, whether from interacting with the Argentinian family across the street, or the Israeli family whose children I tutored in English. When I broke a bone in my foot at age 12, friends of the family from India explained that I would have fewer problems if I got back to walking as quickly as possible, minimising my use of crutches, quite different advice from what I heard at the doctor's office. Friends in high school often had parents in the foreign service, and had lived in multiple countries as a result, even if they were American, bringing yet more international experiences and perspectives into conversations. It should come as no surprise that I chose International

House of Philadelphia as my dorm in graduate school, where the majority of residents, and thus many of my friends, were from other countries. I learned the most from those who came from countries still unknown to me, such as Iran or Pakistan.

As with most immigrant families, the foods that I grew up with directly reflected what my mother grew up eating, in either Germany or Cuba. The former led to a lot of innards, as well as lamb and veal; the latter led to fruits still uncommon in most homes in the USA in the 1960s, such as mangos. On the rare occasions that we ate out, we had our choice of international restaurants in DC.

Remembering family history was always highly valued. When my mother refused to memorise the 400 years of her family's time in Germany, for example, her grandfather wrote it all up as a book, printing enough copies to share with extended family, just to ensure the stories would not be forgotten. Decades later, as a graduate student, I worked with several professors who wrote disciplinary history themselves, and learned the value of documenting the history of a research tradition as a way to stop and examine why we study the topics we do, and in the ways we take for granted.

Much of what we typically teach within intercultural communication involves the recognition that there can be more than one way of organising a culture, and then going on to learn the ways in which others are both different from, and similar to, ourselves. There will always be multiple languages, traditions, foods, objects, clothing, health care, rituals, etc. This is something I never had to learn in school, since I had already learned it within my family. When I published a book on semiotics and culture, emphasising the ways in which people grant meaning to material culture (food, clothing, and objects), that was something I had first learned at home. When I published a book about how it was possible to combine different cultural rituals, such as weddings, that again was not something I had learned in school but at home. Later, comparing notes with a colleague on teaching our children family languages (Hebrew in my case, Chinese in his), I realised intercultural scholars had been ignoring the question of how cultural identity gets passed down through generations and decided it would be appropriate to spend time editing a book on the topic. Who we are, and what we learn at home, thus can be as important as what we learn in formal education contexts, or what we experience after we complete our formal education. Clearly formal education matters as well. And my later narrowing from intercultural communication understood broadly to intercultural dialogue specifically has been about building an international network of scholars willing to share what they know with the larger public.

So, what does my history imply for others? I would suggest three lessons. First, think about what you can learn from your family, friends, neighbours. Not everyone grows up in an intercultural context, but there are other ways to learn the value of interculturality. Intolerance, for example, demonstrates the value of tolerance. If what you experience is narrow or negative, look for the broader view, the positive inverse of that negative. Second, think about what you learn from teachers, as well as peers, in college and graduate school. Some of what they show you will be new and useful – hold on to that and build on it. Other times, you'll discover gaps in what is being taught, and these are places where you can fill in the gaps to expand the common knowledge base. This works across all topics: look to see what questions have not been asked and attempt to answer them. And third, think about how to apply and extend what you learn in formal education to the wider world.

Value Added: ROI in This Journey Through Intercultural Spaces

There is a general principle in investing that suggests in order for an investment to be successful you should expect some kind of return on your investment (ROI). In our busy lives if we elect to invest our time and attention in something, we should expect to get something in return. The underlying motivation that prompted you to look into intercultural communication will no doubt differ from others' motivations, but we can generate a few common ROIs if you commit to learning more about this topic. In fact, consider this our promise to you for the time you invest in journeying through intercultural spaces with us.

Preparation for Career

First, let's get the most pragmatic concern out of the way, unless of course you expect to eventually be independently wealthy – your career. Most of us want to know what the occupational pay-off will be from our effort. It's an important need, and fortunately yields substantial, concrete value from intercultural communication studies. From a professional standpoint, communicating entails an essential skill set that will affect whether you get the job, how well you do in your position, and how far you progress in your career. From the initial interview to making the big sale, your ability to present yourself, convey ideas effectively in a multicultural setting, relate well with your co-workers regardless of ethnic or cultural background, motivate and engage diverse clients, and a host of other communication issues dominate the professional environment. As Arasaratnam-Smith (2020) observed, in an increasingly diverse world, the ability to communicate effectively and appropriately across cultural differences is a marketable skill, no matter your area of technical expertise. In this book we will focus on developing skills that contribute to intercultural competency, such as empathy, active listening, positive attitude towards diversity, etc. that will prepare you for living and working in diverse communities.

Preparation for Relationships

A second need most of us have is more personal – getting along with others. Intercultural trainer Patty Lane (2002) observed that most people living in the tension of cultural conflict are "searching for successful ways to live and work together," they just don't know how to do it (p. 14). A significant by-product of studying intercultural communication is a two-dimensional improvement in our relating habits. The first dimension pertains to our level of self-awareness. Time spent exploring other cultures and ways of being opens the door to understanding our own cultural identity and implicit biases (Arasaratnam-Smith, 2020). As we understand ourselves more completely, it paves the way for the second dimension of our relationships: empathy. Empathy is a relational behaviour and has little to do with your personality. Psychologist and author Alan McGinnis (2004) noted that we are all endowed with personalities that are fairly static throughout our lives, but we can develop relational skills that improve our ability to bridge cultural gaps, build rapport, and enhance collaboration potential. We can all cultivate these habits over time, even if we have negative habits to overcome. As McGinnis said, it's not about changing *who* you are, but changing *how* you are. The ROI of overcoming toxic cultural attitudes and behaviour is perhaps the most difficult investment, but offers the greatest potential return, of our journey.

Preparation for a Broader Outlook

A third value added is one of perspective. We all possess sets of biases which affect how we see particular situations and interpret various circumstances. Through exploring features of intercultural communication you can avail yourself of alternative perspectives. For example, a classic area of study within intercultural communication dealing with perception is attribution theory (Heider, 1958). It is estimated that most of the cross-cultural conflict we encounter is a result of misattribution. When we make an attribution, we offer an explanation to ourselves for why something happened. In essence, we provide (attribute) meaning to the situation. In any given situation, we can assign cause to the people involved, the environmental circumstances involved, or the particular relationship(s) involved. Our tendency to assign cause to one feature over another constitutes our bias. The value of accessing alternative perspectives is not only relevant to interpersonal attributions in diverse settings, but contributes to the broader development of a global mindset. We won't offer you freedom from your biases, but we will promise you the means to step outside of them and view them from alternative vantage points.

Take It to the Bank

These are just a few of the returns you can expect on your investment in the study of intercultural communication. Because communicating is so central to our personal and professional lives, its applications are endless. A bonus is that the skills, attitudes, and motivations you will acquire are not just applicable to one setting or cultural environment. That's the exceptional thing about the approach offered in this book – it's what we call "culture-general" learning. No matter what your particular setting, the principles and concepts we will explore will enhance your ability to interact with, adjust to, and enjoy the people and contexts around you. We hope it awakens a sense of curiosity and adventure to explore unfamiliar places and people groups. As you grow more expert in the particular skills required for a specific environment, those skills in turn feedback on and enhance the culture-general skills that will translate into more adaptability to new, future socio-cultural settings. Whether you take your newly acquired knowledge and skill base into for-profit work, volunteer arenas, or home life, you will be enriched and enriching others in the process; your ROI in that case is as great as what you're willing to invest!

In this chapter we have invited you to begin your quest to develop intercultural competence by providing you with a glimpse into the increasingly multicultural environments in which you will likely live and work due to globalisation, advancements in technology and transportation, and exponential growth in human migration. We close this chapter with an idea that Dr Martin Luther King, Jr shared with an audience at Cornell College in Mt Vernon, IA on October 15, 1962, during the height of the US Civil Rights movement. Dr King said, "I am convinced that men hate each other because they fear each other. They fear each other because they don't know each other, and they don't know each other because they don't communicate with each other, and they don't communicate with each other because they are separated from each other."

In Conversation: Intercultural Scholarship

Lily: We've been talking about the origin of the field of intercultural communication and looking at stories of how some of the intercultural scholars got interested in the field. The answer to this question might be obvious, but why do you think the work we do as intercultural scholars is important?

Ripley: Well, as we mentioned at the beginning of the chapter, many of our global problems require collaborative solutions. And collaboration has often proven difficult across cultural lines.

Lily: So, you think the work we do has something to offer to facilitate better collaboration across cultural differences... I suppose that's implied. But let me ask you the question differently. Many of the scholars, although not all, who have influenced our thinking have their origins in Westernised contexts. That being the case, do you think our work has a built-in ethnocentric bias?

Ripley: Ah, now you've gotten to the rub (do you understand that idiom?). Yes, I am conscious of the fact that the vast majority of "literature" in our field is generated from Western perspectives and published in English. It absolutely runs the risk of biased thinking, but also hegemonic access. As someone who grew up in South Asia, but educated in the US, how do you receive/understand the potential ethnocentric perspectives in our field?

Lily: I think some of the conversations we have had in working together on this project have highlighted different aspects of our cultural differences as well as concepts that are perceived differently by us, such as words and phrases we use to describe things (like the conversation we have in Chapter 3 for instance). But the interesting thing to note is that a significant group of migrant and refugee people from other parts of the world have been educated in the West, like me. Our contributions, too, shape intercultural scholarship in whatever blended way we understand things.

Ripley: Yes, but couldn't that just be one more instance of imperialism? Sometimes people go along in order to get along. Were you ever agitated or frustrated by a persistent presentation of "facts" that just didn't correspond to the way you understood a subject from your heritage culture?

Lily: Sure! [laughs]. Actually, I do often come across situations where someone presents something as a fact when I know that it is "fact" from a certain (cultural) point of view. But I must be careful not to perpetuate ethnocentrism by bringing some of my own biases into the mix. What I have learnt in my own journey of studying intercultural communication is that recognising ethnocentrism in others or myself is one step of the process – the following, and important, step after that is to find a gracious way forward to course-correct without being judgemental in a way that impedes relationship.

Ripley: I appreciate your relational emphasis, that is not necessarily my first instinct as a Euro-American; but if ethnocentrism is endemic, then isn't all knowledge ethnocentric at a certain level? And, aren't you accommodating the dominant voice at the expense of your voice?

Questions for Reflection

1. How do you think Lily would answer that last question?
2. What are other implications of dominant languages and cultural perspectives for non-dominant voices?
3. Where do you see yourself placed in the spectrum of dominant to non-dominant in your society? How does this conversation relate to your experiences?
4. How does understanding the origins of the discipline of intercultural communication help you to understand its purpose, goals, and methods?

Notes

1 Certainly the histories as told by the conquerors and "explorers" offer a somewhat rose-coloured version of the tale, but in any dyadic encounter, there are at least two ways to understand an event.
2 Jonathan Haidt has a wonderful discussion of the difference between individual motivations and truly collective behaviour, or what he calls a shared moral matrix. As part of his argument he draws upon Emile Durkheim's idea of social sentiments that produce a collective effervescence that marks a community and serves to bond them together over time.
3 Like most technological inventions, the telegraph concept was being worked on by multiple scientists around the globe simultaneously. British inventors Cooke and Wheatstone filed a patent on one system in 1837, while American Samuel Morse obtained his patent in the same year. But almost one hundred years earlier in 1753, Scotsman Charles Marshall authored a paper outlining an electrostatic messaging system. Likewise, Swiss physicist Georges-Louis Le Sage built a functioning electric telegraph in his home as early as 1774.

4 The terms *emic* and *etic* are abbreviations from the words phon*emic* and phon*etic*. Someone who studies phonemics is interested in the meanings attributed to words, which requires an insider's understanding of a particular language. Whereas phonetics is the study of sounds contained within a given language, which can be ascertained even by an outsider's observations. Thus, an emic perspective is from within, whereas an etic perspective assumes an outsider's vantage point.

5 Cohen reminds us that the modern discipline of *speech communication* originated as a splinter organisation from the National Council of Teachers of English in 1914. There were 17 "dissidents" that weren't happy with the direction of speech education, so they broke off and formed their own association in order to "escape domination." Since they did not have any research tradition or training, they observed and borrowed from other disciplines (p. x). Of course, Cohen makes clear that the ancient origin of communication studies in the form of Aristotle's rhetoric was actually positioned at the centre of the academy, and instrumental to the effectiveness of all other disciplines.

References

Arasaratnam-Smith, L. A. (2020). Developing global graduates: Essentials and possibilities. *Research in Comparative and International Education, 15*(1), 20–26. https://doi.org/10.1177/1745499920901945

Aristotle. (1998). *Politics* (C. D. C. Reeve, Trans.). Hackett.

Bateson, G. (1936). *Naven: A survey of the problems suggested by a composite picture of the culture of a New Guinea tribe drawn from three points to view*. Stanford University Press.

Bateson, G. (1972). *Steps to an ecology of mind: Collected essays in anthropology, psychiatry, evolution, and epistemology*. University of Chicago Press.

Beattie, J. H. M. (1984). Objectivity and social anthropology. In S. C. Brown (Ed.), *Objectivity and cultural divergence* (pp. 1–20). Cambridge University Press.

Beattie, J. H. (2004). *Other cultures: Aims, methods and achievements in social anthropology*. Routledge. https://doi.org/https://doi.org/10.4324/9781315017648

Benedict, R. (1934). *Patterns of culture*. Houghton Mifflin Company.

Bennett, M. J. (2010). A short conceptual history of intercultural learning in study abroad. In W. Hoffa & S. Depaul (Eds.), *A history of US study abroad: 1965–present* (pp. 419–449). Forum on Education Abroad.

Berry, J. W. (1980). Introduction to methodology. In H. C. Triandis & J. W. Berry (Eds.), *Handbook of cross-cultural psychology: Methodology* (Vol. 2, pp. 1–28). Allyn and Bacon.

Berry, J. W. (2013). Global psychology. *South African Journal of Psychology, 43*(4), 391–401. https://doi.org/10.1177/0081246313504517

Berry, J. W., & Lonner, W. J. (1975). *Applied cross-cultural psychology*. Swets and Zeitlinger.

Bhawuk, D., & Brislin, R. (1992). The measurement of intercultural sensitivity using the concepts of individualism and collectivism. *International Journal of Intercultural Relations, 16*(4), 413–436. https://doi.org/10.1016/0147-1767(92)90031-O

Bhawuk, D., & Brislin, R. (2000). Cross-cultural training: A review. *Applied Psychology, 49*(1), 162–191. https://doi.org/10.1111/1464-0597.00009

Boas, F. (1911). *"Introduction" to the handbook of American Indian Languages*. Government Printing Office.

Borderwich, F. M. (2006). Odyssey's end? The search for ancient Ithaca. *Smithsonian Magazine*. www.smithsonianmag.com/history/odysseys-end-the-search-for-ancient-ithaca-112739669/

Brislin, R., Lonner, W. J., & Thorndike, R. (1973). *Cross-cultural research methods*. Wiley.

Burgueño Salas, E. (2022). *Global airline industry passengers*. Statista. www.statista.com/statistics/564717/airline-industry-passenger-traffic-globally/

Carbaugh, D. (Ed.) (1990). *Cultural communication and intercultural contact*. Lawrence Erlbaum.

Chua, A. (2007). *Day of empire: How hyperpowers rise to global dominance – and why they fall* (Vol. 1). Doubleday.

Cohen, H. (1994). *The history of speech communication: The emergence of a discipline, 1914–1945*. Speech Communication Association.

Durkheim, E. (1961). *The elementary forms of the religious life*. Collier Books.

Eckensberger, L. (1972). The necessity of a theory for the applied cross-cultural research. In L. J. C. Cronbach & P. J. D. Drenth (Eds.), *Mental tests and cultural adaptation* (pp. 99–107). Mouton.

Friedman, T. L. (2000). *The Lexus and the olive tree* (1st Anchor Books ed.). Anchor Books.

Galaskiewicz, J., & Wasserman, S. (1994). Introduction: Advances in the social and behavioral sciences from social network analysis. In S. Wasserman & J. Galaskiewicz (Eds.), *Advances in social network analysis* (pp. xi–xvii). Sage Publications.

Gudykunst, W. (Ed.). (2003). *Cross-cultural and intercultural communication*. Sage Publications.

Gudykunst, W., & Mody, B. (2002). *Handbook of international and intercultural communication* (2nd ed.). Sage Publications.

Gygli, S., Haelg, F., Potrafke, N., & Sturm, J.-E. (2019). The KOF Globalisation Index – revisited. *The Review of International Organizations*, *14*(3), 543–574. https://doi.org/10.1007/s11558-019-09344-2

Haidt, J. (2012). *The righteous mind: Why good people are divided by politics and religion*. Vintage Books.

Hall, E. T. (1959). *The silent language*. Doubleday & Company.

Hall, E. T. (1966). *The hidden dimension*. Doubleday & Company.

Hanvey, R. (1979). *Cross-cultural awareness: An attainable global perspective*. Global Perspectives in Education.

Harre, R., Clarke, D., & Decarlo, N. (1985). *Motives and mechanisms: An introduction to the psychology of action*. Methuen.

Heider, F. (1958). *The psychology of interpersonal relations*. Wiley.

Hofstede, G. (1984). *Culture's consequences*. Sage.

Honley, S. A. (2017). The Foreign Service Institute at 70: Recalling a proud history. *The Foreign Service Journal*. https://afsa.org/foreign-service-institute-70-recalling-proud-history

IOM. (2022). *World Migration Report*. International Organization for Migration. https://worldmigrationreport.iom.int/EN

Johnson, T. M., & Bellofatto, G. A. (2012). Migration, religious diasporas, and religious diversity: A global survey. *Mission Studies: Journal of the International Association for Mission Studies*, *29*(1), 3–22. https://doi.org/10.1163/157338312X637993

Kluckhohn, C. (1972). The gift of tongues. In L. Samovar & R. Porter (Eds.), *Intercultural communication: A reader* (pp. 101–114). Wadsworth.

Kupchan, C. (2003). *The end of the American era: US foreign policy and the geopolitics of the twenty-first century*. Vintage Books.

Leeds-Hurwitz, W. (1990). Notes in the history of intercultural communication: The Foreign Service Institute and the mandate for intercultural training. *Quarterly Journal of Speech*, *76*, 262–281.

Lane, P. (2002). *A beginner's guide to crossing cultures: Making friends in a multi-cultural world.* InterVarsity Press.

Lonner, W. J. (2015). Half a century of cross-cultural psychology: A grateful coda. *American Psychologist, 70*(8), 804–814. https://doi.org/10.1037/a0039454

Maliknowski, B. (1956). The problem of meaning in primitive language. In C. K. Ogden & I. A. Richards (Eds.), *The meaning of meaning: A study of the influence of language upon thought and of the science of symbolism* (pp. 296–336). Harcourt Brace.

McGinnis, A. (2004). *The friendship factor.* Augsburg Press.

McLuhan, M. (1962). *The Gutenberg galaxy: The making of typographic man.* McGraw-Hill.

Mead, M. (1930). *Growing up in New Guinea: A comparative study of primitive education.* William Morrow & Co.

Melosi, M. V. (1971). *American amateur diplomats during the administrations of Woodrow Wilson: An evaluation.* Publication Number 5192, University of Montana. https://scholarworks.umt.edu/etd/5192

Monroe, J. (1823). Message of President James Monroe at the commencement of the first session of the 18th Congress (The Monroe Doctrine). In US Senate (Ed.), *Presidential messages of the 18th Congress ca. 12/02/1823 – ca. 03/03/1825* (Vol. Record Group 46). National Archives: Records of the United States Senate 1789–1990.

Musgrave, P. (2020). The Beautiful, Dumb Dream of McDonald's Peace Theory. *Foreign Policy,* 26 November. https://foreignpolicy.com/2020/11/26/mcdonalds-peace-nagornok arabakh-friedman/

Penalosa, F. (1981). *Introduction to the sociology of language.* Newbury House Publishers.

Quan-Haase, A. (2020). *Technology and society: Social networks, power, and inequality* (3rd ed.). Oxford University Press.

Sapir, E. (1949). *Selected writings of Edward Sapir in culture, language, and personality.* University of California Press.

Segall, M. H., Lonner, W. J., & Berry, J. W. (1998). Cross-cultural psychology as a scholarly discipline: On the flowering of culture in behavioral research. *American Psychologist, 53*(10), 1101–1110. https://doi.org/10.1037/0003-066X.53.10.1101

Smith, L. R. (1992). Media-networking: An intercultural communication model for global management of socio-cultural change. In F. Korzenny, S. Ting-Toomey & E. Schiff (Ed.), *Mass media effects across cultures* (Vol. 16, pp. 201-228). Sage Publications.

Smith, L. R. (2016). Courageous compassion and the immigration crisis: A response to Barz, Darr, Lewis, & Ebertz. *Character and... courageous compassion, 2*(1), 78–94.

Triandis, H. C., Malpass, R. S., & Davidson, A. R. (1971). Cross-cultural psychology. *Biennial Review of Anthropology, 7,* 1–84.

Triandis, H. C., Malpass, R. S., & Davidson, A. R. (1973). Psychology and culture. *Annual Review of Psychology, 24*(1), 355. https://doi.org/10.1146/annurev.ps.24.020173.002035

Trudgill, P. (1974). *Sociolinguistics: An introduction to language and society.* Penguin Books.

UNHCR (The UN Refugee Agency). (2022). Figures at a glance. www.unhcr.org/en-us/figures-at-a-glance.html

3   Perception and Cultural Lenses

Lily once had to play mediator in a disagreement between colleagues. After she listened to one person's version of the events, she surmised, "So, you perceive that..." The colleague in question immediately corrected Lily, saying, "This isn't my *perception*. I'm telling you facts."

There is a long tradition in research of distinguishing between different kinds of reality. Natural or "objective" reality has been studied through scientific, or empirical, methods; social or "subjective" reality is often studied through interpretive, rhetorical, and other methods. Another way of framing this is to note that empirical methods attempt to address causal questions ("what variables contribute to fear of public speaking?"), interpretive methods ask questions about situated meanings ("what do we understand as fear?"), rhetorical methods ask questions about motive, and systems methods ask questions about the interaction between macro and micro levels.

Anderson (1996) identifies four types of empiricism – the study of reality through sensory data – namely, traditional, perceptual, constructive, and postmodern. Traditional empiricism engages with the natural world, assuming an objectiveness to reality that is not present to the same extent in other types of empiricism. Perceptual empiricism recognises a distinction between objective reality and one's interpretation of it; in other words, it recognises the potential for bias in the process of interpretation. Constructive empiricism acknowledges the role of subjectivity and construal in the very nature of the reality that is perceived. Postmodern empiricism not only acknowledges the subjective nature of reality, but also emphasises the contextual and temporal nature of reality such that what was real yesterday in a particular context is no longer real today. In critical approaches to research, social and power dynamics come into focus, particularly how power inequities influence social phenomena. Understanding the different approaches to empirical enquiry is essential to understanding the role of perception in communication.

Perception is the only mechanism through which we understand our reality, social or physical. Just as we perceive our physical surroundings through our bodily senses, we make meaning of our social reality through our cultural lenses. Our sense of sight tells us that our neighbour is wearing a black outfit, while our cultural values tell us whether the outfit is appropriate for the occasion or not.

DOI: 10.4324/9781003318415-4

Although the metaphor of cultural "lenses" is used here, it should not be seen as a static one. As we discussed in Chapter 1, we may elevate different parts of our cultural self in different circumstances.

There are many occasions in which we conflate physical and social realities – like Lily's colleague did, in the response to her comment about perception. Several conversations about identity (Macioce, 2018) also use this conflation by implying that a person's subjective reality ("my" reality) supersedes all other types of reality or even renders any other reality irrelevant. An example is when someone's own "lived experience" is used as counterevidence to contradict the finding of an empirical study or series of studies. Research might show that a particular disease is serious, but someone could say, "I had that disease, and I hardly felt anything. I don't believe it's serious at all." Anderson (1996) argues that subjectivity is both evoked and invoked:

> As invoked, it is called into place by the actions of other, the power of society, or the force of culture. The degree of anonymity in the evocation and the view of the imposed subjectivity as oppression separate the lines of thought that use evocation... Subjectivity can also be invoked in opportunistic attempts to position oneself... One's invocation is often coupled with a concomitant evocation of the other. (pp. 79–80)

People may evoke and invoke subjectivity for many reasons, but the point is that subjective reality plays a powerful role in the meaning-making processes in which we participate daily. As we discussed in Chapter 1, our cultural values and the influences of the various thought communities to which we belong (such as our discipline, our profession, faith, interests) also influence the way we see or perceive the world. Therefore, it is nearly impossible to talk about perception without talking about the cultural lenses through which we perceive things. In this chapter, we will discuss how we process and understand the world around us and how our (cultural) values and beliefs colour the way we engage with the world.

Perception

The process of perception involves selecting and interpreting the various stimuli that surround us (Arasaratnam, 2015). For example, on your way to class, you may pass the cafeteria, the library, park bench, and many other places, but you bypass these stimuli and only select the building in which your class is held and interpret it as relevant to your current destination. In this case, the process of selection and interpretation is influenced by your goal or what is "in focus" for you in that moment, and reflects an important figure-ground phenomenon relevant to intercultural communication (Bennett, 2013). The Gestalt school of psychology suggests that our socio-cultural lenses inform us about what stands out in any given situation and what fades into the background of obscurity.

Culture influences our perceptions in several other ways that mirror Gestalt principles. First, we often impose unseen frameworks over stimuli we perceive in our environment, similar to how the principle of closure works. That is, our socio-cultural conditioning trains our brains what to expect in certain situations, and we "fill in the gaps" using our cultural lenses. Second, we sometimes see things, or attribute meanings to objects and events that are not present. Similar to philosopher Alfred North Whitehead's fallacy of misplaced concreteness, the Gestalt principles of continuity and connectedness suggest that our minds tend to see discrete or abstract objects as connected or seamless wholes, just as when we interpret an image from a constellation of stars, like a bear or a hunter with a bow. The opposite is also true in that our cultural filters sometimes prevent us from seeing meaning that is present in a situation, because we are not attuned to picking out certain details as "relevant."

There have been several attempts to conceptualise the process of social perception (DiDonato et al., 2011; Kopytowska, 2016). One way to understand perception is by breaking the process into steps of *description, interpretation,* and *evaluation* (Wendt, 2009). For example, let's assume you come across two people speaking at a high volume to each other in a library. If you were to *describe* what's before you, the description might go something like this: two people, speaking at a volume that could be heard above all other sounds in the library, frowning at each other, gesticulating with their arms. You may *interpret* what you see and hear as, "they're having an argument." Your *evaluation* of the situation might be, "they're being rude" (disturbing the others in the library).

Description is the straightforward recounting of what our senses pick up (or is it? We will pick this up in Chapter 4). Often, however, we are not always aware of the description phase of perception because we quickly move to interpretation, in which our mind compares the data from the description with our past experiences and knowledge, and makes sense of what we're seeing/hearing. In other words, because our experience has taught us that when people argue they often raise their voices and frown and gesticulate, when we see those behaviours we interpret the collective behaviours as an "argument." Once we interpret that an argument is taking place in the library, we evaluate that this is inappropriate or rude behaviour, based on our existing knowledge of acceptable behaviour within a library. As you can imagine, our culture and the way we were brought up play a big role in what we see as appropriate or inappropriate behaviour, and how we interpret a situation.

De Lange et al. (2018) describe the process of perception, saying that humans "construct predictive models of themselves and their environments, allowing them to quickly and robustly make sense of incoming data" (p. 2). In other words, as we accumulate knowledge of our environment through experience, we become reliant on what we expect of a situation (more on this in Chapter 4). We antici-pate or predict what's happening in a given situation. Within the familiarity of our own (cultural) environment, it is easy to see how this process of perception works fairly efficiently. For instance, people who have grown up in countries where a Westernised version of Christmas is celebrated would not be confused by fairy lights, snowflakes, and reindeer figures appearing in shops and public places in November. These are immediately interpreted as "Christmas decorations" in our minds, based on the time of the year, and our past experience of seeing those lights appear regularly at "Christmastime." If, however, someone who grew up in the West travels to another country in which they see decorative lights appear in shop windows in April, they might not have an immediate interpretation of the meaning of those lights. They might need to ask a local person to find out what they mean, although, based on their experience of seeing lights during festival time, they may deduce that the lights mean a celebration or festival of some kind (e.g., decorative lights on Muslim homes during Ramadan).

Perception is influenced not only by cultural background, but also by language. There are many studies that explore how language influences the way we perceive the stimuli we receive from our senses (e.g. Li, 2022; Whorf, 1956). We mentioned earlier that perception involves comparing the input that we get from our senses with our past knowledge to interpret what's happening. That is, when we get new input from our senses, we try to recognise this input by comparing it to what we know. Lupyan et al. (2020) note, "to recognize is to categorize" (p. 2). We will discuss the significance of categorisation in the process of perception shortly, but the point to note here is that language is the tool we use to put things in categories. For example, unless we know the word "aqua," we would categorise "aqua" as "green" or "blue" or perhaps "greenish blue," still relying on the limitation of the words at our disposal to describe what we see. People who are mono-lingual arguably perceive the world within the limitations of the language to which they have access. People who speak more than one language have more tools at their disposal when it comes to categorising what they perceive (more on language in Chapter 4). In sum, our culture, our experiences, and the language(s) we speak influence our perception or our subjective reality, and in turn influence the way we communicate in intercultural spaces.

Symbolic Interaction

The importance of understanding perception and subjectivity in understanding communication is highlighted in the underlying assumptions of Symbolic Interaction Theory (SIT) (Blumer, 1969; Mead, 1934) which states that a person's behaviour towards others is shaped by the meaning others assign to that person, that meaning is co-created in interaction or communication, and that meaning is modified through a process of interpretation. In other words, in a culture that reveres a person with great wealth, that person might go through life as if she owned the city, because she knows that people would give her preferential treatment because she's rich, and the way she carries herself and how she talks to people reinforces that impression further. SIT says that our self-concept is developed through interaction with others, self-concept being a "relatively stable set of perceptions people hold about themselves" (West & Turner, 2004, p. 89). It is easy to see how the way others treat us influences the way we behave towards other people, and that in turn further shapes the way others behave towards us and how we see ourselves in relation to other people.

The implication of SIT on intercultural communication merits further discussion because there are cultural differences in the way we place social value on things. For example, some cultures value their elders such that being an older person means you automatically command respect from those who are younger. In such cultures, an elderly person would be used to receiving deference from others and this expectation of deference would shape her sense of self as someone who has inherent value in society due to the perceived wisdom she carries with age. If she moves to another culture in which ageing is not revered, she would experience the unsettling reality of being treated no differently to others, and perhaps even treated with impatience or indifference *because* she is elderly. She would need to adjust her self-concept in this new environment.

Similarly, another concept proposed by SIT is the concept of the *looking-glass self* which describes the sense of self we get based on how we think others see us, and how we feel about how we think others see us. For example, in a culture that equates physical fitness with attractiveness ("gym body"), a man who is carrying a few extra kilos around his middle might think others don't perceive him as attractive and might feel bad about himself because of that. That is an aspect of his looking-glass self. The looking-glass self is arguably unreliable in intercultural spaces. For example, if the man in the above example interacts with someone from a culture in which extra weight around the middle is a sign of wealth and success, the man's assumption that the other person sees him in an unfavourable light would be incorrect. Intercultural spaces provide us with opportunities to re-evaluate our self-concept and re-imagine how others see us.

To fully appreciate the range of cultural lenses at play in intercultural spaces, it is helpful to review some frameworks with which to understand culture. Although some scholars have proposed certain predictors of cultural patterns such as population size and geographical conditions, as we examine these frameworks, it is important to note that such frameworks are helpful tools for describing cultural behaviour, not prescribing behaviour. Such frameworks are generalisations derived from observations of behavioural patterns. As we mentioned before, it is inaccurate to apply a "mean" or indicative observation derived from a group of people to an individual. Generalised patterns may help us understand why people from certain cultural backgrounds behave a certain way, but they should not be used to predict someone's behaviour because that person is from a particular culture. Bearing that in mind, we will discuss some of the commonly known frameworks that help us understand how cultural values influence behaviour.

Basic Human Values

One of the earliest concepts to emerge in the social sciences as a focal point in the articulation of socio-cultural differences, as well as their evolution over time, is that of values. Cultural values are often put forward as the primary conceptual framework for explaining personal, group, organisational, and societal attitudes and behaviour and are thought to play a central role in various forms of social control (Parsons, 1951, 1978). Values can be defined as the desirable characteristics and goals of a culture. Some values pertain to terminal goals like living in harmony with others or having a sense of accomplishment; and other values are instrumental in helping you get to those ultimate values, such as being honest, cheerful, and working hard (Rokeach, 1973). Of course, not everyone within a given culture group subscribes to the set of common values with the same intensity, and some may even attribute a negative quality to values that others perceive as positive. Overall, however, cultures will reflect normative values and expectations. For example, in the United States, it is codified into national documents that people are equal individuals with God-given rights to life, liberty, and the pursuit of happiness and believed that these values are effectively preserved within institutions that ensure their freedom of expression and safety.

Schwartz's (1992) Theory of Basic Values emerged as a response to existing cultural values frameworks that were either exclusionary in the sense that they dichotomised cultural positions or they failed to capture the relational structure and range of factors necessary to describe cultural similarities *and* differences (e.g., Kluckhohn & Strodtbeck, 1961; Rokeach, 1973). Schwartz (1992) identified ten distinct types of values and described an underlying conflict/congruence structure with interrelationships between two primary axes: 1) self versus social focus; and, 2) conservation versus expansion/change. In Schwartz's (2012) scheme, contradictory or competing values are juxtaposed in a pie shape, while proximate values within the pie are more congruent and reflect a "continuum of related motivations" (p. 9). The ten universal values identified in more than 85 distinct cultures include self-direction, stimulation, hedonism, achievement, power, security, conformity/tradition, benevolence, and universalism (see Figure 3.1).

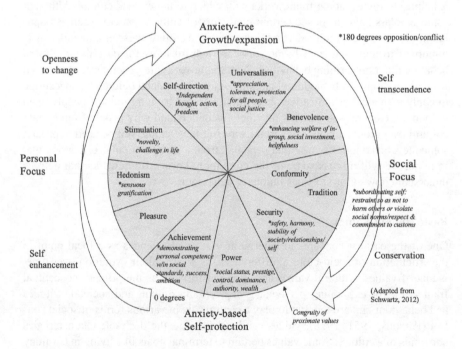

Figure 3.1 Schwartz Basic Values, adapted from Schwartz (2012).

Schwartz's theory posits that internal conflicts are an inherent part of value systems when they are expressed in actions. When a person holds a set of values, certain behaviours that are motivated by a particular value will produce consequences that conflict with other core values. Cultural differences emerge in how separate groups prioritise the ten values and deal with the cognitive dissonance produced by that dynamic tension (Bilsky et al., 2011; Schwartz, 2011; Vauclair et al., 2011). Studies have shown that benevolence, universalism, and self-direction are the most important values across numerous samples while power and stimulation are the least important (Schwartz, 2012).

Dimensions of Culture

One of the well-known frameworks with which to understand culture is commonly known as Hofstede's (1984, 1991) dimensions of cultural variability, although many researchers have contributed to our current knowledge of these dimensions. Based on research within corporate culture in 53 countries and three additional global regions, Hofstede proposed that there are certain discernible cultural patterns or dimensions, each operating as a continuum along which countries fall in their orientation towards that dimension. The initial dimensions identified by Hofstede's research are power distance, individualism, masculinity, uncertainty avoidance, and long-term orientation (see Figure 3.2 for an example country comparison).

Power distance is a culture's orientation towards how social power, particularly power based on position or institutional role, is distributed in society. Cultures that fall towards the higher end of the power distance spectrum are ones in which unequal distribution of social power is accepted and "normal" whereas cultures oriented towards low power distance exhibit more evenly distributed power amongst its members. Examples of high power distance values in social behaviour are addressing people by their title (instead of first name), attention to social hierarchy, and showing deference to people in perceived positions of authority. Higher power distance has been demonstrated to be correlated with collectivism (Ghosh, 2011). Cultures high in power distance also seem to respond better to benevolent paternalistic types of leadership (e.g., Islam et al., 2022).

Individualism is a culture's orientation towards autonomy and individual agency. At the opposite end of the spectrum is collectivism which values harmony, obligation, and the collective good above individual agency. Examples of individualism can be seen in parenting behaviour, for instance, where parents in individualistic cultures encourage children to think for themselves, work towards financial independence, and forge their own path, whereas parents in collectivistic cultures encourage children to defer to parents/elders for decision-making and work towards contributing to the collective wellbeing of the family, even at the expense of one's own personal preferences or goals (Triandis, 2001). Despite its critics (Voronov & Singer, 2002), individualism/collectivism is a framework that has been widely used in research to understand cultural behaviour (Lomas et al., 2023; Na et al., 2021; Wang & Lou, 2022).

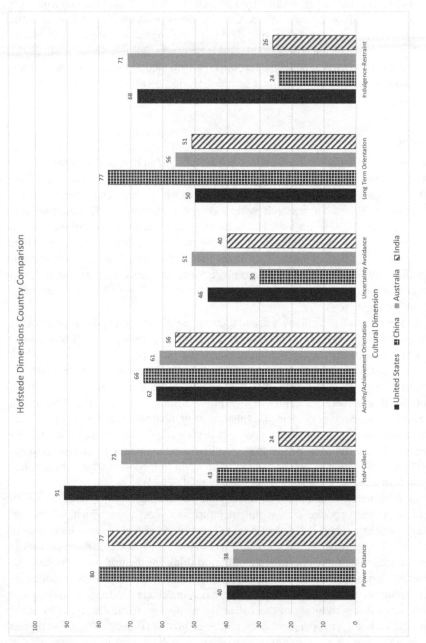

Figure 3.2 Hofstede Cultural Dimension Comparison, adapted from Minkov and Kaasa (2022).

Masculinity refers to the distribution of sex roles within a culture where there are clearly defined roles and an orientation towards behavioural traits that Hofstede found were overwhelmingly endorsed by males (e.g., assertiveness, exhibition, competitiveness, and dominance). At the opposite end of the spectrum, feminine cultures have more distributed gender roles and orientation towards stereotypically feminine traits such as nurturing, humility, and caring. Masculine or feminine cultural orientation is shown to affect perception of advertising material, for example, with masculine cultures responding better to egoistic motivators and feminine cultures responding better to altruistic motivators (Nelson et al., 2006). In the 50 years since Hofstede's original research, discussions around sex and gender have caused some scholars to refer to these kinds of role characteristics as activity orientations rather than sex-defined traits, thereby recognising that what motivates an individual is not necessarily incumbent upon a certain combination of chromosomes.

Uncertainty avoidance refers to a culture's level of comfort with ambiguity. Cultures low in uncertainty avoidance tend to be risk-takers, innovators, and have certain high tolerance for people with behaviours that deviate from social norms (Hancıoğlu et al., 2014; Hofstede, 1984; Yeganeh, 2023) while cultures high in uncertainty avoidance tend to prefer tradition and established ways of doing things as well as rely more on experts than lower-level personnel for certain tasks. There is some evidence to suggest that in countries lower in uncertainty avoidance, there is greater sense of wellbeing associated with older age (Lawrie et al., 2020).

Long-term orientation refers to cultures that value perseverance, thriftiness, and subordination for the purpose of harmony whereas short-term orientation is characterised by fulfilment of present obligations, quick results, and social pressure (Bond & Hofstede, 1989; Hofstede & Minkov, 2010; Merkin, 2004). Venaik et al. (2013) make a distinction between long-term orientation and future orientation (Smith, 2006) in which they note that long-term orientation focuses on "tradition" versus "thrift" whereas future orientation focuses on planning practices that have a focus on the present or the future. Other authors draw a cultural distinction in time orientation between cultures that view time as abundant versus those that view time as limited (Hall, 1983; Lane, 2002). More on this topic in Chapter 4.

Hofstede's Dimensions of Culture framework has inspired much research in understanding cultural behaviour across different contexts (for example, Bouziane et al., 2023; Tetteh et al., 2023; Vollmann et al., 2023). It is a helpful tool for navigating intercultural spaces because it helps us to understand why someone may see the world in a particular way. For example, the power distance dimension helps explain why someone from a high power distance value-system might take offence to being addressed by their first name (instead of their title or rank) because it is perceived as disrespect, whereas being addressed by the first name may imply camaraderie to someone with low power distance values. Like Hofstede's dimensions, another helpful framework for navigating intercultural spaces is Hall's (1976) high and low context.

High and Low Context

As we mentioned in Chapter 2, Edward T. Hall presents the premise that culture is communication (Hall, 1960; Hall & Hall, 1990). Noting that communication always happens within a context, Hall identifies two types of communication: high context and low context. In high context communication, the meaning of the message is almost entirely contained in nonverbal and contextual cues whereas in low context communication, the meaning of the message is explicitly verbal. For example, a mother could simply raise an eyebrow, communicating displeasure to a son who, based on past experience and longstanding relationship with the mother, entirely understands what a raised eyebrow means when he does something of which she doesn't approve. This type of high context communication isn't effective in the absence of shared history and/or familiarity with shared contextual cues. Although early research shows that people from certain cultures show certain cultural preferences for low (e.g., Americans) or high (e.g., Japanese) context communication, other research highlights more nuanced cultural differences (Hooft, 2011; Kapoor et al., 2003) and the need to understand the high/low context framework as a way of communication rather than a prescribed cultural trait, especially given that national labels ("Australian") increasingly encompass diverse cultural groups.

In communication between two people, if both communicators are communicating in high context or both in low context, arguably there wouldn't be significant context challenges in understanding each other. The potential for misunderstanding becomes significant when one person is communicating in high context and the other in low context (Jokinen & Wilcock, 2006). For example, consider the conversation between two low context communicators:

LC1:   I'd love to have you over for dinner on Tuesday. (Thinking: my poor friend can't afford much right now; she should have at least one decent meal this week.)

LC2:   That's so nice of you, considering how busy you are at work. What time should I be there? (Thinking: she'll let me know if she needs a hand with anything.)

LC1:   Come around 6. I'll just get takeaway because I need time before dinner to finish my work project. Actually, do you mind picking up dinner on your way in if I order and pay for it ahead of time?

LC2:   Sure, sounds good. Thanks again! See you Tuesday.

LC2   picks up dinner that LC1 had previously ordered and turns up at 6 to LC1's place, and they enjoy a meal together.

* * *

Now, the same conversation between two high context communicators:

HC1:   I'd love to have you over for dinner on Tuesday. (Thinking: my poor friend can't afford much right now; I need to ensure she has at least one decent meal this week.)

HC2:   That's so nice of you, considering how busy you are at work. What time should I be there? (Thinking: she probably needs a hand with things. I'll turn up early to help.)

HC1:   Come around 6. (Thinking: She'll probably come at 5 to give me a hand. I'll order takeaway when HC arrives, and she can pick it up for us while I finish my work project in time for dinner at 6.)

HC2:   Sure, sounds good. Thanks again! See you Tuesday.

HC2   turns up at 5 to HC1's place, HC1 orders takeaway and asks HC2 to pick up the food while HC1 finishes working on her project, and they both enjoy a meal together afterwards.

* * *

Let's see this conversation unfold between a low context and high context communicator:

HC: I'd love to have you over for dinner on Tuesday. (Thinking: my poor friend can't afford much right now; I need to ensure she has at least one decent meal this week.)

LC: That's so nice of you, considering how busy you are at work. What time should I be there? (Thinking: she'll let me know if she needs a hand with anything.)

HC: Come around 6. (Thinking: She'll probably come at 5 to give me a hand. I'll order takeaway when LC arrives, and she can pick it up for us while I finish my work project in time for dinner at 6.)

LC: Sure, sounds good. Thanks again! See you Tuesday.

LC   turns up at HC's house at 6, and finds a harried HC who feels let down because LC hadn't arrived early to help with picking up the food. LC is hungry and slightly annoyed because HC seems disorganised and the food is nowhere to be seen, even though HC had invited LC for dinner at 6.

* * *

As the example illustrates, the same conversation, when had by two LC communicators or two HC communicators, unfolds without misunderstanding because both communicators are operating on the same assumptions and communication rules. Whereas when the conversation is between LC and HC communicators, there is a breakdown in expectations and interpretation of meaning.

Hall's framework of high context (HC) and low context (LC) communication is helpful in intercultural spaces where cultural differences come into focus. A HC communicator may be sending out cues that are missed by a LC communicator while picking up cues that are not being communicated by the LC communicator. It is important to also note that people can switch from HC to LC mode or vice versa depending on the situation. As we said before, HC communication is conducive to situations where there is established shared history/familiarity such that many things do not need to be explicitly verbalised. People often use LC mode in professional settings where there is low familiarity between people and HC mode in personal contexts where there is shared history and familiarity.

Loose and Tight Cultures

Another framework with which to understand cultures is presented by Pelto (1968), who described societies as falling on a continuum of "tight" and "loose" depending on strength of norms and the level of tolerance for deviant behaviour. Gelfand et al. (2011) explain:

> The strength of social norms and tolerance of deviant behavior is also afforded by and reflected in prevailing institutions and practices. Institutions in tight nations have narrow socialization that restricts the range of permissible behaviour, whereas institutions in loose nations encourage broad socialisation that affords a wide range of permissible behavior. (p. 1104)

A number of studies have used the tight-loose culture framework to understand a range of concepts such as immigrants' experiences, for example (Komisarof & Leong, 2016; Leong et al., 2020). Addressing international education in Japan, Komisarof (2020) noted that tight cultures, like Japan, need to be more inclusive in their expectations of "outsiders" if they are to promote diverse communities. Peltokorpi and Froese (2014) noted that loose cultures are better positioned for change because of their more flexible views on conformity to social norms.

The loose-tight cultural framework is helpful to understand social contexts within which people are raised and their orientation to behavioural expectations not only of themselves, but also of others who may come to cohabit their communities, such as immigrants and sojourners. As referenced in the previous paragraph, Adam Komisarof and Chan Hoong Leong are a couple of researchers who have done work on social markers, such as tight-loose cultures, that influence immigrant experiences. Their personal narratives of how they became interested in intercultural research are shared below.

The way in which differences in cultural values affect people's lived experiences is best understood through first-hand stories of people. We have shared two such stories below, from two intercultural scholars whose work has been cited in this book. These stories give you not only a glimpse of cultural differences at play, but also a perspective on the personal experiences of researchers whose scholarly work continues to shape our understanding of intercultural communication.

Reconciling Disparate Values in Different Cultural Contexts: Belonging and Ingroup Membership

Adam Komisarof

I have a dream that my four little children will one day live in a nation where they will not be judged by the color of their skin but by the content of their character. I have a dream today. (Reverend Dr Martin Luther King, Jr, *I Have a Dream* speech)

As a 16-year-old high school student, these words gave me chills – they still do. I have always tried to understand the prejudices that I carry so that their grip on my thinking and behaviour is weakened, and I have tried to reach others through my university teaching and intercultural workshops to do the same. The values of diversity, equity, and inclusion have always been close to my heart both personally and professionally, and a great deal of my research has been devoted to the topic of belonging: what it means, how it is achieved, and facilitating its realisation and enjoyment for others.

When I first arrived in Japan in 1990, I was a fresh graduate in Educational Studies from Brown University and proud of my training as a teacher. I had already taught inner city high school students at Temple University and interned in English and social studies classes at a middle school in Harlem, New York. I couldn't wait for my first full-time job in the classroom waiting for me in the suburbs of Tokyo, where I would teach English as a Foreign Language. I had never been abroad before, but was eager to delve into Japanese culture and experience the challenges of living in a place so different from where I had been raised in suburban Philadelphia. I expected to be treated as the well-trained, professional, young teacher that I was.

Almost immediately, I realised that many of my goals, or at least how I had originally conceived them, were not coming to fruition. I imagined that I would learn Japanese, live "the Japanese way," and be accepted – perhaps even adopted – among the locals. But it was quickly obvious that this was not to be. While some of my students were excited to make contact and welcomed me with gifts of cassettes of their favourite music, others cringed when I spoke to them, as they hated English, or they literally quaked with fear or were otherwise viscerally uncomfortable when I approached them.

As the months passed and I became more fluent in Japanese, I noticed other patterns: some Japanese engaged me in rudimentary conversation, while others – often those who were most fluent at English and considered to be "internationalised" – responded to me only in English, as if to say either my Japanese was not good enough or they had been conditioned only to speak English with foreigners, as foreigners could never be Japanese. This was confusing and hurtful, especially when I thought about Martin Luther King's dream of people being accepted regardless of their race, and by extension, their ethnicity or nationality.

One day, I was sitting in the teachers' room when one of my fellow English teachers tapped me on my shoulder and wanted to talk to me outside. As we left, I noticed the principal starting a meeting for those who remained. In the hallway, my colleague self-consciously explained that the principal had asked him to escort me away, as the meeting was only for "full-time Japanese teachers." While I was full-time, I was neither Japanese nor certified in the government-mandated teacher training programme which was only available to Japanese. My Ivy League education and my teaching experience in two of America's toughest inner-city environments meant nothing here.

After two years in Japan, I had made many friends in the community and among my colleagues, and I loved teaching my students, but I often felt like an outsider, particularly when people seemed to see a non-Japanese face first and related to me on the level of being a "foreigner" instead of a more complex individual who might contradict some of their stereotypes about Caucasian American males. These experiences of being othered made me weary, as I had not grown up with them like so many of my non-White friends in the US where such experiences were part of their daily existence.

I returned to the US, teaching in a private school near Seattle, where I began to process the meaning of my time in Japan. To further this, I enrolled in a master's programme in intercultural relations. Fortuitously, I attended a speech by Karen Hill Anton, a long-term resident of Japan and a journalist, who said of Japanese society, "In order to be a member, you've got to act like one." Inspired, in my master's thesis I tried to identify key norms and values expected of Japanese teachers to be accepted among their colleagues, which encompassed not only profession-specific criteria but also more general ones for building relationships within Japanese society.

Soon after completing my master's, I discovered John Berry's work on acculturation strategies, which helped me to understand people's psychological relationship to acculturation, or more specifically, their relationship to many of the criteria for gaining acceptance that I had identified in my master's thesis. I discovered that even if people recognised that such criteria existed, they might choose not to engage with them and instead behave as they would in their native cultures. Others, like me, would try to assimilate, or adjust to those criteria wholeheartedly to gain acceptance.

In 2015, I began my research of national identity and social markers of acceptance. This further helped me to identify in Japan and other countries what types of criteria are used in society to decide who is "one of us" and why some host national groups may be more accepting or exclusionary towards non-native born migrants. People who tend to be more accepting believe that national identity can be acquired and that their criteria for becoming a member of the nation and society are readily achievable among migrants, while those who think that only specific groups (usually that of a certain ethnicity) can become insiders tend to be less accepting towards migrants. This is exactly where I found myself when I was first teaching in Japan. But I was also fortunate to meet many Japanese who didn't feel that way: they were open to me becoming an ingroup member. In my 25 years in Japan, I have found many such people in my workplaces, neighbourhoods, friends, and most importantly, my wife and her family.

Over the past ten years, I have also continued to refine theories of how belonging is achieved – both in work organisations and groups constructed around national cultures. The conflict between my ideal that everyone should be accepted regardless of their racial or ethnic background and my encounters in Japan in which people presumed group membership based on immutable, largely inborn characteristics has fuelled my research for many years. My advice to those living abroad or starting careers in intercultural research and/or practice would be to take in everything you can, even if it makes you uncomfortable. Try to grasp deeply the meaning of the unfamiliar and comes to terms with it. In that process, you will become more accepting of such differences, and you may also gain insight into how to be a culturally sensitive change agent.

Understanding cultural differences is not the same as endorsing them, although in some cases, that can be the result. In other instances, the differences may run so deep that they fundamentally contradict who you are. However, the same line from *I Have a Dream* still inspires me, and I will always hold dear and work towards Dr King's vision. When we cannot agree with the differences that we encounter, we can be compassionate and patient in their presence, engaging with them with the hope – not the demand – to gradually transform them. That is, perhaps, my own modest dream.

What Egalitarianism Means to Individuals from Unequal Societies

Chan-Hoong Leong

While both Singapore and New Zealand are immigrant receiving societies, the socio-political compact is markedly different. The former is a collective state that expects deference to authorities, assigns priority to allocentric interests over those of the individuals, and strict compliance to established rules and social norms. The latter is a vibrant democracy with a robust track record in human rights protection, respects for autonomy, and assigns a premium to idiosyncratic goals when there is a conflict of interest.

More crucially, Singapore is a high power distance culture where people generally accept some form of inequality, and that the individuals are stratified according to their respective status in the hierarchy, albeit reluctantly for some. The New Zealanders, on the other hand, are staunch defenders of equal rights and opportunities, they would stand up for what they believe is rightfully theirs, or what is considered fair for everyone.

Indeed, it was a baptism of fire for our first day in Wellington, the capital city. I vividly remember my family and I arrived a week shy of Christmas in December 2001. It was summer in the southern hemisphere, but the weather was terribly cold, windy, and unusually wet. Prior to our departure, we received an accommodation close to the campus that was advertised as family friendly. As part of the contractual requirement, a non-refundable deposit was paid to secure the accommodation.

On arrival at the apartment, our hearts sank. The house was damp, and one wall was mouldy. We left and opted for a nearby hotel for temporary abode, and the deposit was forfeited.

I did not think much about losing the deposit but weeks later, my PhD supervisor suggested that I write in to seek a refund as the accommodation was not deemed to be acceptable. I wrote in, and expectedly, my appeal was turned down.

In the three years that I lived in New Zealand's capital city I was never once judged for the clothes I wore when I walked into a shop. New Zealanders would respect my scholarly opinions even if they disagreed. In my daily conversations with people, there was little need to contextualise my articulation – clarity and brevity are warmly welcomed. For most New Zealanders, generosity is a part of their DNA, and it means lending a helping hand to people who need it, whatever their background.

To be sure, New Zealand is not a utopian state. Liberal democracies have their limitations. For Singaporeans like me who grew up under a tight culture, a semi-authoritarian regime where protests are outlawed, and essential public works are given a short runway for implementation, it was mind-boggling to observe how national development could sometimes end up in a political stalemate. For me, the history of the Wellington motorway bypass in the city centre is the epitome of this conundrum.

The motorway project was first conceptualised in 1963, connecting several remote zones across Wellington city using a mix of overbridges and underground tunnels. The road work was put on hold due to budgetary constraints in 1974 but was revived in 1980 albeit with a scaled-down model. Further changes to the motorway's design were proposed in 1994, linking the city centre to the regional airport. The development of the city bypass would clearly improve the quality of life of the majority of Wellingtonians. When the project was eventually announced in 2001, hundreds of residents took to the streets, many of them students and small business operators around the affected area. The protesters were upset that some of the gentrified neighbourhoods and historical buildings would be demolished to make way for the bypass. According to them, these buildings were landmarks of Wellington city and should be preserved at all costs. After a protracted debate, a compromise was reached. Sixteen heritage houses were uprooted and relocated. The construction finally began in March 2005, and the motorway bypass became fully operational two years later.

In the three years that I studied and lived in Wellington this controversial project dominated local headline news. It took a staggering 44 years from inception to completion, a period that is considerably long for similar developments in most parts of Asia. For those who are more familiar with living in a fast-paced, high octane environment where a decisive resolution trumps over-deliberative engagement, this new cultural norm is befuddling.

There is, however, a deeper lesson that intercultural scholars can draw from this incident and the personal anecdote. Specifically, egalitarianism as a cultural value is evident at both individual and collective levels. It means empowerment to the average person in making discrete decisions, and how dissent should be handled when the individual's or subgroup's interests do not align with the broader collective goals. Managing plurality in an egalitarian, low power-distance society precipitates the recognition that all individuals and parties have equal rights to shaping the discourse.

Even in a transaction that favours one party over the other (e.g., my forfeited deposit), all is not lost. In taking a clear stand in our communication (e.g., seeking a refund for a misleading accommodation), we derive a stronger sense of personal agency that could eventually culminate into a movement that drives actions and change. At the very least, taking control to initiate actions is an important aspect to nurture intercultural competence, particularly in countries that emphasise independence.

In the ensuing years after my PhD education, I often ask myself how people from egalitarian societies would respond to domestic and global calamities where a unified and decisive collective response is sometimes warranted. What are the New Zealanders' answers to global migration, tribal identity politics, and the growing hostility between the US-led Western democracies and China's autocracy? Would that be vastly different for people living in collective-centric, high power distance societies?

I do not have all the answers.

The world is reeling under the cumulative weight of climate change, geo-political conflicts, and global supply chain disruptions. While our behaviours and reactions to these crises may be driven by different cultural values and priorities, the end goal is seemingly the same.

We all want to live a peaceful and fulfilling life.

We hope the reflections of researchers like Adam Komisarof and Chan-Hoong Leong give you insight into the personal experiences that inspire intercultural research. Continuing our discussion of perception, in order to understand social perception fully, it is necessary to understand the process of how we categorise new information. Understanding categorisation is also essential for understanding how stereotypes are formed, which we will discuss shortly.

Social Categorisation

Social categorisation is a fundamental process within intercultural relations. It refers to our automatic tendency in complex social and psychological environ-ments to categorise people and objects into groups (Fiske & Taylor, 1991). We process new information by comparing it to existing information and categorising the new information (Fiske & Neuberg, 1990). Socialisation and past experiences play a part in this process. For example, a dog can be a pet, a security measure, or food, depending on one's cultural experiences. When it comes to categorising people, there is evidence to suggest that race and gender are prominent criteria, or criteria we first notice (Weisman et al., 2015). Humans also have the unique ability not only to put others in categories, but also to place ourselves within an existing group or category (Bodenhausen et al., 2012). By doing so, we then have the ability to see other people as belonging to "our" group or not – in other words, we have the ability to evaluate others based on whether they are part of our ingroup or whether they are in an outgroup (Tajfel, 1981). Perhaps unsurprisingly, research shows that we are predisposed to seeing our ingroup members more favourably than those perceived to be in an outgroup (Jacoby-Senghor et al., 2015), although there is some evidence to suggest that in members of devalued groups, the ingroup bias is negative. For example, March and Graham (2015) found that amongst female Hispanic participants, ingroup members were perceived less favourably than outgroup members. The authors suggest that this could be because social groups that are typically perceived negatively might internalise these negative perceptions and apply them to their own ingroup. In a study of children and their ability to categorise people based on race, Lee and Setoh (2022) found that we develop a positive ingroup bias before developing a negative outgroup bias.

Understanding categorisation as an integral process of perception is essential because categorisation helps us to understand not only why stereotypes exist, but also that they serve an important function in helping us understand the world around us. When we put things (or people) into mental categories, we group them based on certain similarities. For example, we group chair, table, sofa, desk, bed, etc. into the category of "furniture" based on the similarity of their functional purpose even though these items are shaped differently and often made of different materials. We may have sub-categories within the broader category of "furniture" based on types of furniture or the functionality of the rooms in which the furniture is found (e.g., "bedroom furniture"). The more complex or nuanced the categories, the more precise the categorisation. These same principles of categorisation apply to categories of people.

In broad terms, we may group people in terms of nationality (Australians, Kenyans, Indonesians, etc.). Within these nationalities, we may make distinctions between regional, language, religious, or other types of ethnic groups. But the more we get to know someone, the more information we have about that person, and the more we are able to categorise them in a nuanced way. For example, when you meet a new classmate from a different country, you might have put her in the generic category of "international student." As you get to know more about her, you may find out her country, her ethnicity, her likes, dislikes, etc. and eventually she may cease being a generic international student and become Amy, your friend. But when you first met Amy, you had to fit her somewhere in your categories. And that "somewhere" is inherently a broad, general category because you didn't know much about Amy other than what you could observe or presume based on superficial knowledge. These broad, generic categories are where stereotypes live. In fact, stereotypes are generalised behavioural expectations we have about a group of people.

Stereotypes

The coining of the word stereotypes is credited to Walter Lippmann (1922), who described stereotypes as mental pictures that help us think of human groups in simplified terms. Hilton and Von Hippel (1996) define stereotypes as "beliefs about characteristics, attributes, and behaviors of members of certain groups" (p. 240). Operario and Fiske (2004) identify three broad principles of stereotype content. First, stereotypes contain a mixture of negative and positive attributes – in other words, ambivalent beliefs. Secondly, stereotypes exaggerate or augment negative behaviour, highlighting extremes. Thirdly, the content of stereotypes favours ingroups at the expense of outgroups.

Based on the premise that all stereotypes are not created equal, Fiske et al. (2002) propose the Stereotype Content Model (SCM) which identifies warmth and competence as two dimensions of stereotypes. The authors argue that stereotypes could be a mixture of these two dimensions. The authors further suggest that the (perceived) status of a group predicts competence, high status being associated with high competence, and competition predicts warmth, with high competition associated with low warmth.

For example, imagine a scenario where a smart Arab student joins a class of pre-dominantly White students in a small town where people haven't interacted much with people from other cultures. At first, the Arab student may be seen as an exotic addition to the class, clever and interesting. There is perceived high status here due to the student's exhibited intelligence, but also high warmth because the student is not seen as a threat but a curiosity. However, imagine if that student then invites 20 of her friends to join the class. Suddenly, the intelligent and "exotic" Arab students outnumber the local students and start competing with the local students for scholarships and other accolades. In that scenario, while the Arab students' intelligence may still give them perceived high status, the increased competition would lower their perceived warmth. Instead of being a curiosity, they now pose a threat to the local students' goals of earning the highest marks in class or winning a competitive scholarship. You can see how this pattern may apply to immigrant groups in a community too. When a group is small, it may be perceived as warm, but once it grows larger to the point of being seen as competing for jobs and resources, then the perceived warmth decreases.

In further research, Cuddy et al. (2008) propose warmth and competence as universal dimensions of social perception. Based on research involving participants from multiple cultural groups, Cuddy et al. (2009) observe that the SCM can be used to predict stereotype content in different (intercultural) contexts, although some researchers suggest that warmth should be nuanced as morality and sociability and competence should be nuanced as ability and assertiveness (Abele et al., 2016). Yet others have proposed that the SCM doesn't account for a range of predictors of stereotype content such as socio-economic status or belief systems (Koch et al., 2020) as well as emotions, health, geography, appearance, etc. (Nicolas et al., 2022). The point to note is that stereotypes serve an important function in social cognition, and the content of stereotypes is influenced by a number of variables. In other words, stereotypes are neither pre-existing or fixed ("that's just the way they are, can't be helped"), nor disposable ("everything will be fine if we just get rid of stereotypes").

Stereotypes influence behaviour in a number of ways. For example, Muntoni et al. (2021) found that gender stereotypes (i.e., "girls are better at reading than boys") not only contribute to better reading efficacy and motivation in girls compared to boys but also contribute to poorer reading outcomes in boys. In other words, when there are shared stereotypes in a group, that influences our behaviour as well as reinforces the stereotype. Similarly, Vos et al. (2023) found that gender stereotypes about maths performance (i.e., "boys are better at maths than girls") contributed to poorer results from female students in arithmetic and cognitive reflection tests. Stereotypes can also influence behaviour in that negative stereotypes about a group of people could influence the way we treat them. For example, Carlana and colleagues (2022) found that teachers who had negative stereotypes about immigrants tended to recommend lower quality high schools to immigrant students compared to native students with similar capabilities.

Although stereotypes are an integral and inevitable part of social perception, the extent to which we rely on stereotypes is mitigated by certain variables. One of those variables that merits further discussion is cognitive complexity. People who have the ability to form multiple, nuanced categories are better equipped to be more accurate in their perception of others. This capacity to understand stimuli in differentiated and multi-faceted ways is known as cognitive complexity. Higher cognitive complexity is "indicated by... more differentiation and integration" of information and "less concrete episodic descriptions" (Benet-Martínez et al., 2006, p. 388), or more abstractness. There is evidence to suggest that cognitively complex people are not only able to think complexly, but are also motivated to do so (Woodard et al., 2021).

Understanding how stereotypes assist and influence our perception is important in understanding communication in intercultural spaces because the perception of differences is an essential factor in the creation of an intercultural space, as Proposition 1 in Chapter 1 states. We will further discuss stereotypes and prejudice in Chapter 5.

To recap what we discussed in this chapter, we engage with social reality through the process of perception which involves selection and interpretation of stimuli. And the way we select and interpret stimuli as important or relevant (or irrelevant, for that matter) is influenced by contextual and cultural variables. We examined some frameworks with which cultural behaviour can be described, and we identified the significance of stereotypes in the process of categorising and processing information. The frameworks discussed in this chapter will be helpful points of reference as we delve into new material in other chapters. For example, when we discuss intercultural conflict navigation in Chapter 5, we will refer back to cultural differences in approaches to conflict using some of Hofstede's Dimensions of Culture as a frame of reference. One of the important perceptual tools at our disposal is language. We will delve into that in the next chapter.

In this chapter, we have talked about how our social, cultural, and experiential "lenses" influence the way we see the world. As we conclude this chapter, we share with you below an excerpt of a conversation between the two of us as we planned this project, which highlights how perceptual lenses play a role even in the very construction of this book.

In Conversation: Cancel Culture

Ripley: A current source of tension in many societies has to do with people expressing ideas that are perceived as inappropriate or unfavourable ideologies based upon certain perspectives. What is your take on the whole cancel culture phenomenon?

Lily: The trouble with disengaging with ideas with which you disagree is that there's really nowhere to go from that point of disagreement. Disagreement becomes self-perpetuating when people start isolating from those with whom they disagree, making the chasm bigger and not resolving anything.

Ripley: There are certain groups of people and certain topics that seem to be excluded from public sphere conversations. Certain markers and articulation of "unacceptable perspectives" denies those groups the opportunity to express their positions.

Lily: The groups you mention could be White, male, could be female, but anyone who expresses a view that's perceived unfavourably, right? And the categorisation as "unfavourable" may even be a minority perception, right? It could be a small but very vocal group's perspective.

Ripley: Yes, I suppose so. What I find problematic is that it effectively reproduces what took place in previous eras, where your race, your education or lack thereof, or literacy or lack thereof, cancelled you from the conversation… we've just flipped it to some different markers, but are still omitting people from important conversations.

Lily: But it's in the premise of correcting a historical wrong… that's the premise of cancel culture, that we're correcting a wrong that has been done. However, that approach has created new challenges of inequity instead of creating space for constructive dialogue.

Ripley: Right. I believe those that are shouting down certain perspectives believe they are serving the cause of justice; but in a pluralistic society, it seems equivalent to saying two wrongs make a right.

Lily: Exactly. The point I want to make is, let's be constructive in our language. Inflammatory language doesn't accomplish much except to put people's back against the wall, so that they're not even engaging in the conversation.

Questions for Reflection

1. What is your experience of, or reaction to, cancel culture?
2. Do you agree or disagree that in a pluralistic society everyone should have a voice, even if you find their opinions offensive?
3. How can we preserve freedom of expression while also maintaining civil discourse?

References

Abele, A. E., Hauke, N., Peters, K., Louvet, E., Szymkow, A., & Duan, Y. (2016). Facets of the fundamental content dimensions: Agency with competence and assertiveness – Communion with warmth and morality. *Frontiers in Psychology*, 7, 1810.

Anderson, J. A. (1996). *Communication theory: Epistemological foundations*. Guilford Press.

Arasaratnam, L. A. (2015). Perceptions. In J. M. Bennett (Ed.), *The SAGE encyclopaedia of intercultural competence* (pp. 662–664). Sage.

Benet-Martínez, V., Lee, F., & Leu, J. (2006). Biculturalism and cognitive complexity: Expertise in cultural representations. *Journal of Cross-Cultural Psychology*, *37*(4), 386–407.

Bennett, M. J. (2013). *Basic concepts of intercultural communication* (2nd ed.). Intercultural Press.

Bilsky, W., Janik, M., & Schwartz, S. H. (2011). The structural organization of human values – evidence from three rounds of the European Social Survey (ESS). *Journal of Cross-Cultural Psychology*, *42*, 759–776. https://doi.org/10.1177/0022022110362757

Blumer, H. (1969). *Symbolic interactionism: Perspective and method*. Prentice Hall.

Bodenhausen, G. V., Kang, S. K., Peery, D., Fiske, S., & Macrae, C. N. (2012). Social categorization and perception of social groups. In S. T. Fiske & C. N. Macrae (Eds.), *The SAGE handbook of social cognition* (pp. 311–329). Sage.

Bond, M. H., & Hofstede, G. (1989). The cash value of Confucian values. *Human Systems Management*, *8*(3), 195–199.

Bouziane, A., Bouziane, K., & Tahri, W. (2023). The role of national cultural dimensions in the quality of legal audit missions. *International Journal of Society, Culture & Language*, *11*(1), 160–170.

Carlana, M., Ferrara, E. L., & Pinotti, P. (2022). Implicit stereotypes in teachers' track recommendations. In *AEA Papers and Proceedings* (Vol. 112, pp. 409–414). American Economic Association.

Cuddy, A. J., Fiske, S. T., & Glick, P. (2008). Warmth and competence as universal dimensions of social perception: The Stereotype Content Model and the BIAS map. *Advances in Experimental Social Psychology*, *40*, 61–149.

Cuddy, A. J., Fiske, S. T., Kwan, V. S., Glick, P., Demoulin, S., Leyens, J. P., … & Ziegler, R. (2009). Stereotype Content Model across cultures: Towards universal similarities and some differences. *British Journal of Social Psychology*, *48*(1), 1–33.

De Lange, F. P., Heilbron, M., & Kok, P. (2018). How do expectations shape perception? *Trends in Cognitive Sciences*, *22*(9), 764–779.

DiDonato, T. E., Ullrich, J., & Krueger, J. I. (2011). Social perception as induction and inference: An integrative model of intergroup differentiation, ingroup favoritism, and differential accuracy. *Journal of Personality and Social Psychology*, *100*(1), 66.

Fiske, S. T., Cuddy, A. J., Glick, P., & Xu, J. (2002). A model of (often mixed) stereotype content: Competence and warmth respectively follow from perceived status and competition. *Journal of Personality and Social Psychology*, *82*(6), 878–902.

Fiske, S. T., & Neuberg, S. L. (1990). A continuum of impression formation, from category-based to individuating processes: Influences of information and motivation on attention and interpretation. *Advances in Experimental Social Psychology*, *23*(C), 1–74.

Fiske, S. T., & Taylor, S. E. (1991). *Social cognition* (2nd ed.). McGraw-Hill.

Gelfand, M. J., Raver, J. L., Nishii, L., Leslie, L. M., Lun, J., Lim, B. C., … & Yamaguchi, S. (2011). Differences between tight and loose cultures: A 33-nation study. *Science*, *332*(6033), 1100–1104.

Ghosh, A. (2011). Power distance in organizational contexts – a review of collectivist cultures. *Indian Journal of Industrial Relations*, *47*(1), 89–101.

Hall, E. T. (1960). The silent language in overseas business. *Harvard Business Review*, *38*(3), 87–96.

Hall, E. T. (1976). *Beyond culture*. Doubleday.

Hall, E. T. (1983). *The dance of life*. Anchor Press/Doubleday & Company.

Hall, E. T., & Hall, M. R. (1990). *Understanding cultural differences*. Intercultural Press.

Hancıoğlu, Y., Doğan, Ü. B., & Yıldırım, Ş. S. (2014). Relationship between uncertainty avoidance culture, entrepreneurial activity and economic development. *Procedia-Social and Behavioral Sciences*, *150*(8), 908–916.

Hilton, J. L., & Von Hippel, W. (1996). Stereotypes. *Annual Review of Psychology*, *47*(1), 237–271.

Hofstede, G. (1984). Cultural dimensions in management and planning. *Asia Pacific Journal of Management*, *1*, 81–99.

Hofstede, G. (1991). Empirical models of cultural differences. In N. Bleichrodt & P. J. D. Drenth (Eds.), *Contemporary issues in cross-cultural psychology* (pp. 4–20). Swets & Zeitlinger Publishers.

Hofstede, G., & Minkov, M. (2010). Long-versus short-term orientation: New perspectives. *Asia Pacific Business Review*, *16*(4), 493–504.

Hooft, A. V. (2011). A comparison of Mexican and US American students' perceptions of high-low context business communication style. *ITL-International Journal of Applied Linguistics*, *161*(1), 68–89.

Islam, T., Sharif, S., Ali, H. F., & Jamil, S. (2022). Zooming into paternalistic leadership. Evidence from high power distance culture. *European Journal of Management and Business Economics*. https://doi.org/10.1108/EJMBE-05-2021-0149

Jacoby-Senghor, D. S., Sinclair, S., & Smith, C. T. (2015). When bias binds: Effect of implicit outgroup bias on ingroup affiliation. *Journal of Personality and Social Psychology*, *109*(3), 415.

Jokinen, K., & Wilcock, G. (2006). Contextual inferences in intercultural communication. *SKY Journal of Linguistics*, *19*, A Man of Measure: Special supplement, 291–300.

Kapoor, S., Hughes, P. C., Baldwin, J. R., & Blue, J. (2003). The relationship of individualism–collectivism and self-construals to communication styles in India and the United States. *International Journal of Intercultural Relations*, *27*(6), 683–700.

Kluckhohn, F. R., & Strodtbeck, F. L. (1961). *Variations in value orientations*. Row, Peterson & Co.

Koch, A., Imhoff, R., Unkelbach, C., Nicolas, G., Fiske, S., Terache, J., … & Yzerbyt, V. (2020). Groups' warmth is a personal matter: Understanding consensus on stereotype dimensions reconciles adversarial models of social evaluation. *Journal of Experimental Social Psychology*, *89*, 103995. https://doi.org/10.1016/j.jesp. 2020.103995.

Komisarof, A. (2020). Global education's outcomes and improvement: The role of social markers of acceptance in constructing Japanese identity and ingroup boundaries. In N. Doerr (Ed.), *The Global Education Effect and Japan* (pp. 98–118). Routledge.

Komisarof, A., & Leong, C. H. (2016). Acculturation in East and Southeast Asia. In D. L. Sam & J. W. Berry (Eds.), *The Cambridge handbook of acculturation psychology* (pp. 248–271). Cambridge University Press.

Kopytowska, M. (2016). Mediating identity, ideology and values in the public sphere: Towards a new model of (constructed) social reality. *Lodz Papers in Pragmatics*, *11*(2), 133–156.

Lane, P. (2002). *A beginner's guide to crossing cultures: Making friends in a multi-cultural world*. InterVarsity Press.

Lawrie, S. I., Eom, K., Moza, D., Gavreliuc, A., & Kim, H. S. (2020). Cultural variability in the association between age and well-being: The role of uncertainty avoidance. *Psychological Science*, *31*(1), 51–64.

Lee, K. J., & Setoh, P. (2022). The developmental trajectories of racial categorization and explicit racial biases in Singapore. *Acta Psychologica*, *229*, 103694.

Leong, C. H., Komisarof, A., Dandy, J., Jasinskaja-Lahti, I., Safdar, S., Hanke, K., & Teng, E. (2020). What does it take to become "one of us?" Redefining ethnic-civic citizenship using markers of everyday nationhood. *International Journal of Intercultural Relations*, *78*, 10–19.

Li, C. (2022). Foreign language learning boredom and enjoyment: The effects of learner variables and teacher variables. *Language Teaching Research*, 13621688221090324.

Lippmann, W. (1922). *Public opinion*. Harcourt Brace.

Lomas, T., Diego-Rosell, P., Shiba, K., Standridge, P., Lee, M. T., Case, B., ... & VanderWeele, T. J. (2023). Complexifying individualism versus collectivism and West versus East: Exploring global diversity in perspectives on self and other in the Gallup World Poll. *Journal of Cross-Cultural Psychology*, *54*(1), 61–89.

Lupyan, G., Rahman, R. A., Boroditsky, L., & Clark, A. (2020). Effects of language on visual perception. *Trends in Cognitive Sciences*, *24*(11), 930–944.

Macioce, F. (2018). Asymmetrical recognition. Group vulnerability and group rights, beyond cultural identities. *International Journal on Minority and Group Rights*, *25*(1), 132–151.

March, D. S., & Graham, R. (2015). Exploring implicit ingroup and outgroup bias toward Hispanics. *Group Processes & Intergroup Relations*, *18*(1), 89–103.

Mead, G. H. (1934). *Mind, self, and society*. University of Chicago Press.

Merkin, R. (2004). Cultural long-term orientation and facework strategies. *Atlantic Journal of Communication*, *12*(3), 163–176.

Minkov, M., & Kaasa, A. (2022). Do dimensions of culture exist objectively? A validation of the revised Minkov-Hofstede model of culture with World Values Survey items and scores for 102 countries. *Journal of International Management*, *28*(4), 1–17. https://doi.org/https://doi.org/10.1016/j.intman.2022.100971

Muntoni, F., Wagner, J., & Retelsdorf, J. (2021). Beware of stereotypes: Are classmates' stereotypes associated with students' reading outcomes? *Child Development*, *92*(1), 189–204.

Na, J., Kim, N., Suk, H. W., Choi, E., Choi, J. A., Kim, J. H., ... & Choi, I. (2021). Individualism-collectivism during the COVID-19 pandemic: A field study testing the pathogen stress hypothesis of individualism-collectivism in Korea. *Personality and Individual Differences*, *183*(3–4), 111127. doi:10.1016/j.paid.2021.111127.

Nelson, M. R., Frédéric, F. B., Magne S., & Rajesh, V. M. (2006). Effects of culture, gender, and moral obligations on responses to charity advertising across masculine and feminine cultures. *Journal of Consumer Psychology*, *16*(1), 45–56.

Nicolas, G., Bai, X., & Fiske, S. T. (2022). A spontaneous stereotype content model: Taxonomy, properties, and prediction. *Journal of Personality and Social Psychology*, *122*(6), 1243–1263.

Operario, D., & Fiske, S. T. (2004). Stereotypes: Content, structures, processes, and context. In R. Brown and S. Gaertner (Eds.), *Blackwell handbook of social psychology: Integroup processes* (pp. 22–44). Blackwell Publishers.

Parsons, T. (1951). *The social system*. The Free Press.

Parsons, T. (1978). *Action theory and the human condition*. The Free Press.

Pelto, P. J. (1968). The differences between "tight" and "loose" societies. *Trans-action*, *5*, 37–40.

Peltokorpi, V., & Froese, F. (2014). Expatriate personality and cultural fit: The moderating role of host country context on job satisfaction. *International Business Review*, *23*(1), 293–302.

Rokeach, M. (1973). *The nature of human values*. The Free Press.

Schwartz, S. H. (1992). Universals in the content and structure of values: Theoretical advances and empirical tests in 20 countries. *Advances in Experimental Social Psychology*, *25*, 1–65.

Schwartz, S. H. (2011). Studying values: Personal adventure, future directions. *Journal of Cross-Cultural Psychology*, *42*(2), 307–319. https://doi.org/10.1177/0022022110396925

Schwartz, S. H. (2012). An overview of the Schwartz Theory of Basic Values. *Online Readings in Psychology and Culture*, *2*(1). https://doi.org/10.9707/2307-0919.1116

Smith, P. B. (2006). When elephants fight, the grass gets trampled: The GLOBE and Hofstede projects. *Journal of International Business Studies*, *37*(6), 915–921.

Tajfel, H. (1981). *Human groups and social categories*. Cambridge University Press.

Tetteh, S., Dei Mensah, R., Opata, C. N., & Agyapong, G. N. Y. A. (2023). Beyond monetary motivation: The moderation of Hofstede's cultural dimensions. *International Journal of Productivity and Performance Management*, *72*(1), 156–179.

Triandis, H. C. (2001). Individualism-collectivism and personality. *Journal of Personality*, *69*(6), 907–924.

Vauclair, C.-M., Hanke, K., Fischer, R., & Fontaine, J. (2011). The structure of human values at the culture level: A meta-analytical replication of Schwartz's value orientations using the Rokeach value survey. *Journal of Cross-Cultural Psychology*, *42*(2), 186–205.

Venaik, S., Zhu, Y., & Brewer, P. (2013). Looking into the future: Hofstede long term orientation versus GLOBE future orientation. *Cross Cultural Management*, *20*(3), 361–385.

Vollmann, M., Todorova, I., Salewski, C., & Neter, E. (2023). Stresses of COVID-19 and expectations for the future among women: A cross-cultural analysis according to the femininity/masculinity dimension. *Cross-Cultural Research*, *57*(4), 327–351. https://doi.org/10693971221149783.

Voronov, M., & Singer, J. A. (2002). The myth of individualism-collectivism: A critical review. *The Journal of Social Psychology*, *142*(4), 461–480.

Vos, H., Marinova, M., De Léon, S. C., Sasanguie, D., & Reynvoet, B. (2023). Gender differences in young adults' mathematical performance: Examining the contribution of working memory, math anxiety and gender-related stereotypes. *Learning and Individual Differences*, *102*, 102255.

Wang, H., & Lou, X. (2022). A meta-analysis on the social relationship outcome of being compassionate towards oneself: The moderating role of individualism-collectivism. *Personality and Individual Differences*, *184*, 111162.

Weisman, K., Johnson, M. V., & Shutts, K. (2015). Young children's automatic encoding of social categories. *Developmental Science*, *18*(6), 1036–1043.

Wendt, J. R. (2009). Die: A way to improve communication. *Communication Education*, *33*(4), 397–401.

West, R. L., & Turner, L. H. (2004). *Introduction to communication theory: Analysis and application*. McGraw-Hill.

Whorf, B.L. (1956). *Language, thought, and reality: Selected writings*. Technology Press of Massachusetts Institute of Technology.

Woodard, S. R., Chan, L., & Conway III, L. G. (2021). In search of the cognitively complex person: Is there a meaningful trait component of cognitive complexity? *Personality and Social Psychology Review*, *25*(2), 95–129.

Yeganeh, H. (2023). Culture and innovation: A human emancipation perspective. *International Journal of Sociology and Social Policy*. https://doi.org/10.1108/IJSSP-07-2022-0185

4 Language, Symbols, and Contexts

One of Ripley's favourite *Star Trek: Next Generation* episodes is "Darmok," which aired in September of 1991. Captain Jean Luc Picard and the crew of The Starship Enterprise venture into an uninhabited system, near the territory of an enigmatic race known as *The Children of Tama* with whom the Federation has previously failed to establish communication. This "incomprehensible" race requests a rendezvous with the Federation which generates some anxiety, but Picard says confidently, "communication is a matter of patience and imagination." After several unsuccessful attempts to communicate, the leader of the Tamarians, Captain Dathon, eventually abducts Captain Picard in an effort to forge some kind of alliance. Even in person, his style of communicating is perplexing, despite the fact that Tamarian phrases seem to be composed of known English words and phrases. Immediately before the abduction, Dathon solemnly states, "Darmok and Jalad at Tanagra!" The Enterprise's counsellor, Deanna Troi, observes that, "a single word can lead to tragedy; one word misspoken or misunderstood..." Troi's observation is prophetic as Picard fears for his life on the surface of the nearby planet. Despite appearances otherwise, Captain Dathon continues efforts to get through to Picard and communicate the reason for their coming together, but Picard's bewilderment remains. Again, it wasn't that they didn't understand the language construction, they just lacked the appropriate contextual referent.

The entire episode is a wonderful illustration of the complexity of communication, and the relationship of language to culture. In fact, the episode's writer came up with the concept from reading Julian Jaynes' *The Origin of Consciousness in the Breakdown of the Bicameral Mind* (Jaynes, 1976). He was fascinated by the idea that different cultures could possess distinct styles of consciousness. We, too, are intrigued by the way human language works, not least of which is because our use of language appears to set humans apart from all other species. The creation and transmission of messages between people is a complex phenomenon that involves simultaneous encoding and decoding processes across multiple channels. In a very simple scenario, it involves verbal codes (language) and nonverbal signals (behaviours) conveyed at varying levels of consciousness. Because of the complexity and murky conscious connections, we have to admit that communication is often imperfect, or, as John Durham Peters (1999) observed, always at a distance:

DOI: 10.4324/9781003318415-5

Our sensations and feelings are, physiologically speaking, uniquely our own. My nerve endings terminate in my own brain, not yours. No central exchange exists where I can patch my sensory inputs into yours, nor is there any sort of "wireless" contact through which to transmit my immediate experience of the world to you. (p. 4)

In this chapter, we will explore the relationship between culture and language, both verbal and nonverbal. We will examine its symbolic nature, and the way in which it both defines and reflects the contexts in which we use it, with the end goal in mind of coordinating our interactions as successfully as possible. What we hope you will come to realise is that language is "more than a tool for communication of facts between two or more persons," but is also a fundamental expression of culture and identity (Lippi-Green, 2011, p. 3). Unfortunately, as Hall (1976) pointed out, it shares a paradoxical relationship with culture:

Language, the system most frequently used to describe culture, is by nature poorly adapted to this difficult task. It is too linear, not comprehensive enough, too slow, too limited, too constrained, too unnatural, too much a product of its own evolution, and too artificial. (p. 57)

What Is Language?

In Chapter 1 we introduced the idea that communication is a symbolic activity. We need to dive into that idea more deeply as an umbrella concept to understand how language operates. Remember that a symbol, like a national flag, is something that represents something else. By definition, symbols are arbitrary when they are created. A symbol that is assigned to an object or referent is neutral. For example, what picture comes to your mind when we use the English word, "rose?" That label is not organically connected to the flower that just popped into your mind. Some English-speaking ancestors invented that label and assigned it to represent the flower. In Greek it is "ρόδο" (Rhodon), and in Turkish it is "Gül." That is the subtle language game that Juliet is playing in Shakespeare's *Romeo and Juliet* when she asks Romeo, "What's in a name? That which we call a rose, By any other name would smell as sweet." Juliet's words underscore the point that, in natural reality, an object exists and exhibits its inherent properties, independent of the name we assign to it.

The name, or symbol, does not in fact carry any inherent meaning – meaning is assigned by people. Communication theorist David Berlo (1960) famously, and somewhat controversially, said, "meanings are in people, not in words." Berlo was advancing an idea that seems to have originated with Herbert Spencer in his book, *The Philosophy of Style* (1852), where he made the argument that the meaning of a message is created by the receiver due to his or her unique frame of reference, and categorisation/conceptualisation of symbols. His ideas were the precursors of symbolic interactionists who view people as symbol-using creatures (Mead, 1934). Language, in its essence, is a symbolic system that relates meaning to a written code and sound.

The symbolic nature of language leads to the question, how do symbols operate in our thinking, or cognition? To answer that question, let's return to our flag example. Your national flag is a symbol of your country. French philosopher Roland Barthes thought of symbols like that as *signs*, composed of two dimensions: *signifiers* and *signifieds*. The cloth of the flag with shapes and colours is the set of signifiers, while what each of those colours and shapes represent is the set of signifieds. Together, they are two sides of the same coin and "stand for" a nation. Of course, national flags provoke patriotic emotions in many people. In fact, shared symbols like that often evoke a sense of mutual identity, especially in times of war or national threat (DiMaggio, 1997; Haidt, 2012).

When sets of symbols come together to form a coherent system that we implicitly rely upon to infer meaning or make assumptions about the nature of things, they represent cognitive schemata. For example, when we see a group of people in a park clustered around balloons and cake, we think, "Ah, it must be someone's birthday" because balloons, cake, and people gathering fit within our schema for a "birthday party." These schemata are essentially the knowledge structures in our brain that inform the meaning-making process, and when shared with others they create the thought communities we introduced in the first two chapters. DiMaggio (1997) noted that one of the things schemata do for us is simplify our thought processes by introducing efficiencies. And when those efficiencies are held in common by groups of people, they become thought communities, or what he calls "institutionalised culture... in schematic cognition we find the mechanisms by which culture shapes and biases thought" (p. 269). To restate it plainly, the "essences" we apply to words are in the end products of culture and convenience; they do not inherently derive from those symbols (Zerubavel, 1991).

One of the more interesting things schemata do is cause us to perceive, or focus on, objects and information that fits with our community of thought (Konecki, 2021). That is, they predispose us to see the world in a certain way. Our perception of events, objects, people, and situations is socially framed to some degree. What that means is that out of all of the stimuli coming at us, our inherited cognitive frames (schemata) predispose us to select or identify certain of those stimuli and ignore others, as well as interpret those preferred stimuli in ways that are consistent with our thought communities. In a later chapter we'll explore the subject of how we can overcome those implicit cognitive biases, but for now, it's important that we see how they are connected to our language and meaning-making system. Zerubavel (1991, pp. 5–32) referred to this as the process of carving up chunks of reality into islands of meaning. When we do that, he argued, we transform the natural world into a social construction that in turn brings order to our lives and shapes the way we live and relate to others. But in the process, we take a continuous stream of stimuli, or reality, and break it into arbitrary units and associations that fit with our thought communities' schemata. The connection of this process to language is a fundamental component in the creation of intercultural spaces.

Linguistic Relativity

One of the most important insights to emerge from the field of linguistics in the 20th century is that human brains seem to be hard-wired for language acquisition:

> The fact that all normal children acquire essentially comparable grammars of great complexity with remarkable rapidity suggests that human beings are somehow specially designed to do this, with data-handling or "hypothesis-formulating" ability of unknown character and complexity. (Chomsky, 1959, p. 62)

It turns out the FOXP2 gene in the human DNA structure facilitates the production of speech as it interacts with some one hundred other genes (Lippi-Green, 2011, p. 5). The interesting caveat behind that seemingly universal capability observed by Chomsky is that those group-specific grammars seem to reflect distinctive patterns. While humans are universally programmed to acquire language, we are socialised into a particular first language (L1). And much to the chagrin of Enlightenment authors like Jonathon Swift, there is no superior language, nor even an *idealised* form of a given language (Lippi-Green, 2011, p. 55). Languages are the products of communities that use them, and they use them in different ways. In the decade between 1929 and 1939 American linguist, Edward Sapir, and his student Benjamin Lee Whorf, a chemical engineer who moonlighted in anthropology, developed a hypothesis about the relationship between language, culture, and thought that garnered significant attention. The Sapir-Whorf hypothesis put forward the idea that:

> Language is a guide to "social reality." It powerfully conditions all of our thinking... the fact of the matter is that the "real world" is to a large extent unconsciously built up on the language habits of the group... The worlds in which different societies live are distinct worlds, not merely the same world with different labels attached. (Sapir, 1949, p. 162)

Sapir and Whorf's hypothesis built upon the work of Franz Boas' analyses of Native American languages and eventually evolved into the less deterministic theory of *linguistic relativity* which argues that language exerts an *influence* on thought, rather than constraint, and is consistent with the notion of inheriting cognitive biases from our thought communities (Hoijer, 1991; Holtgraves, 2002; Martin & Nakayama, 2010). It was Boas (1850–1942) who saw that a full description and understanding of culture without the study of language was not possible, and that languages ought to be studied anthropologically.

Philosophers outside of anthropology and linguistics have also argued for a *historico-linguistic bias* in our thinking. Martin Heidegger and Hans Georg Gadamer suggested that language shapes the very core of, or expresses itself through, one's identity (*DaSein*). Gadamer (1975) phrased it this way:

Similar to the act of making, the act of speaking one word brings another with it and so thoughts are eventually set forth. It is truly a speech that emerges from the background, usage of language and space are already schematized in advance. We speak and the word or artefact goes beyond to consequences and ends which we have not perhaps conceived of. When you take a word in your mouth you must realize that you have not taken a tool that can be thrown aside if it won't do the job, but you are fixed in a direction of thought which comes from afar and stretches beyond you. (p. 497)

What he meant is that our subconscious understanding of the world is linguistically mediated.[1] The conventions and traditions embedded (handed down to us) in our L1 means that our words frame and construe, capture and liberate, reify and reinvent, and together provide continuity of understanding, all without our witting agency. Heidegger went so far as to say language precedes us in our speaking; it speaks its (cultural) identity through us. Sapir (1931) seemed to concur, writing that language "actually defines experience for us by reason of its formal completeness and because of our *unconscious projection of its implicit expectations* in the field of experience" (emphasis added; Sapir, 1931, p. 578). Sapir and Whorf were convinced that different languages *index* various aspects of experience differently. And if our languages are expressing historico-cultural biases through us, then civil rights essayist James Baldwin was correct when he wrote in his *Notes of a Native Son* that "People are trapped in history and history is trapped in them" and we should endeavour to make ourselves aware of those fore-meanings (Baldwin, 2002, p. 82).

As we conclude the conversation about the symbolic nature of language, we want to make clear that just because the relationship between words and their referents is arbitrary, that does not mean they aren't real in their consequences. As Wolfe (1992) asserted, "the social world is as real as the natural world. Cognition is as real as behaviour. If a distinction is called into being, acted upon for centuries, incorporated into people's mental maps, predicts how people behave, and becomes an essential aspect of self and identity, does it make sense to call it arbitrary" (Wolfe, 1992, p. 378)? Likewise, we will also want to keep in mind that just as there is variation in how strongly individuals pledge allegiance to their flag, there is also considerable flexibility in the way people actually subscribe to particular thought communities and use a particular language.

Language Variety and Functions

According to current estimates there are 7,168 languages spoken in the world among approximately 650 ethnic groups and some 16,000 constituent people groups (Eberhard et al., 2023).[2] Those numbers are *estimates*, yet on the face of it they seem to make intergroup communication and any sort of global cooperation impossibly complex. However, despite the *polysystemic variation* and dynamic nature of language throughout the world due to regional, socio-political, historical, and contextual factors, all languages serve a set of fairly universal functions within most cultural communities.[3]

Language in its various forms serves a variety of functions (Fiedler & Freytag, 2009). First, it is the primary vehicle of social interaction.[4] As illustrated previously, it also serves a significant identity function and provides solidarity to the speakers of the language (Jackson, 2015). For example, Uganda is typical of an African tri-lingual system where language serves to delineate local, regional, and national affiliations. As a country of approximately 46 million people, there are at least three languages spoken in most communities – a local tribal language like Luganda, English (a colonial language), and Swahili (an East African lingua franca). Driving across Uganda, it is possible to unknowingly cross into one of more than 43 active tribal language communities that have distinct greetings, marketplace traditions, and mannerisms. The narrative by Professor Jane Jackson below is a powerful example of language identity and community in/exclusion.

Yes, But Where Are You *Really* From?

Jane Jackson

I was born and raised in the English-speaking region of New Brunswick, Canada, in a small town on the border with the United States. As a secondary school student, I joined summer French immersion programmes in the French-speaking region of my home province. Immersed in the French language and Acadian culture, I began to think more about my place in the world. Like many border crossers before me, I soon discovered that exposure to unfamiliar ways of being can serve as a powerful stimulus for identity awakenings (e.g., cultural, ethnic, gender, linguistic, national, regional, religious, personal) and personal growth *if* you take the time to step back and really think about what you are seeing, experiencing, and feeling.

At this juncture, many of the messages that I received in the world around me emphasised cultural difference and the "culture as nation" approach, whereby individuals from a particular country (or cultural community) are assumed to possess similar characteristics (e.g., identities, values, beliefs, communication styles). While participating in the French immersion programmes, I became more aware of the close connection between language, culture, and identity, and the negative consequences of putting people into boxes. Exposure to Acadian culture and the friendships I made with people from different linguistic and cultural backgrounds enhanced my appreciation of diversity and the complexity of identities, which, in turn, helped me to push past existing stereotypes.

As a university student, I continued my French studies and majored in bilingual (French-English) education at a university in my home province. In my third year, I joined a "Junior Year Abroad" programme in Québec; all of my coursework was in French and for much of the time I lived with Québécoises. I again experienced the natural ups and downs of adaptation, including the challenge of expressing my ideas, emotions, and personality in a second language on a daily basis. This process was both exhilarating and exhausting.

When interacting with locals, I was reminded that I was not a native speaker. More often than not, when I met Québécois, after a few minutes, I was asked where I was from, and in some situations the speakers switched to English, which was rather frustrating as I wished to fit into the local scene and live in French. This experience prompted me to think more about the strong emotions and sense of alienation that can arise when one's preferred self-identities are contested or not understood.

After finishing my undergraduate studies, I started off my career as a French as a Second Language (FSL) teacher in New Brunswick and later taught in French immersion or bilingual (French-English) programmes in several provinces in western Canada.

By this time, I had developed close friendships with some Arab students and immigrant families. As I had begun to consider working in the Middle East, I studied Arabic in both formal classes and individual tutoring sessions. As I interacted with my Arab friends and observed their struggles to adjust to life in Canada, I became sensitised to the powerful role of the media in shaping local people's views about the Middle East and Arabs in general. I frequently witnessed the detrimental consequences of stereotyping and otherisation. While a multiculturalism policy can promote positive intercultural relations and discourage overt racism, biases can persist and manifest themselves in subtle ways.

When I returned to Canada after a year of travelling internationally, I taught French immersion in Vancouver and also taught English as a Second Language (ESL) to adults in the evening. By this stage, I'd become very interested in cross-cultural adaptation and the experiences of migrants, and also recognised there would be more international job opportunities in English.

After teaching at universities in Egypt, Oman, the USA, and Canada, in 1995 a job opportunity at the Chinese University of Hong Kong brought me back to Asia. Many of my students (mostly applied linguistics majors) carried out projects that dealt with language, identity, and cultural issues, including cross-cultural adaptation.

Intrigued by language use and identities, "Mandy," a Hong Kong Chinese undergraduate, conducted multiple interviews with a middle-aged woman of Indian ethnicity. Even though the interviewee was a second-generation resident of the city who spoke conversational Cantonese, Mandy did not view her as a Hong Konger as she was not Chinese. When I reviewed the interview tapes/ transcripts, I could see that the woman repeatedly stressed that she was a local and had not set foot in India for decades. Despite this, my student persisted in asking her questions about her "homeland, India." The woman's preferred identities were contested over and over again, and by the end of the interviews her frustration was evident in the tone of her voice.

I witnessed similar experiences in Hong Kong with American-born, British-born, or Canadian-born Chinese, especially those who were not fully fluent in Cantonese or Putonghua (Mandarin). Although I had been in Hong Kong for 25 years and felt very much at home, my self-identities were also contested both in the city and away. When people asked me where I was from, if I said that I was a Hong Konger, this was inevitably followed by something like this: "Yes, but where are you *really* from?"

"Where are you from?" seems like such an innocent question; however, it can cause offence and negatively impact relationship-building, especially if it is asked within a few seconds of meeting and the person is a minority member, immigrant and/or second language speaker. Instead of immediately asking questions of identity and belonging when meeting people for the first time, it's important to spend time getting to know them as individuals. Listen attentively to gauge what they seem to be willing to share and notice nonverbal behaviours as they can provide clues about their comfort level. While we may have no intention to cause offence when asking identity-related questions, it matters if it is causing harm to our communication partners. Besides critical self-awareness, recognising and respecting the identities of the people we interact with is essential for mutually satisfying intercultural relations.

In some cases, languages also function to represent separatist or resistance identities such as Yiddish, Catalan, Flemish, Lhasa Tibetan, or Euskara which is spoken in the Basque region on the border between Spain and France. Not only does language serve social interaction, identity, and solidarity functions, but it encodes the implicit structures for reasoning and persuasion. Robert Kaplan demonstrated in a study of student essays that one's first language predisposes the writer to construct an argument with a specific logical form (Kaplan, 1988). Writers whose L1 was English preferred a direct, linear logic whereas speakers from Sino-Tibetan L1 backgrounds preferred an indirect, tangential logic. Thus, a language serves as a structure, or code, with grammars and forms. It also serves to shape communal identity and reflect and reinvent the cultural context in the moment of conversation (Philipsen, 1987).

The Relationship of Language to Culture

Counsellor Troi and the Enterprise crew eventually deduced that the Tamarian language is entirely built upon metaphorical expressions drawing from the culture's historical narratives and mythology, which renders the language virtually opaque to cultural outsiders. Idiomatic expressions in language are metaphorical in the sense that they require a deep understanding of history and word play in a given culture in order to understand the meaning of a phrase. For instance, "he is a chip off the old block" (which means, the boy is a lot like his father or mother). In order to understand the expression we would have to be very familiar with the context and how language is used. The idea that metaphor is at the heart of language systems was most convincingly put forward by Charles K. Ogden and Ivor A. Richards in their book, *The Meaning of Meaning: A Study of the Influence of Language Upon Thought and of the Science of Symbolism*. Metaphors, like idioms, they concluded, require that we understand the context of the expression in order to derive the meaning of the words-in-use (Ogden & Richards, 1923/1989). And so it is with language. It wasn't until the Enterprise crew understood how deeply culture and language are intertwined, that they could grasp what the Tamarians wanted from Picard and the Federation. In the following paragraphs we will explore some of the ways in which culture reveals itself in language.

So far, we have suggested that language is a symbolic system that on the face of it arbitrarily relates meaning to words and serves a variety of functions. However, from the perspective of a given language community, the meaning of words is agreed upon (shared) and undergoes a process of reification. For example, the fruit we know as "banana" is called that because that's the name people have collectively assigned to it such that, over time, the name "banana" is inseparable from the fruit to which we have assigned that name. Every language is structured by sets of rules, or *grammars* (Jackson, 2015). You probably remember when you were first learning to spell, read, and eventually write in your first language that you had to wrestle through the ins and outs of all those rule systems. A fundamental assumption of any sociology is that human behaviour is not entirely random, but is, within certain limits, predictable and patterned.

Sociolinguistics assumes language is rule governed and that these rules affect, and are affected by, social context. In other words, social meaning is created by linguistic forms above and beyond their referential meaning. For example, Stewart and Bennett (1991) suggest that American English forces causality and a fixed understanding of the relationship between nouns and their attributes upon its users with expressions like "it is raining" (who is "it"?) and "the sky *is* blue" (really? always?). As we unpack sociolinguistic rules, we are able to look into the "how" of interaction – phenomena like dialects, styles, word choice (lexicon), aspects of meaning (semantics), sounds and pronunciation (phonology), the way in which words are combined to form sentences and expressions (syntax), and the way in which language is used in specific contexts (pragmatics). Both separately and together, these rule systems reflect culture in varying ways.

Rules related to pronunciation fall under the study of *phonetics* and *phonemics*. For example, in English the letter T can be pronounced with a number of subtle variations and one not so subtle voicing. The traditional T sound (or allophone) has a hard, staccato sound as in telephone, bat, or stop. Notice where your tongue is hitting the top of your mouth, just behind your front teeth in that articulation. It can also have a non-fricative, or glottal stop voicing as in beaten, curtain, or kitten. With this allophone the tongue doesn't even really touch the roof of your mouth until after you say the letter. Rather it is formed by cutting off the air in the back of your throat; in other words, a glottal stop. The not-so-subtle difference is the kind of T we've used in two different words in these past few sentences: "traditional" and "articulation." The second T in each of those words uses a soft sound that doesn't even resemble the other allophones for T. The phonetic rules, or grammar, for the letter T's various allophones describe the conditions under which each pronunciation occurs. The letter T has the distinction of having the most allophones of all the letters in the English alphabet. Depending on how you count them and the dialect in use, the English language uses 35–40 allophones. When we are referring to the letter T without regard to its pronunciation, but rather to the meaning it has across all pronunciation cases, then we are dealing with *phonemic* rules. So, for instance, the very first letter in the English dictionary is "A." The phonemic rule tells us that it is an indefinite article, as opposed to the definite article "the," and is used to refer to objects. Understanding the idiosyncrasies of our first language helps us to be aware of idiosyncrasies in other languages, such that we are mindful of ways in which idiosyncrasies in language may influence (mis)understanding in intercultural spaces.

Language rules that relate to the meaning of words fall under the study of *semantics*. One of the more interesting cross-cultural areas of study in semantics concerns idiomatic expressions. While Ripley was in graduate school, he conducted a study among international students on campus and asked them to define common American-English expressions like "Sherri is a bookworm," or "Bill is up a creek without a paddle," and "keep a stiff upper lip." The students that came from non-English L1 backgrounds had a difficult time trying to discern the meaning behind those expressions. It was a similar case when he presented US-American students with the following excerpt from a letter to an American student from her Australian friend, written in "Strine:"

> I met a bloke from down the street and we decided to walk down to the river to sunbake. We dressed like dags, put on sandshoes, grabbed an icypole and left on the footpath. This cheeky kid in a ute heard me talk and started to knock me in a pom accent. I needed the time to relax, I was stuffed because we were moving flat-out. We had a barbie, played footy, and eventually filled out papers for uni.

That paragraph is filled with slang and *connotative* meanings that confuse American English speakers. Here is a "translation" for non-Strine speakers:

> I met a man/guy from down the street and we decided to walk down to the river to lie in the sunshine. We dressed down in old/unfashionable/extremely casual clothes, put on walking shoes, grabbed a popsicle and walked down the side-walk. This disrespectful kid in a utility vehicle heard me talk and started to talk down to me in a British accent. I needed time to relax, I was tired because we were moving fast. We had a barbeque, played football, and eventually filled out application forms for university.

These kinds of idiomatic problems trip up international businesses as well. Any number of idiom-related faux pas have occurred in product and marketing situations over the years. For example, Kentucky Fried Chicken's slogan "Finger Lickin' Good" translated poorly into Mandarin, resulting in, "Eat your fingers off." Coors, the American brewing company famous for its fresh Rocky Mountain origin, launched a "Turn It Loose" campaign in Spain. Unfortunately, the equivalent Spanish tagline was a common expression for those suffering from diarrhoea. British banking powerhouse, HSBC, was forced to undergo a multimillion-dollar rebranding effort in 2009 to correct a long-running "Assume Nothing" campaign that translated as "Do Nothing" in multiple markets around the world. Or, the former American Motor Corporation's *Matador* model did not sell well in Puerto

Rico as expected, because it conjured up the equivalent of "killer," which ended up not being a great branding image for a car. As you can see from these examples, idiomatic mistranslation is a challenge when communicating in intercultural spaces. Although avoiding idioms or perhaps pausing to explain idioms might be a good thing in intercultural spaces, idioms aren't always obvious for those who are immersed in a sociolinguistic context, unless we are mindful – more on that in Chapter 7.

Similar to idiomatic expressions that are dependent on context for their meaning, problems with *lexical equivalence*, or lexical gaps, also reveal culture-specific meanings. A lexical gap occurs when a word or phrase exists in one language, but the equivalent word does not exist in another. An example is the French word, *detente*. It captures an easing of tensions between nations, but there is no single English word with that meaning. Zerubavel (2018) adds that these gaps also occur when our language contains subtle assumptions that often hide alternative possibilities from our view. A poignant example of lexical equivalence/gaps is given in Anne Fadiman's book, *The Spirit Catches You and You Fall Down*. In her story, a Hmong family grapples with the California medical system when their young daughter is diagnosed with epilepsy. The Hmong language does not have a word for epilepsy as a serious medical condition. Instead, it is culturally perceived as *qaug dab peg*, or an honourable ability of a person to temporarily communicate with the spirit world. The plot of the story revolves around the misunderstandings and tension between the medical community and the family's beliefs about what is taking place in their daughter. These kinds of lexical discrepancies are not just about abstract labels applied to material realities, but strike at the very core of our experience of the world. Communication in intercultural spaces often involves one or more persons speaking in a language other than their first language. As such, lexical gaps become particularly relevant if the communicators are not sufficiently familiar with the language or contextual use of the language.

Semantic differences are built into the grammatical structure of our languages as well. For example, languages like Spanish and Hindi that encode gender into certain nouns influence the way in which we experience certain kinds of phenomena or what we are forced to declare to our listeners. For example, if I tell you in English that, "I went to see my doctor today," you have no idea whether my doctor is male or female. But, if I tell you the same thing in Spanish, "Fui a ver a mi doctora hoy," I am obliged to let you know that my doctor is a female. On the other hand, I *am* obligated to be time-conscious in telling you about my doctor visit in English (I went, I am going, I will go, etc.). Whereas in many Sino-Tibetan languages, like Chinese, I am not forced to declare the timing of verbs by using tense because a single form can be used for past, present, and future cases, emphasising the interconnectedness of events. For example, in Chinese, the verb forms for "to buy," including "buy," "buying," and "bought," are all communicated with the same form, *mǎi*. Instead of conjugation, speakers, readers, and writers must rely on the context in order to ascertain the intended meaning in Chinese.

Deutscher (2010a) provides additional compelling examples of how the structure of our language cultivates "habits of mind" like assigning gender to inanimate objects such as bridges and beds. More importantly, there is a growing body of research that suggests structural and semantic associations have far reaching consequences; "once gender connotations have been imposed on impressionable young minds, they lead those with a gendered mother tongue to see the inanimate world through lenses tinted with [particular] associations and emotional responses" (Deutscher, 2010a, p. 42). Sociologist Antonio Gramsci was concerned about the implications of these kinds of language associations as well, believing that "culture, embedded in language and everyday practices, constrains people's capacity to imagine alternatives to existing arrangements" (DiMaggio, 1997, p. 268). For example, speakers of German, Spanish, and French divide up the world linguistically between the familiar and unfamiliar, or by status and authority, due to the formal/plural and informal pronouns (e.g., Du/Sie in German). If you are familiar to me, or you occupy a lower status (e.g., a child) I will address you with the Spanish *tu* rather than the formal *usted*. Whereas in the world of English, I am not obligated to overtly (linguistically) acknowledge status and familiarity. The language forms the foreground, or brings to conscious awareness, a social relationship as part of most interactions. Once more, the relevance of semantic differences in intercultural spaces is self-evident, especially if you contemplate the scenario wherein speakers whose first language is not gender encoded have to speak in a common language that *is* gender encoded.

The characteristic of language to highlight certain elements of our environment and relationships and obfuscate other features has implications for sociopolitical power relationships. For centuries, appending certain professional titles with the word "man" in English speaking societies had very real implications for women's career opportunities. Titles like "chairman of the board," "clergyman," "policeman or fireman," "salesman," "longshoreman," "handyman," "stuntman," "councilman," and "anchorman" all implicitly suggested that the person occupying that job should be a man. And when those words become normative, we end up not seeing what we're leaving out, which has meaningful consequences (Zerubavel, 2018, p. 69). Through our language system we often conform to the status quo and perpetuate *ignorance* until we step outside of the system and *recognise* our blind spots. As Konecki (2021) pointed out, "socialised language is vital for reproducing social structure and power" (p. 1151).

We mentioned earlier that language serves a primary function in constructing our identities. It is equally true, then, that one's ability to mirror the dominant speech style demarcates a line of inclusion and oppression. From casual interpersonal interaction to housing, education, the media, the criminal justice system, or finding a job, sociolinguistic identity can quickly become a marker within the public sphere that comes with expectations to accommodate or enforce the normative linguistic standard (Lippi-Green, 2011).

We hope it is clear by now that language shapes culture in multiple ways, influencing how individuals perceive and interact with the world around them, and reflecting cultural values and practices. Many of those practices and expressions are also encoded nonverbally. We can illustrate that by returning to our opening Star Trek scenario with Captains Picard and Dathon. Almost immediately upon arriving on the planet's surface, Captain Dathon begins gesturing emphatically towards Picard with a dagger in either hand. He then throws one dagger at Picard's feet and urges him to pick it up. Picard interprets the behaviour as an invitation to fight the other captain. He imagines that he has been abducted in order to be matched in battle with Captain Dathon, with the winner possibly taking possession of the other captain's vessel and crew. In addition to his attempts to speak with Captain Picard in the metaphorical Tamarian language, Captain Dathon was desperately trying to convey his feelings and meaning through the language of behaviour. Next, we'll turn our attention to the ways in which the "silent language" of nonverbal expression reflects cultural values and patterns.

Out of Awareness Communication and Culture

In Chapter 2 you were introduced to Edward T. Hall, the anthropologist at the US Foreign Service Institute that popularised the need to examine "unconscious culture" because behaviours like gestures, eye contact, and our use of space and time are subconsciously patterned by culture. His point was made in the first sentence of the first chapter of his ground-breaking book, *The Silent Language*: "Time talks. It speaks more plainly than words" (Hall, 1959, p. 1).

The truth of those first two words is evident, albeit in different ways, in every culture. In the United States, being "on time" for a dinner engagement conveys courtesy and respect for the host. In England, it is appropriate to be 5–15 minutes late for an invitation to dinner, arriving too punctually gives the appearance of rushing the host to feed you. In Australia, it is better to arrive a few minutes early for a business meeting. In Ecuador, arriving a few minutes late for a business meeting conveys power and status. Unlike verbal language with its layers of grammar, however, there are very few formal, stated rules when it comes to nonverbal expression. There is no playbook describing the myriad different behaviours. Likewise, because nonverbal behaviour is by nature high context, relying on signs and analogues to convey its message, it is both more ambiguous and more efficient than verbal communication. For example, it is quicker to flash a smile at someone than to explain to them that they made you happy. And a grimace could suggest frustration or perseverance or even pain. But those same properties of ambiguity and efficiency open the door to misinterpretation as well. Nonverbal codes serve several important communication functions, such as complementing a verbal message (smiling while saying "I'm so happy to see you"), contradicting a verbal message (frowning while saying, "That's great!"), substituting for a verbal message (nodding instead of saying "yes") or reiterating a verbal message (holding up four fingers while saying "four").

Unfortunately, nonverbal intercultural communication isn't as simple as translating from one coding language to another where there is an agreed upon transformation from one set of symbols to another (Cherry, 1978). Implicit in Hall's terse initial insight is that nonverbal codes are not only silent, but they are *culture-specific*. Hall's second sentence captures the organic, behavioural quality that is distinct from verbal communication. Nonverbals suffer less from the arbitrary symbol–referent relationship we discussed earlier related to verbal codes.

Nonverbals are more viscerally connected to our emotive meanings or internal states, and therefore some conclude that they communicate, at least with respect to our relational messages, more accurately than verbal codes (Anderson, 1991).

Similar to our investigation of verbal language, our primary question with respect to nonverbal behaviour is how does culture express itself? The literature surrounding nonverbal communication has formed a soft consensus around the following categories of nonverbal behaviour: time (chronemics), space (proxemics), body movement (kinesics, including facial expressions and gestures), touch (haptics), eye contact (oculesics, including gaze), paralanguage (vocalics), smell (olfactics), silence, and artefacts and personal appearance (Anderson, 1991; Hall & Knapp, 2013). Through these varied channels we communicate things like intimacy, affirmation, affection, understanding, and displeasure or frustration. One of the burning questions that consumed early scholars' attention in this area had to do with the universality of nonverbal expressions of emotion. Anthropologists like Margaret Mead (1975) and Ray Birdwhistell (1970) claimed that Darwin (1872) had it wrong when he concluded that all humans shared a common set of facial expressions. And for a time, it seemed they were right since studies in the first half of the 20th century were inconclusive.

But later research would demonstrate that, indeed, at least seven emotions expressed through our faces *are* universally recognised. These are, anger, contempt, disgust, fear, happiness, sadness, and surprise (Matsumoto & Hwang, 2013). Thus, the shared FOXP2 gene may have some influence over the expression of our silent language as well as our verbal codes. The question of culture's relationship to nonverbal expression captured Hall's attention while working at the Foreign Service Institute primarily because he felt it took place outside our conscious awareness, and therefore represented a bigger problem than most people realised.

Time Orientation

In the case of time orientation, Hall couldn't have been more correct. His original observations on cultural uses of time developed into the *monochronic* (M time) to *polychronic* (P time) continuum, similar to Hofstede's long-term orientation introduced in Chapter 3. He argued that this *micro time* continuum is culture-specific and operates almost entirely outside of our conscious awareness (Hall, 1983, p. 24). Cultures that operate on a monochronic orientation see time as fixed, limited, and linear. In this orientation it is normally appropriate to undertake one activity at a time in order to "concentrate," because time is tangible to the extent that it can be measured, managed, wasted, saved, and spent. M-time cultures emphasise schedules, punctuality, and a zero-sum mentality, because you can only increase your number of activities or involvements by decreasing the time allotted to each. To some extent the M-time orientation can also be associated with a future orientation insofar as planning and scheduling are required elements of segmenting a limited resource and responding to change (Condon, 2015; Hall, 1983; Kluckhohn & Strodtbeck, 1961).

In contrast, a polychronic orientation experiences time as abundant, non-linear, and as intangible as the air that surrounds us. P-time lends itself to multi-tasking and generally focuses on what is immediate and present within a deep appreciation for the historical context of people, places, and events. A P-time orientation places the stress on the sacredness of a particular moment, not the list of appointments that must be adhered to religiously. For example, a manager oriented towards monochronic time would perceive a knock on the door by an employee as an interruption to the scheduled activity presently in progress, and may ask the employee to wait until she completes the activity. If the manager's time orientation was polychronic, she would see the conversation with the employee as part of the day, even if the conversation makes her late for her next meeting. While the example is an oversimplification of time orientation, it highlights how, for persons with polychronic time orientation, what is immediate takes precedence over what is to come, as well as the non-zero-sum mentality where multiple things can take place at the same time.

The contrast between M-time and P-time orientations is profoundly illustrated in culture-specific musical forms. In common Western music theory the performers in an ensemble all abide by a shared time signature and metre, 3/4 triple metre for example. Everyone has a common down beat and follows the "map" of the chart or score (monochronic). But in some non-Western music like Gregorian chants, Native American flute music, or West African drumming, time signature and metre are fluid or *polyrhythmic*. In traditional Ewe dance drumming found in Ghana, Togo, and Benin, there are multiple time signatures integrating with one another in a juxtaposed call-response sequence.[5] Rather than playing a predetermined pattern of notes, each musician performs "what he perceives as the expectancies of the integration" (Anku, 1997, p. 213). Musicians don't count the beats in a measure in Ewe drumming, instead, they figure out how they relate to the timeline (sometimes even requiring the performer to momentarily disassociate from the existing rhythms). And the *emergent* rhythm is not the product of one particular player but the integration of the performers' contributions, requiring a high level of intrinsic awareness of the interplay between emergent and resultant rhythms (Anku, 1997; Dor, 2006).

The contrast between the unconscious M-time and P-time worldviews really can't be exaggerated. As Kubik (2008) observed,

> We can attempt to *translate* African musical phenomena into [Western harmonic concepts like rhythm, melody, and harmony,]... but we have to recognize that they have no linear equivalents in African languages. Even phenomenologically, the Western categorisations do not match up with what they purport to describe, because there is also in most African styles... an acute awareness of... not just "rhythm"; [but] it can be much better understood as... a delicate web of timbre-melodic and melodic-rhythmic patterns. (p. 138, emphasis in the original)

Such fundamental differences in cultural orientation to time have far reaching consequences on everything from organisational structures and bureaucratic complexity to the layout of work spaces and business meeting norms (Hall, 1983, p. 44ff). Certainly there are pros and cons to both time orientations. Hall (1983) noted that "the blindness of the monochronic organisation is to the humanity of its members. The weakness of the polychronic type lies in its extreme dependence on the leader" (p. 52).

The relevance of the monochronic/polychronic time orientation to communicating in intercultural spaces is evident when considering how orientation towards time could be misinterpreted as disrespect or lack of responsibility. For example, consider two friends bumping into each other on the sidewalk after a long absence. Friend A's response is to pause and ask how things have been, whereas Friend B keeps walking by, saying, "Sorry I can't stay and chat as I'm on my way to a meeting, but let's definitely schedule a time to catch-up properly." If Friend A's orientation is polychronic, he might view Friend B's response as rude or lacking in warmth because the present moment with a friend should have taken precedence over other things. Likewise, if Friend A had kept on talking and "delayed" monochronically oriented Friend B, the latter may have considered Friend A to be inconsiderate because Friend B had explicitly said he was on his way to another appointment. As in other frameworks, orientation to time should also be understood as a descriptive framework helpful for understanding behaviour rather than a prescriptive one intended to expect certain types of behaviour from certain cultural groups ("she must be monochronic because she's American").

There is evidence to suggest a connection between monochronic/polychronic time orientation and high/low context cultures (Ursu & Ciortescu, 2021). Polychronic cultures are more attuned to social relationships and strong, high context people bonds, while monochronic cultures feature a low context calibration to tasks, schedules, and processes (Hall, 1983, p. 53). Finally, it is important to note that variation in time orientation does occur across life sectors; for example, people could be monochronic in their orientation to formal time, such as "work" time, and more polychronic in orientation to informal or leisure time. However, Hall notes that even a compartmentalisation between work and leisure is itself a subtle adumbration of M-time (p. 175).

Kinesics and Silence

Some years ago, Ripley had an international student in his office who was distraught because she thought none of the US-American students liked her.

"Why on earth would you think that?" he asked.

She replied, "Because, when I try to talk to them, they pull away and avert their eyes. I get the feeling they don't like me."

As they continued talking, it became clearer that her Venezuelan posture, gestures, use of touch, and preferred social distance were perhaps sending unfamiliar signals to the host country students. They didn't know how to interpret her behaviour, and she didn't know how to interpret their interaction posture and social spacing. Consequently, her construal of their responses as unfriendly was a classic example of misplaced attribution.[6] Upon further inquiry with some of the local students in her classes, Ripley confirmed that students did indeed like her, found her interesting, and had nothing but positive things to say. Part of the issue was that her preferred social distance was a bit closer than the typical Midwestern US student felt comfortable with, so they were changing their body orientation and reducing eye contact in order to re-establish a comfortable spacing. It was not a conscious signal of displeasure or disliking. Her interpretation wasn't without basis, body orientations like leaning in towards others and facing people directly do communicate involvement, warmth, and immediacy in US settings (Andersen et al., 2013). She just hadn't recalibrated her behaviour and understanding to her new environment yet.

Body movement, or *kinesics*, is a broad area of nonverbal communication that includes posture, various body movements, gestures, facial expressions, and even conversational regulators like minimal vocalised responses to let people know we're still listening. The inability to accurately interpret the composite of these cues can lead to what is known in Japan as "kuuki yomenai," or the inability to read the atmosphere (Meyer, 2014). A great deal of research has been conducted in this fascinating area that explores how things like power, intimacy, persuasion, inclusion, and immediacy are communicated with our bodies in differing ways across cultures (Andersen et al., 2013; Matsumoto & Hwang, 2013). In particular, gestures can be difficult to interpret across cultures. A particular message, like greetings, can take many forms, from a firm handshake, to bowing, to prostrating oneself. Some gestures mirror what is spoken, known as *illustrators*, as when a person "speaks with their hands" while talking on the phone. Research suggests that these kinds of gesticulations are closely connected to universal biological impulses and happen largely outside our conscious awareness. In fact, a study among congenitally blind children demonstrated that even when they were speaking to other blind individuals, they continued to gesture with their hands, suggesting an innate coordination impetus behind these nonverbal expressions. Other gestures, known as *emblems*, replace speech, or occur independent of a verbal code, like the "okay" sign or the various ways of signalling "you're crazy." These kinds of gestures tend to be more culture-specific. Misunderstandings in reading these myriad kinaesthetic cues can cause significant relational difficulties in business, educational, and healthcare settings (Smith, 1993; Ursu & Ciortescu, 2021).

Another out-of-awareness and unspoken posture that complicates intercultural interaction is silence. From a Western-European perspective we often think of communication as the absence of silence. In this conceptualisation, silence is simply the "background to speech" (Nakane, 2007, p. 1). But in many non-Western cultures, silence is a complex and sophisticated part of the meaning-making process. Certainly there are unique grammars of silence taught to children in Western cultures, some of which give evidence to the environmental factors that circumscribe context-specific speech conditions. Rules like "A child should be seen and not heard." Or, "Don't speak unless spoken to." Or, "I know it's not my place to talk, but…" Or, "Shh, you're in a library!" And the function of silence can vary as well, such as when your significant other is giving you the "silent treatment" or you choose to "plead the 5th amendment" in order not to incriminate yourself. What should be noted in these Western grammars of silence is that most of the rules distinguish silence from *meaningful* communication. That is, silence is the absence of *communicare*, the Latin root meaning to share together. There are many conditions under which people refrain from speaking. Even the Western "silent treatment" is not so much making a statement, as it is withholding communication and highlighting dysfunction, resulting in the chastised partner crying out, "just tell me what I did for crying out loud!" The non-Western use of silence goes beyond that sense of absence, and instead becomes an important symbolic resource (Braithwaite, 1990). Such an approach to silence was made clear by the following student's story.

One of our students grew up on the Leech Lake Reservation of the Leech Lake Band of Ojibwe Native Americans in the American Midwest. He went away to college for his freshman year several hundred miles away and did not return home until Christmas break. When he came back home, several of his Ojibwe friends came by his house and hung around, keeping their distance for several days as he went about helping his father attend to work around their farm. He thought it was strange that his friends didn't come up to greet him or talk to him. It wasn't until several days had passed that his friends approached him and struck up conversations. He asked them what had been going on the last few days, referencing their lurking about his place but not saying hello. Their response was that they were waiting to see if he had changed before they engaged him directly. He found it curious that their means of finding out if he had changed was through passive observation, silence. Basso (1970) found a similar behaviour among the Western Apache of the United States where silence is appropriate in situations where "the status of the focal participant is marked by ambiguity" (p. 226). Silence takes many forms across cultures, and fulfils social, affective, and discursive functions (Albert & Ha, 2004; Ambele & Boonsuk, 2018; Carbaugh & Berry, 2006; Fujio, 2004; Ha & Li, 2014; Kim, 2002; Pietikäinen, 2018). For example, silence can be an indirect speech act that reveals, and sometimes conceals, information, or it can be a strategic tactic in impression management (Nakane, 2007, p. 8).

Proxemics and Culture

During trips to Japan, Taiwan, and China, Ripley became acutely aware of what Hall (1966) called *infraculture*. It consists of subconscious perceptual frameworks that underlie culture and have their roots in our biological origins. They in turn influence our experience of micro-cultural processes like territoriality, or our use of space. What struck him in those respective cross-cultural experiences were the distinctive architectural forms and city plans that reflected local values and philosophies on a grand scale. Proxemics is the study of how humans use space and create extensions that mark territory, both visible and invisible. It is used variously to signal status, ownership, and relationship characteristics (Matsumoto & Hwang, 2013). Hall made the remarkable claim that proxemic behaviour demonstrates that "people from different cultures not only speak different languages but, what is possibly more important, *inhabit different sensory worlds*" (p. 2). Ripley noticed East Asian sympathies towards collectivism, high context, and holistic interrelationship of spiritual and physical realities (*Dào*) in everything from building design and city plans to address systems. Hall devised a three-level model of territorial markers and refers to this level of proxemics as fixed feature space, meaning cultural design principles that get embedded into permanent structures. For example, it is not uncommon to see tall office buildings in Taiwan and China with large voids or cut-outs in them. And while they are aesthetically pleasing, that doesn't begin to capture the entire function. There is a subtle, yet profound, social and environ-mental logic in the design that resonates with its infraculture origins in *fēngshuî* (Almodovar-Melendo & Cabeza-Lainez, 2018).

Almodovar-Melendo and Cabeza-Lainez (2018) write that the requirements of *Dào* produce "a correlative way of thinking through which architecture becomes a human creation, which must reproduce the supernatural through cosmological ideas and thus remain in balance with the natural order" (p. 2). That philosophy emerges time and again in East Asian fixed-feature spaces (Gudykunst & Kim, 1997, p. 143ff). In Japan, it expresses itself through the old *Chiban* system of house addresses that were based on longevity of land ownership in the neighbourhood. Houses were numbered, or related, based upon the time they were built. The result was a neighbourhood of addresses that appear "out of order" from the standpoint of the British or American sequential system based upon linear proximity or loca-tion. Finding an address in a Japanese *chiban* neighbourhood therefore requires an insider's high context familiarity with the residents of that community. We grow accustomed to our familiar fixed-feature spaces. Does the room feel too big or too small, the ceilings expansive or oppressive, the road too wide or too narrow? As Hall (1966) observed, our use of, and markers for, territory "is in every sense of the word an extension of the organism" (p. 103). In each case, the externalities affect and betray our interiorities.

The cultural influence on spaces extends to *semi-fixed features* as well. How you arrange the furniture in your rooms or where specific activities "normally" take place in your homes and workplaces communicate silent relational messages. Sometimes we arrange our spaces to cordon off private areas or keep people at a distance. Hall (1966) called that kind of behaviour *sociofugal* space within this second level of his model. For instance, placing a desk between you and your office door creates a barrier, quietly saying "please keep your distance." *Sociopetal* space brings people together, invites intimacy, and communicates "my defences are down." Neither kind of space is intrinsically good or bad, and a configuration that is sociofugal in one culture can be considered sociopetal in another.

As a case in point, on a trip to Tokyo Ripley was visiting with a former stu-dent that played soccer for him once upon a time. They got together with some of the former student's Japanese friends to make potstickers and have dinner at their flat. Something you must know about Japan, and Tokyo in particular, is that given the relatively small size of the island and the high population density, the average living quarters are "economical." The result is an interesting semi-fixed space phe-nomenon. His friends' flat was a one-bedroom unit with a total living space of not more than 900 square feet. Three of his friends lived in the flat, which required that the "living room" double as a sleeping space. The fact is, multi-purpose spaces are quite common in Japanese homes, sometimes even accompanied by movable walls that allow you to adjust the size and configuration of the space to suit the activity. We prepared and ate the food in what my Western sensibilities called the living room, but which one of his friends also called their "bedroom." The flexible config-uration allowed the space to vacillate between sociopetal and sociofugal depending upon the situation. The important thing to remember is that these manipulable space characteristics affect and reveal our internal states and have the potential to promote or inhibit communication.

The third level of Hall's (1966) model pertains to what he calls *informal space*. Growing up, Ripley spent a lot of time in wilderness areas of the American West, Colorado, Wyoming, and Montana specifically. It was always exciting when they would come across tracks indicating a predator had passed through, or a bear's marking tree with tell-tale claw marks. Animals are by nature territorial, and humans are no exception. We have a series of concentric boundaries that demar-cate intimacy, comfort, and inclusion. Hall (1966) identified four zones of informal space by which we manage personal encounters, the size of which varies by cul-ture. The zone which arguably possesses the greatest cultural significance is what Hall called intimate space. In US-American culture, intimate space ranges from dirty dancing to about 18 inches. On an individual level, it is the space that a person maintains in order to feel comfortable during interactions, relying on a range of multi-sensory input from vocal volume and smell to posture and touch. The second zone Hall referred to as personal distance; it regulates social interaction and ranges from 18 inches to 4 feet. A society's norm results from the socialisation of com-munity members into largely unspoken rules that seem "innate," such that most are able to walk down a crowded street without "violating" spatial boundaries of passers-by. When you stop to think about it, that's a small miracle.

In addition to preserving personal comfort, spatial zones also serve to identify in-group from out-group members, with the latter unable to invade these first two zones without some kind of behavioural response that works to restore the com-fort level. It is important to note that while there are certainly cultural differences in these two informal spatial zones, research shows that there are also significant similarities in proxemic behaviour across cultures. From family interactions to sexual relationships and child rearing, some degree of universal behaviours like hugs, hand-holding, and breastfeeding exist in our proxemic and tactile behav-iour (Andersen et al., 2013, p. 312). Differences often emerge in these universal expressions in relation to when, where, and how these behaviours are exhibited.

The final two zones refer to average social distance (4–12 feet) and public interactions (greater than 12 feet). Subsequent research on these zones in numerous cultures around the world has confirmed the universality of the Hall's four zones, but has found that the relative size of the zones varies by culture and situational factors. He hypothesised that warmer climate cultures appear to be higher *con-tact* cultures with somewhat smaller preferred social distances and more frequent touching while cooler climate cultures appear to be *non-contact* cultures (Watson, 1970). However, subsequent research has pointed to additional factors other than longitude and latitude, like immediacy behaviours, that appear to account for differences (Andersen, 2011). It is important to point out that even though culture does play a role in both preferred social distances and touch (haptics), the primary factor is the relationship between the people involved (Matsumoto & Hwang, 2013). In general, close friends and family will enjoy smaller social distances than acquaintances and strangers. Having said that, there is a fascinating line of research that demonstrates how occasional violations of social distance norms can actually communicate interest, immediacy, and liking under the right conditions (Andersen et al., 2013; Burgoon, 2015).

Just as time orientation has implications for organisational hierarchies and corporate mission drift, so too proxemic patterns affect everything from community attachment to road rage. There is also an interaction effect between time orientation and proxemic preferences. Specifically, M-time people compartmentalise time, but they also compartmentalise space in order to achieve the former. P-time people are more likely to prefer open floor plans and sociofugal features in order to promote interaction and simultaneous involvement across activities (e.g., Japanese homes). On the community level for example, city plans in predominantly M-time cultures often feature grid layouts with parallel streets that never intersect. Two neighbours living one block apart can start out for a walk and never intersect. In contrast, many P-time cultures layout their neighbourhoods in concentric circles with streets that all eventually lead to the piazza, or city centre. Interaction with one's neighbours is almost guaranteed.

Finally, Deutscher (2010b) described compelling implications of the interaction between our verbal and nonverbal codes in our conceptualisation of space. He reported evidence that structural features of language predispose their speakers to particular experiences of space and direction. For example, speakers of English experience space *egocentrically*, employing self-centred directional terms like "left," "right," "in front of," "behind," "after," and "beside." All of these terms are implicitly dependent upon the location of self. Alternatively, an Australian Aboriginal language, Guugu Yimithirr spoken north of Queensland, uses fixed *geographical* coordinates to communicate directions and situate self in space. Guugu Yimithirr is not alone in using cardinal direction terms like north, east, south, and west for spatial orientation; various language communities in Mexico, Namibia, Polynesia, and Bali have been found to use the same method. The surprise to native English speakers that assumed their manner of spatial orientation was universal is that all of these languages necessitate that their speakers be constantly aware of cardinal directions; like having true North emblazoned on your consciousness, speakers of these *geographical* languages appear to have an instinctive awareness of their location with respect to the compass. This research appears to corroborate Gadamer (1975) and Zerubavel's (2018) historic-linguistic bias thesis in the formation of our thought communities.

Nonverbal communication is particularly salient in intercultural spaces because the various cues and expressions are out-of-awareness. It is important, therefore, to exercise increased awareness in these settings; as noted in Proposition 6, mindfulness is necessary for perceiving an intercultural space.

Hazards to Superficial Study of Verbal and Nonverbal Behaviour

A common theme throughout our discussion of language, both verbal and nonverbal, is that our symbolic encoding marks out territories of affiliation and separation, in-groups and out-groups, boundaries that carve up islands of meaning. If we're not careful, especially in our assessment of unfamiliar nonverbal codes, we can *overgeneralise* the practices of a particular culture group and generate stereotypes based upon a mythical average person. Because cultural differences are often interesting, even entertaining, we can also fall into the error of *exaggerating differences*. The result can be a harmful or hurtful caricature rather than an accurate description of a particular behaviour. Both of these errors play into our natural *ethnocentrism* and *prejudices* (based upon social categorisation effects). We need to remember that not all verbal and nonverbal cues are created equal, and that individuals within a particular culture group may or may not manifest particular behaviours to varying degrees. Finally, every culture is dynamically perpetuated by its members, and therefore is constantly evolving (Martin, 2015; Martin & Nakayama, 2010; see Judith Martin's narrative about her journey towards intercultural understanding). For these reasons, an attitude of conscious-competence mindfulness is recommended when interacting in intercultural spaces in order to sidestep these hazards (more on this in Chapter 7).

My Journey Towards Intercultural Understanding

Judith Martin

I grew up in a Mennonite/Amish cultural tradition. All my grandparents were Amish, and my parents were Mennonite, so I grew up within that tradition. My father was a pastor and he planted a church in Wilmington, Delaware, right in the city, but all of our connections were very much to our extended family. So, my grandparents were completely Amish in appearance and behaviour. They did have cars because at one point they had left the Amish church and went more towards the Mennonite tradition, but they never changed their church affiliation. They belong to what's called the Amish Mennonite church, so they weren't that far from the Amish in cultural beliefs.

The Amish don't believe in proselytising, rather the way to get to heaven is to be separate from the world and live the way they believe the Bible tells them to live. My dad still wore what they called the "plain suit," consisting of a narrow jacket made from dark fabrics, and my mother never cut her hair and wore a white net hair covering. So when I went to visit my relatives that's the way I had to dress, and when I went to the Mennonite boarding school, I had to wear a special "cape dress" and I had to wear the hair covering and I couldn't cut my hair. We didn't watch movies. We didn't have a TV. We didn't go to proms, we didn't have any of that. Occasionally missionaries would come to our church and show us pictures of Africa and different places, and so those were some of my early cross-cultural connections.

From an early age, and I don't exactly know why, I was more curious than some of my brothers and sisters. I wanted to know what it was like out in the secular world. And so, one year I was too young to go to the Mennonite boarding school, but had finished my Christian school grades, I had to go to the local public school for eighth grade. That experience opened my eyes. I don't think it was any accident that I fell into a little group of very diverse friends who were from different socio-economic backgrounds, religious backgrounds, etc. There was a Jewish girl, and there was me, and there was an Italian-American Catholic girl and a Greek-American girl. I went on to finish high school at a boarding school in Virginia that's associated with Eastern Mennonite University, which is where I eventually graduated from. So I also think that's something that played a role; I had this curiosity about cultures and how the world lives.

Right after college, I went to Algeria through the Mennonite church for two years to teach English in a high school. It was preceded by a year of preparation in France, where we learned French. I think through that experience I realised how complicated intercultural interaction is. I think I thought, because I had studied sociology as an undergraduate, that I kind of understood cultures; in some sense I just didn't expect it to be so hard. I had severe culture shock in Algeria; I mean, I managed, and I'm glad I was young, but when I came back, of course that's what I studied. We study what we're not good at, right? I studied intercultural adaptation, and in particular, re-entry. I had a really tough re-entry, so that's how I got into it.

I also realised overseas how American I was. I thought I had this big global outlook and everything because I was a "citizen of the world," and all that hippie stuff from the 70s. But then, oh my goodness, Christmas came around and nobody celebrated Christmas in Algeria since it's a Muslim country. I started to come to understand my identity a bit more, that I wasn't just a Mennonite or Amish or female, but I was American in my cultural identity. That led to my work on the sojourner phenomenon and later my work on ethnic and racial identity and whiteness and racial hierarchies. A real pivotal moment came as I worked alongside Thomas Nakayama, because I never, I mean it's hard to believe now, but I had never thought about what being White meant. That we label others, but whites are not labelled, which reveals a racial hier-archy. That was kind of the beginning of the second part of my career, where I moved a little bit away from acculturation, although that's very related, and moved more towards social and racial identity and hierarchy. I realised in hind-sight that while I was at Temple University for one year in college and living in an African American neighbourhood, I thought I understood things, but then I realised how much being White allowed me to simply not think about race. I thought a lot about my religious identity, my Mennonite identity, but never my racial identity.

For example, given my upbringing, I was not an "American" in a pop-culture sense – I was always embarrassed that I didn't know what people were talking about related to popular music, TV, and films – and yet, nobody challenged me like they did my co-author, Tom Nakayama, asking him where he was from – even though he grew up in Georgia. What they were really saying to him is, you're not really American, because you can't be from Georgia. The bells went off for me. I realised he had a very different experience in the world than I. That was a significant part of my evolution, to realise that intercultural adaptation wasn't just individual factors or influences, but it is a complex, dynamic process of understanding people's different experiences in the world.

Language as Invitation into Thought Communities

As we conclude, we return to our interaction between Captains Picard and Dathon. Picard begins to understand the mythological nature of Captain Dathon's metaphorical language as they struggle to relate to each other on the planet's surface. In a last-ditch effort to avert a crisis, he shares a mythological story from Earth about the *Epic of Gilgamesh*. In the story Gilgamesh, king of Uruk, and Enkidu, an enemy warrior, forged a bond of friendship while facing hardship together. His story ends up mirroring their circumstances and foreshadowing Dathon's death. But more importantly, Picard realises his *positionality* within his sociolinguistic landscape and the artificiality of socially constructed boundaries (Zerubavel, 1991). As with any topological space, the horizon within intercultural spaces is continuously being remapped as we negotiate shared and unique spaces with those we meet (Klyukanov, 2005, p. 143). Within each of those meetings, we enjoy the opportunity of adjusting our *cultural gaze* and learning to see the world in a slightly different manner. Picard learns that Captain Dathon didn't abduct him in order to work on a mutual translation project, or teach him a lesson, but rather to invite him into an experience that would mirror Dathon's style of consciousness, and perhaps provide Picard a pathway towards understanding other cultures that appear to be "incomprehensible" (trekdocs, 2016). In the end, intercultural spaces are in part discursive spaces where meaning is constructed through language, both verbal and nonverbal (Martin & Nakayama, 2010).

In Conversation: The Language of Racialisation

Ripley: When I referenced people of colour in this chapter… you didn't seem to like that term.

Lily: I had highlighted it and said, "I wouldn't use that term," didn't I?

Ripley: Yes, why is that? I had mentioned that APA actually prefers that expression now over other terms that refer to the composite of non-White racial groups.

Lily: Yes, I wasn't aware that it was a sanctioned phrase in the common vernacular in the US. To me it's problematic on two levels. One is that it homogenises everyone who is "quote-unquote" of colour; and the second is, it doesn't recognise Caucasian or white-skinned people as people who have a colour, which… white is a colour [laughs].

Ripley: The origins of that category are interesting in and of themselves. It has a long history of usage dating back nearly to the beginnings of the US

African slave era as a term embraced by non-White communities to express divergence and solidarity. But its related category "coloured" was also used by dominant communities for purposes of exclusion.

Lily: Yes, in contrast it is a form of ownership of the "otherness" as well... to say "I'm coloured" or whatever else... I get that, but I think it's very much contextualised within the US. It's not a phrase we use in Australia.

Ripley: It is a paradoxical expression. As late as 1960 in the US civil rights movement the category "coloured people" was a symbol of racial pride (e.g., NAACP), but by the 1980s it accrued negative connotations in popular usage, and by the early 2000s "people of colour" became the more respectful descriptor of aggregate non-White communities.

Lily: But it still doesn't address the homogenisation of a variety of people who are not White. So, I wouldn't want to use a label that dichotomises White people on one side and everyone else on the other... which is deeply divisive, I think.

Ripley: So, if we're not going to use "people of colour" because it perpetuates the conflation of race with power and discrimination, what are some alternatives to that expression?

Questions for Reflection

1. Do categories like "people of colour" or "non-white" perpetuate racialised thinking? What do you think of Lily's feeling that it homogenises ethnic communities and creates division? Is it an example of minimisation (see the DMIS model in Chapter 7)?
2. What insights occurred to you by reading about the influence language has over the way you perceive the world around you (e.g., gendered nouns, implied agency, propensity for dichotomisation, etc.)?
3. Do you have a story about your own experience of nonverbal, out-of-awareness culture like the ones mentioned in this chapter?

Notes

1 Gadamer means something very specific by this expression and has an extended treatment of it in *Truth and Method*, a subject to which he returns repeatedly. He says, "The linguisticality of understanding is *the concretion of historically effected consciousness*" (loc 5903). Clarifying that "The essential relation between language and understanding is seen primarily in the fact that the essence of tradition is to exist in the medium of language... Linguistic tradition is tradition in the proper sense of the word – i.e., something handed down... What has come down to us by way of verbal tradition is not left over but given to us, told us –" (loc 5915). Thus, "the continuity of memory" is where tradition resides; "Through it tradition becomes a part of our own world..." And "It is the tyranny of hidden prejudices that makes us deaf to what speaks to us in tradition" (loc 4200). Later he indicates that "conventions of meaning... become sedimented in language" (loc 6079).

2 The self-reported nature of census operations and the dynamic nature of language communities that are affected by migration and mortality makes determining exact numbers challenging.

3 The psychological explanation of polysystemic variation rests in part in our behaviour of accommodating our language use to perceived contexts and referent groups (Giles, 2008).

4 Given the importance of that function, some linguists like Noam Chomsky have theorised that humans are programmed for language, suggesting that there is a universal grammar underlying all languages.

5 "Drums are generally considered the most important musical instrument of Africans… they are symbols of political power, … embodiment of black spirituality, galvanising tools, uniting forces, speech surrogates, and exquisite artefacts" (Dor, 2006, p. 356).

6 An attribution is an interpretation of the meaning and motivations of behaviour or the inferences about the causes of behaviour. Our goal in intercultural communication is to make isomorphic attributions with the host culture, meaning that we would explain a given behaviour approximately the same way the cultural other would. Heider, F. (1958). *The Psychology of Interpersonal Relations*. Wiley.

References

Albert, R. D., & Ah Ha, I. (2004). Latino/Anglo-American differences in attributions to situations involving touch and silence. *International Journal of Intercultural Relations*, 28(3), 253–280. https://doi.org/10.1016/j.ijintrel.2004.06.003

Almodovar-Melendo, J.-M., & Cabeza-Lainez, J.-M. (2018). Environmental features of Chinese architectural heritage: The standardization of form in the pursuit of equilibrium with nature. *Sustainability*, 10(7), 2443.

Ambele, E. A., & Boonsuk, Y. (2018). Silence of Thai students as a face-saving politeness strategy in a multicultural university context. *Arab World English Journal*, 9(4), 221–231.

Andersen, P. (2011). Tactile traditions: Cultural differences and similarities in haptic communication. In M. J. Hertenstein & S. J. Weiss (Eds.), *The handbook of touch: Neuroscience, behavioral, and health perspectives* (pp. 351–371). Springer Publishing.

Andersen, P., Gannon, J., & Kalchik, J. (2013). Proxemic and haptic interaction: The closeness continuum. In J. A. Hall & M. L. Knapp (Eds.), *Nonverbal communication* (pp. 295–329). De Gruyter.

Anderson, P. (1991). Explaining intercultural differences in nonverbal communication. In L. A. Samovar & R. E. Porter (Eds.), *Intercultural communication: A reader* (6th ed., pp. 286–296). Wadsworth Publishing.

Anku, W. (1997). Principles of rhythm integration in African drumming. *Black Music Research Journal*, 17(2), 211–238. https://doi.org/10.2307/779369

Baldwin, J. (2002). Stranger in the village. In J. N. Martin, T. K. Nakayama, & L. A. Flores (Eds.), *Readings in intercultural communication: Experiences and contexts* (pp. 81–87). McGraw-Hill.

Basso, K. H. (1970). "To give up on words": Silence in Western Apache culture. *Southwestern Journal of Anthropology*, 26(3), 213–230.

Berlo, D. K. (1960). *The process of communication*. Holt, Rinehart, and Winston.

Birdwhistell, R. (1970). *Kinesics and context*. University of Pennsylvania Press.

Braithwaite, C. A. (1990). Communicative silence: A cross-cultural study of Basso's hypothesis. In D. Carbaugh (Ed.), *Cultural communication and intercultural contact* (pp. 321–327). Lawrence Erlbaum Associates Publishers.

Burgoon, J. K. (2015). Expectancy violations theory. In J. M. Bennett (Ed.), *The Sage encyclopedia of intercultural competence* (1st ed.). Sage Publications. https://search.cre doreference.com/articles/Qm9va0FydGljbGU6NzY5OTU3?aid=107283

Carbaugh, D., Berry, M., & Nurmikari-Berry, M. (2006). Coding personhood through cultural terms and practices: Silence and quietude as a Finnish "natural way of being". *Journal of Language and Social Psychology, 25*(3), 203–220. https://doi.org/10.1177/0261927X06289422

Cherry, C. (1978). *On human communication: A review, a survey, and a criticism* (3rd ed.). MIT Press.

Chomsky, N. (1959). Review of *Verbal Behavior* by B. F. Skinner. *Language, 35*(1), 26–58.

Condon, J. (2015). Value dimensions: Kluckhohn and Strodtbeck value orientations. In J. M. Bennett (Ed.), *Sage reference publication: The Sage encyclopedia of intercultural competence*. Sage Publications.

Darwin, C. (1872). *The expression of the emotions in man and animals*. Oxford University Press.

Deutscher, G. (2010a). Does your language shape how you think? *New York Times Magazine, 42*, 26 August. www.nytimes.com/2010/08/29/magazine/29language-t.html

Deutscher, G. (2010b). *Through the language glass: Why the world looks different in other languages*. Metropolitan Books.

DiMaggio, P. (1997). Culture and cognition. *Annual Review of Sociology, 23*, 263–287.

Dor, G. W. K. (2006). Drumming. In A. Prahlad (Ed.), *The Greenwood Encyclopedia of African American folklore* (pp. 356–363). Greenwood Press.

Eberhard, D. M., Simons, G. F., & Fenning, C. D. (Eds.). (2023). *Ethnologue: Languages of the World* (26th ed.). SIL International.

Fiedler, K., & Freytag, P. (2009). Attribution theories wired into linguistic categories. In H. Pishwa (Ed.), *Language and social cognition: Expression of the social mind* (pp. 349–369). De Gruyter.

Fujio, M. (2004). Silence during intercultural communication: a case study. *Corporate Communications, 9*(4), 331–339. https://doi.org/10.1108/13563280410564066

Gadamer, H. G. (1975). *Truth and method*. Seabury Press.

Giles, H. (2008). Communication accommodation theory. In L. A. Baxter & D. O. Braithwaite (Eds.), *Engaging theories in interpersonal communication* (pp. 161–174). Sage.

Gudykunst, W. B., & Kim, Y. Y. (1997). *Communicating with strangers: An approach to intercultural communication* (3rd ed.). McGraw-Hill Companies.

Ha, P. L., & Li, B. (2014). Silence as right, choice, resistance and strategy among Chinese 'Me Generation' students: Implications for pedagogy. *Discourse: Studies in the Cultural Politics of Education, 35*(2), 233–248. https://doi.org/10.1080/01596306.2012.745733

Haidt, J. (2012). *The righteous mind: Why good people are divided by politics and religion*. Vintage Books.

Hall, E. T. (1959). *The silent language*. Doubleday & Company.

Hall, E. T. (1966). *The hidden dimension*. Doubleday & Company.

Hall, E. T. (1976). *Beyond culture*. Anchor Books.

Hall, E. T. (1983). *The dance of life*. Anchor Press/Doubleday & Company.

Hall, J. A., & Knapp, M. L. (Eds.). (2013). *Nonverbal communication*. De Gruyter.

Heider, F. (1958). *The psychology of interpersonal relations*. Wiley.

Hoijer, H. (1991). The Sapir-Whorf hypothesis. In L. A. Samovar & R. E. Porter (Eds.), *Intercultural communication: A reader* (pp. 244–251). Wadsworth Publishing.

Holtgraves, T. M. (2002). *Language as social action: Social psychology and language use*. Psychology Press.

Jackson, J. (2015). Intercultural communication and language. In J. M. Bennett (Ed.), *The Sage encyclopedia of intercultural competence*. Sage Publications.

Jaynes, J. (1976). *The origin of consciousness in the breakdown of the bicameral mind.* Houghton Mifflin.

Kaplan, R. B. (1988). Cultural thought patterns in inter-cultural education. In J. S. Wurzel (Ed.), *Toward multiculturalism: A reader in multicultural education* (pp. 207–221). Intercultural Press.

Kim, M. S. (2002). *Non-Western perspectives on human communication: Implications for theory and practice*. Sage Publications.

Kluckhohn, F. R., & Strodtbeck, F. L. (1961). *Variations in value orientations*. Row, Peterson & Co.

Klyukanov, I. E. (2005). *Principles of intercultural communication*. Pearson Education.

Konecki, K. T. (2021). Distinctions and something between: An inspection of Eviatar Zerubavel's concept driven sociology. *The Qualitative Report, 26*(4), 1150–1156. https://doi.org/10.46743/2160-3715/2021.4780

Kubik, G. (2008). *Africa and the Blues*. University Press of Mississippi.

Lippi-Green, R. (2011). *English with an accent: Language, ideology and discrimination in the United States*. Taylor & Francis Group.

Martin, J. N. (2015). Revisiting intercultural communication competence: Where to go from here. *International Journal of Intercultural Relations, 48*, 6–8.

Martin, J. N., & Nakayama, T. K. (2010). *Intercultural communication in contexts* (5th ed.). McGraw-Hill.

Matsumoto, D., & Hwang, H. C. (2013). Culture and nonverbal communication. In J. A. Hall & M. L. Knapp (Eds.), *Nonverbal communication* (pp. 697–727). De Gruyter.

Mead, G. H. (1934). *Mind, self & society from the standpoint of a social behaviorist*. University of Chicago Press.

Mead, M. (1975). Review of *Darwin and Facial Expression. Journal of Communication, 25*, 209–213.

Meyer, E. (2014). Looking another culture in the eye. *New York Times*, 14 September, p. 8.

Nakane, I. (2007). *Silence in intercultural communication: Perceptions and performance.* John Benjamins Publishing.

Ogden, C. K., & Richards, I. A. (1923/1989). *The meaning of meaning: A study of the influence of language upon thought and of the science of symbolism*. Harcourt Brace Jovanovich.

Peters, J. D. (1999). *Speaking into the air: A history of the idea of communication*. University of Chicago Press.

Philipsen, G. (1987). The prospect for cultural communication. In D. L. Kincaid (Ed.), *Communication theory: Eastern and Western perspectives* (pp. 245–254). Academic Press.

Pietikäinen, K. S. (2018). Silence that speaks: The local inferences of withholding a response in intercultural couples' conflicts. *Journal of Pragmatics, 129*, 76–89. https://doi.org/10.1016/j.pragma.2018.03.017

Sapir, E. (1931). Conceptual categories in primitive languages. *Science, 74*(1927), 578. doi:10.1126/science.74.1927.571.

Sapir, E. (1949). *Selected writings of Edward Sapir in culture, language, and personality*. University of California Press.

Smith, L. R. (1993). Kinesics in the multicultural classroom: An analysis of Hispanics and Anglos. *The Arizona Communication Association Journal, 19*, 193–212.

Spencer, H. (1852/1917). *The philosophy of style*. Allyn and Bacon.

Stewart, E., & Bennett, M. (1991). *American cultural patterns: A cross-cultural perspective*. Intercultural Press.

trekdocs [@trekdocs]. (2016). *Joe's response on Darmok: Fascinating ideas, though only the very core would make it to screen. September 4, 1990*. 15 July. https://twitter.com/trekdocs/status/753986378795450368?s=20

Ursu, O., & Ciortescu, E. (2021). Exploring cultural patterns in business communication. insights from Europe and Asia. *CES Working Papers*, *13*(2), 149–158.

Watson, O. M. (1970). *Proxemic behavior: A cross-cultural study*. Mouton.

Wolfe, A. (1992). Where (and whether) to draw the line [review of *The Fine Line: Making Distinctions in Everyday Life*, Eviatar Zerubavel]. *Sociological Forum*, *7*(2), 375–380.

Zerubavel, E. (1991). *The fine line: Making distinctions in everyday life*. Free Press.

Zerubavel, E. (2018). *Taken for granted: The remarkable power of the unremarkable*. Princeton University Press.

5   The Dark Side of Differences

Introduction

The 70th episode of the original Star Trek series was titled "Let That Be Your Last Battlefield." In the episode, the *Enterprise* crew rescues a suffocating alien pilot trapped on a stolen shuttlecraft from Starbase 4. When they first see the pilot, named Lokai, they are perplexed by his appearance, never having seen such a creature. He is humanoid, but is black on one half of his body, and white on the other. A short time later, a second similarly featured alien appears on the *Enterprise* deck and introduces himself as Commissioner Bele, Chief Officer of the Commission on Political Traitors from the planet *Cheron*. He asserts that he is there to apprehend Lokai as a traitor. It turns out Commissioner Bele has been pursuing Lokai around the galaxy for the equivalent of 50,000 earth years. He claims that Lokai led a revolt against the ruling class on Cheron, though Lokai claims that Bele's class enslaved Lokai's people. The *Enterprise* crew eventually recognise that Bele is black on his right side, while Lokai is white on his right side – that being the only discernible racial difference between the two. In due time, the *Enterprise* arrives at the planet Cheron, but sensors reveal that the planet's entire population has been annihilated in an apparent civil war. Bele and Lokai begin fighting each other on the *Enterprise* control deck, blaming each other for the destruction of their planet. Eventually they beam down to the surface of their devastated planet, and blinded from the insanity of their argument, continue their fight. Captain Kirk notes that all they have left is their hatred.

Proposition 3, introduced in Chapter 1, sheds light on Lokai and Bele's dilemma. It states:

> The lack of shared thought communities or cultural identities debilitate communication in intercultural spaces.

Conflicts between "civilisations" have marked every era of human history because of the inherent connection between culture and identity. However, 21st century network effects from transportation, migration, and globalisation that were described in Chapter 2 have exacerbated societal pluralisation and provoked the realisation of Huntington's (1993) *Clash of Civilization* fault lines, with their tension between

DOI: 10.4324/9781003318415-6

tribalism and globalism (p. 22). The evidence suggests that interethnic hostilities around the world are on the rise and each ethno-culture-related event ratchets up suspicion and violence, and plays into people's natural proclivity for social categorisation and the resulting dark side behaviours it motivates (Chua, 2003; Littler, 2020; Shaukat, 2020).

There are any number of barriers to intercultural communication that represent the dark side of relationships (Jackson, 2024; Spitzberg & Cupach, 2011a). We have touched on the ideas of social categorisation, ethnocentrism, stereotypes, and xenophobia in previous chapters, but in this chapter, we will delve more deeply into the reasons for those dark side phenomena, the ways in which they manifest, and potential avenues for overcoming their influence.

Origins of Bias

The presence of bias may be one of the most universal features of groups (Haidt, 2012). Contemporary societies are dealing with identity threat sparked by increases in migration, growing prejudice and discriminatory practices from dominant groups, and overt and covert violence in response to perceived race-related events, just to name a few. In order to address the root source of these societal concerns, we need to return to a familiar idea that forms the ground of the dark side of intercultural communication. We previously discussed the positive aspects of social categorisation (e.g., Chapter 3). But there is a flip side to that cultural coin, and what serves solidarity also promotes prejudice and discrimination. The sauce that binds people together in groups and provides the foundation for trust and cooperation is also the source of hierarchies, tribal rivalries, and intergroup threat (Kesebir, 2012). And when a human collective gets the idea of "we," the potential for an intergroup dark side is not far away. As the philosopher Willam James (1893) famously observed, "the breaches between [our] thoughts are the most absolute breaches in nature" (p. 153). Our opening scenario between Lokai and Bele depicts the destructive potential of that barrier.

Social categorisation and social identity are the most widely used theories to explain the dark side of intergroup relations (Rowatt et al., 2013; Tajfel & Turner, 1979; Turner, 1985). Social categorisation is a basic sense-making process that is fundamental to intergroup relations (Fiske & Taylor, 1991). It functions to distinguish self from other, and in the process produces attribution biases, stereotypes, prejudices, and can lead to discriminatory behaviours. The social groups to which we belong shape our worldview, behaviour, and experience of the world in powerful ways, often undetected by our conscious mind, demonstrated through implicit biases (Beelmann & Lutterbach, 2020; Somerville et al., 2020). General attribution effects include behaviours like favouritism for in-group members, as well as derogation of, and increased social distance from, out-group members (Hewstone et al., 2002; Tajfel & Turner, 1979).

A common example of such an effect occurs when you are on a long road trip, far away from your home state or province. You pull into a highway rest stop to take a break, and as you pull in, you spot a vehicle from your home state, which is more than a thousand miles away. Of all the people and all the vehicles at the rest stop, you are most likely to engage those "strangers" who just happen to fall into a "we" category for you. The likelihood will be compounded if their vehicle happens to display a decal of your favoured sports franchise on the back window or bumper! Social categorisation has been linked to intercultural barriers such as prejudiced attitudes and social distance (Halperin et al., 2007), identity threat (Cowling et al., 2019), plurality resistance (Wölfer & Foroutan, 2022), and religiosity (Johnson et al., 2012).

Social identity theory (Tajfel & Turner, 1979) pertains more to human needs for belonging and the impact group relations can have on the formation of self. People who share a salient self-categorisation may debate core dimensions of their identity, but they will generally align within a shared label and perceive themselves and others more stereotypically. Our self-categorisation, or group attachments, in turn "transforms self-conception and generates a feeling of belonging and group identification… [and] causes our thoughts, feelings, perceptions, and behavior to conform to our prototype of the in-group" (Hogg & Reid, 2006, p. 11). Our social identification tends to de-individuate others, which causes us to ignore differences and emphasise common in-group characteristics. Group membership also creates an emotional bond influential enough to affect our self-esteem. To boost in-group self-esteem, we often think of other groups as inferior to our own group. The resulting social comparison generates competition, negative attributions, and often hostility due to competing identities (Sherif et al., 1988). Sherif et al.'s (1988) famous "Robber's Cave" experiment was a classic demonstration of how group identity could create hostility between formerly friendly individuals.

A second source of bias is socio-economic class. The American Psychological Association defines socio-economic status (SES) as either a distinction related to material and structural wealth, or social and political power inequalities that set one person or group up for success over another (privilege). Both forms represent demographic disparities, or an explicit hierarchy based on access to, and possession of, material and social resources that affect some of the most basic elements to life like housing, education, healthcare, food, and income. Social class can also have implications for legal status. For example, the US Supreme Court has defined the position of being "socially disadvantaged" based on discrimination in income, education, or cultural opportunity. Very public labour strikes reveal these social class disparities when labour groups criticise the fact that CEOs often make 365 times the annual salary of an average worker.

Alternatively, subjective social status (SSS) is a self-ascribed comparison in relation to others that takes into account human, social, material, and cultural capital. Certainly, there is a direct relationship between measurable economic disparities and the subjective perception of one's "social class," but the latter carries with it the compounding difficulties of in-group/out-group effects. Manstead (2018) noted that social status is often characterised by differences in social capital (e.g., social network connections) as well as engagement in various cultural activities. There is a growing body of research demonstrating that social class and perceived status are primary predictors of beliefs, behaviour, and lifestyle (Henry, 2014; Kraus et al., 2019; Manstead, 2018; Urbiola et al., 2023).

Both SES and SSS have significant, culture-specific effects on our attitudes, prejudices, and behaviours. In other words, growing up in different status contexts produces an indelible effect on who we are and what we think (Stephens et al., 2014). Stephens et al. (2014) suggest in their research that our home, school, and work environments afford and promote different kinds of attitudes. For example, someone growing up in a low-income, working-class family and neighbourhood may have a more interdependent self-construal, realising that one has to rely on social connections in order to survive and get ahead, and that tough knocks are par for the course. Alternatively, someone from a more affluent background may have a more independent self-construal and lack personal resilience in the face of adversity by comparison. In fact, even in supposedly meritocratic environments like schools, certain norms and values that are more familiar to children from middle and upper-class backgrounds may subtly reproduce social inequalities. Thus, what may appear on the surface to be a question of qualifications or merit, may in fact reflect hidden advantages in the form of values and resources due to social class.

Of course, social class intersects with more common cultural and psychological identity markers like ethnicity, nationality, race, and gender (Urbiola et al., 2023). Historically social and cultural psychologists have ignored social class despite arguments by sociologists concerning its influence on identity, attitudes and behaviour (Eidlin & McCarthy, 2020). But recent TEDTalks by Coleman Hughes on colour-blindness and research by Manstead (2018), Stephens et al. (2014), and others is renewing a conversation around social class *as* culture (Dittmann, 2016).

Given these two sources of bias, we can now turn our attention to the repercussions of socio-cultural bias. We will break the bias implications into two types: those for which there is personal, or individual responsibility, and those implications for which there is corporate, or systemic responsibility. We will first survey the range of dark side obstacles that emerge in intercultural spaces before discussing productive ways to navigate your way out of the darkness.

Individual-Oriented Bias Responses

Intergroup bias has direct implications for personal attitudes, stereotypes, and prejudice. Recall the conflict between Commissioner Bele and Lokai in our opening scenario. From Bele's perspective, Lokai and his kind are intellectually, morally, and in other ways inferior to Bele's group. Approached from this angle, Bele exhibited some of the classic bias responses, including ethnocentrism, prejudice, stereotyping, racism, xenophobia, and discrimination. In turn, Lokai also reflected some of the same attitudes, emotions, and behaviours, less the authority to impose systemic discrimination. Together, they were the epitome of what Spitzberg and Cupach (2011b) refer to as "the study of all things depressing, deviant, or disturbing," collectively called the dark side of communication (p. 9). In the late 1990s they opened up a lane of inquiry in communication studies that explored the destructive potential in our communicative interactions. Brian Spitzberg, a professor of communication at San Diego State University for most of his career, takes us behind the scenes on the origin of dark side communication research.

The Personal Professional Scholarly Journey of Brian H. Spitzberg

Brian H. Spitzberg

I competed in drama and debate tournaments in high school; during my junior year, our drama coach asked me if I was going to try out for his end-of-year musical. I said no, and he asked why. "Because I can't sing." He said "Anyone can hum a tune. Try humming this…" He hummed a few notes. I hummed a few notes. He looked at me for a moment, and said: "Have you considered trying out for the debate team?"

I was successful at competitive forensics (policy debate), but not spectacularly so. Upon graduating high school, I chose to attend the University of Texas at Arlington in part because I could commute from my family home in Dallas. I had been a good-but-not-great student, but suddenly both my school and my peers were intellectually challenging and motivating. During my junior year I changed my major to communication because I had been taking those courses anyway since they were taught by my debate coaches. In my senior year, I consulted with my debate coach and mentor at the time about what I wanted to be when I grew up. After some discussion I considered communication consulting, and he recommended six universities where I could pursue a master's degree. I got a graduate teaching assistant position at the University of Southern California (USC) School of Communication. My first day wandering around the USC campus, I met William (Bill) R. Cupach, and we found we had a lot in common, including a background in college debate. Later I met Daniel J. Canary, who already had an MA in hand. My eventual success was actually in large part due to the reinforcements of this network. They were an essential resource, emotionally, socially, and intellectually.

I got interested in interpersonal communication in a fairly strategic move. I surveyed my options for our first assignment and looked for a topic that met certain criteria: (1) It needed to be broad, expansive, and expandable. (2) It needed to be deeply flawed. It had to need fixing. (3) It needed to resonate with me. (4) It needed to be esoteric enough, challenging enough, that not just any featherless biped could come along and beat me to the punch by the next conference. (5) It would help if it was interdisciplinary, as this would benefit from my library research skills honed by debate and might allow me to end up knowing more than my professors knew about the topic.

I chose the topic of interpersonal competence. For about the next 15 years of my life, virtually everything I pursued in my research was somehow intimately related to this topic.

My very first conference paper was about loneliness and interpersonal competence. Small wonder for a graduate student 1,500 miles from home. But increasingly, studying "good" communication seemed mundane. I was particularly intrigued by the conflicts, the dilemmas and predicaments of life, the perplexing, coercive, deceptive, exploitative, intractable contexts of communication in which competent performance was difficult to achieve.

Around the time of these meandering intuitions, I was asked to come in as co-author to revise a basic interpersonal textbook. I soon found myself having to contend with statements such as: an interpersonal communicator should be honest, understandable, cooperative, empathic, trustworthy, assertive, and so forth. Such claims not only seemed too simplistic and scientifically irresponsible, but they seemed intuitively uninteresting. As I started playing with the metaphor of the *dark side*, I realised that much of the discipline already dealt with it, but few had considered their common threads. I spoke to Bill Cupach about the potential of the metaphor, and we started developing a list of topics and scholars we knew who could contribute. By 1994, *The Dark Side of Interpersonal Communication* had emerged as a volume of scholarly topics edited by Bill Cupach and myself, and we eventually co-edited and co-authored four more volumes under this rubric.

The third phase of my career evolved when a political science scholar I had known at San Diego State University invited me for a conversation. He told me he was on a team with a geographic information scientist and a computational linguist, and they needed a good theorist in revising their grant proposal. They were proposing to see how well cyberspace data (e.g., tweets) could be correlated to realspace behaviour. To the extent the contents of such data can be geolocated and correlated to real events (e.g., Arab Spring and civil unrest, disinformation and disease outbreaks, etc.), it would be a significant tool for social scientists and policymakers.

This connection ended up with two large National Science Foundation grants. My new background was expansive – social media, geospatial sciences, computational linguistics, terrorism, civil unrest, public health, and memetics. The result was an entirely new line of studies and publications, including a new communication theory of meme diffusion and an analysis of COVID-19 pandemic misinformation and conspiracy theories.

The most important factors propelling me in the course I eventually took were: (1) loving parents who stuck it out through thick and thin, (2) not being able to sing (see above), (3) becoming active in intercollegiate competitive forensics (debate), (4) having a faculty mentor recommend me to graduate study, (5) having faculty in the graduate programme who envisioned me as an eventual legacy, and (6) forming a deep and trusting friendship with a compatible fellow graduate student, with whom I have now co-authored or co-edited about 40 papers, articles, chapters, and books.

While I do not have children by blood, I have dozens of published progeny that have garnered thousands of citations, and will remain in the digital DNA of humanity as long as humanity survives its existential and technological crises. Rabbi Shira Stutman recounts a saying by Maimonides, the mediaeval scholar, in the Mishna Torah, writing that "in a cemetery, everyone should have a headstone, … except for the scholars; … because their teachings are their lasting memorial; … when someone brilliant and righteous, a *tzadik*, passes away, what lives on are their teachings." May I be so fortunate as to have no headstone but for my teachings.

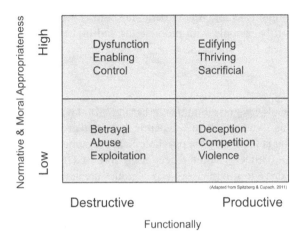

Figure 5.1 Dimensions of Dark Side Communication, adapted from Spitzberg and Cupach (2011a).

Spitzberg and Cupach (2011b) reviewed the characteristic features of dark side communication, which include everything from dysfunction to exploitation, and offered a two-dimensional framework by which to classify these kinds of messages (see Figure 5.1). The first dimension relates to whether people generally approve or disapprove of the behaviour and the second dimension refers to how the behaviour affects people or society at large.

Communication that is obviously abnormal or immoral, for example verbally abusive behaviour, falls into the lower left quadrant and is categorically destructive. There is no defence for exploitation, abuse, bullying, or infidelity. Communicative behaviours in the lower right quadrant are still non-normative or immoral, but can occasionally, or paradoxically, produce productive outcomes. For example, the nearly universal falsehoods of Santa Claus and the tooth fairy that are taught to susceptible young minds around the world, often causing tears, disbelief, and shame when they later realise the truth of these myths. Yet, a case can be made that the joy, imagination, and mystical wonder this deception brings to children around the world actually improves their existence, even if only for a few years. The final dark side quadrant is the upper left where we find communicative behaviours that appear to be normative or moral, but can carry a devious double edge. For example, when we assist refugee families that are resettling in their new host cultures, we want to come alongside and assist them in ways that improve their lives. But if we do too much for these families, we may delay their goal of self-sufficiency and acculturation (see Corbett & Fikkert, 2013).

What Spitzberg and Cupach don't mention is that power plays a role in each dark side quadrant. The role it plays is directly related to communication. As human beings, we wield an extraordinary tool in our words and communicative actions. We have the ability to lift someone up and put a smile on their face, or shatter their expectations and betray their trust, all in a word or gesture. Schultze (2000) called it *symbolic power* – the human capacity to define a situation and influence perception and action. It plays an unmistakable role in dark side communication. We all have some symbolic power, but people with more status and higher social class have more than those with less SES and SSS.

Othering

Another impact from social categorisation is "othering." In layman's terms, othering is creating an "us" versus "them" dynamic between groups with an assumed hierarchy. Othering is fuelled by the psychological phenomenon of *social dominance orientation* (SDO). SDO is a preference for group-based hierarchy such that privileges accorded to one's in-group vis-à-vis out-groups are not seen as problematic (Fischer et al., 2012). Across numerous studies it has been linked to an array of constructs that capture "an individual's *foundational orientation* toward social group relations" (Cargile, 2017, p. 40). We see othering in a pronounced way between fans of different sports franchises. If you are a Manchester United fan, the Manchester City fans constitute "them" in your English Premier League book. And the more a person buys into the social identity of "us," the more likely they will treat the "them" in dehumanising or marginalising ways. Sports fanaticism is a rather superficial example, although it can get carried away during contests depending on how many "beverages" the fans have consumed. But othering can be based upon much more consequential identifiers like race, culture, language, ethnicity, religion, or regional and geographic features. In each case, the distinctions are the basis for inclusivity, exclusivity, inequality, and occasionally conflict.

Ethnocentrism and Xenophobia

Our third set of dark side bias effects will be familiar to you from earlier chapters. Ethnocentrism is the belief that one's cultural customs, traditions, worldview, and norms are superior to those of other cultures. For example, Australians and Americans often tease that the other culture "drives on the wrong side of the road." Even though it might be said in good humour, deep down, the person saying it might really feel like "it just makes more sense to do it *our* way." However, ethnocentrism can move well beyond teasing into disdain and derision. Perhaps even more dangerous is when ethnocentric opinions embody a taken-for-granted superiority that elevates one's own cultural belief or behaviour as the standard by which all others are judged.

Interculturalist James Neuliep devoted a good portion of his career investigating and teaching his students about intercultural communication apprehension and ethnocentrism. He argued that one of the primary communication functions in initial relationships is to reduce uncertainty (as a coping mechanism). Consequently, we need to reduce ethnocentrism and communication apprehension because they both "impede the reduction of uncertainty during initial intercultural communication" (Berger & Calabrese, 1975; Gudykunst & Hammer, 1988; Neuliep, 2012, p. 2). He shares his initial introduction to the questions of communication, culture, and how ethnocentrism interferes with intercultural relationships in the following narrative.

Discovering Culture

James W. Neuliep

I was born and raised in a small rural town in northern Illinois approximately 100 miles west of Chicago and 30 miles south of the Wisconsin border. The town is agriculturally oriented and the home in which I was raised was surrounded by corn fields and bean fields, literally. The town was probably 99% (or more) White. In the summers migrant workers from Mexico were brought into town to work the fields. They were housed in what looked like a prison and were prohibited from interacting with the public. So, for the first 18 years of my life, intercultural communication did not exist. Ironically, beginning in third grade we were taught Spanish. But we learned the language only, not culture.

As an undergraduate, I went to a primarily White private liberal arts college in central Illinois, and I did start to meet students from other cultures. My plan was to become a high school teacher. During my student teaching semester, a few of my students were from other cultures and I started to learn about the different value orientations held by persons from cultures different than my own. I found them fascinating. I decided to pursue a master's degree and continue learning about other cultures. My master's thesis was a cross-cultural comparison of Japanese and American compliance-gaining strategies. My thesis was accepted for presentation at the national convention of the Speech Communication Association where it was awarded the Ralph E. Cooley Memorial Award for the most outstanding paper presented to the Commission on International and Intercultural Communication. I went on to earn my doctorate.

Early in my career at St. Norbert College, the College's president charged the faculty to internationalise the curriculum. In response, I created and developed an intercultural communication course. The course was initially for communication majors only but soon became a General Studies class. Each semester the class closed quickly with long waiting lists.

One of the early lessons I teach in my intercultural communication course is the idea that culture is learned. We are born human and become cultural. This leads to ethnocentrism; that is, the idea that one's native culture is the standard by which other cultures are observed and judged. As we learn our culture, we are taught the "correct" way to think and behave. One of the effects of ethnocentrism is that it clouds our perception of others. We have a tendency to judge others, and their communication, based on the standards set by our own culture. But ethnocentrism is essentially descriptive and not necessarily pejorative. Ethnocentrism often forms the basis for patriotism and group loyalty.

To be sure, ethnocentrism can be problematic. At high levels, ethnocentrism is an obstacle to effective intercultural communication. In 1997, my friend and colleague the late Jim McCroskey and I developed the Generalized Ethnocentrism Scale (GENE) which is considered the valid and reliable self-report measure of ethnocentrism. The GENE has been used in dozens of studies and has been translated into several languages. Future research should document how ethnocentrism evolves, develops, and shifts in individuals over time. A fascinating longitudinal study would be to recruit a sample of individuals who agree to complete the GENE scale at specified intervals over several years along with keeping a diary of their intercultural experiences. We could then trace how, or if, their ethnocentrism shifts over the years.

I've taught my intercultural communication class for over 30 years. Often international students will take my class. I enjoy that immensely because they offer so much to the class. Often international students from Japan and South Korea take my class. And although I encourage them to contribute, they rarely speak up or ask questions in class. One student from Japan told me (after class one day) that she would never raise her hand in class because, to her, that would be interrupting me. She told me that in her culture, "the tallest nail gets hammered down" and that by raising her hand, she would stick out. I told her that in US culture "the squeaky wheel gets the grease" and that by sticking out, you get attention [which is generally seen as positive]. On the final day of class, she approached me and thanked me for the class and all that she had learned. She said that by taking my class and learning so much about other cultures, she now knows what it means to be Japanese. She reduced uncertainty.

In 1948, the painter and writer Wyndham Lewis wrote about a "global village" in his book *America and Cosmic Man*. Several years later, his friend Marshall McLuhan also used the term to describe how technological advances of mass media would eventually disintegrate the natural time and space barriers inherent in human communication. McLuhan predicted that through the elimination of such barriers, people would continue to interact and live on a global scale – but one virtually transformed into a village.

A quarter of the way into the 21st century, McLuhan's vision of a global village is no longer an abstract idea but a near certainty. Technological changes have made Earth a smaller planet to inhabit. The essential effect of technology is its decentralising role in disseminating information across local, regional, national, and international borders. The ease and speed with which people of differing cultures can now communicate is stunning. Moreover, the sheer frequency and quantity of messages sent is baffling compared with only a few years ago. Initiating a relationship with someone from across the globe is much easier now than it was only a few years ago.

Although these technological advances facilitate the initiation and maintenance of cross-cultural relationships, we have to remember the idea of ethnocentrism. Too often when people of diverse cultural backgrounds converge in one place, the outcome is hostility of one group of people towards another, *different*, group of people. Ethnocentrism, the fear or even contempt of that which is foreign or unknown about a person from a different culture, inhibits and prevents the growth and evolution of the global village. Competent intercultural communication is essential. Now more than ever.

It is only a short leap from local ethnocentrism to distancing xenophobia in our global village, as Neulip pointed out. Xenophobia was introduced in Chapter 2 as the unfounded fear of strangers. That fear comes in many shapes and sizes, but there are three typical kinds of fear that are commonly provoked in host nationals by the prospect of immigrant populations. First, there is the fear of cultural change, or intergroup threat. Intergroup threat takes into consideration both real and imagined, or symbolic, fears (Rowatt et al., 2013). Identity threat is a type of intergroup threat and is often based on the false notion that cultures are static when in fact all cultures are dynamic and subject to change via internal and external factors. But the perception of a loss of control, disruption in sense-making and belonging, and the perceived threat to the continuity of one's cultural environment can be very real. Because religion plays a particularly prominent role in social identity threat, faith-based threat may be expressed not only by increasing social distance or holding biased attitudes, but also with outward expressions of violence (Rowatt & Al-Kire, 2021). Research has shown that unfamiliar cultural communication patterns can also increase threat perception, such as unfamiliar indirect or subtle responses in a low context situation, or high in-group boundary conditions in a largely individualistic setting (Rowatt et al., 2013, p. 177). Eskelinen et al. (2021) noted that threat perception is one of the key precipitating factors in the out-group exacerbation effect that occurs particularly in religious intergroup attitudes.

A second kind of fear is economic threat. The perception that immigrants are going to destabilise the economy and compete for limited jobs is a common argument against open borders. The fact that new immigrants contribute billions of dollars to national economies, are disproportionately represented among entrepreneurial ventures, and often work in less desirable industry sectors or manual labour jobs contradicts those perceptions. By some estimates, more than half of the most profitable American technology firms were founded by immigrants or first-generation Americans. For example, Apple co-founder Steve Jobs' father was a Syrian immigrant. Sergey Brin (co-founder of Google) immigrated to the US from Russia. And Amazon founder Jeff Bezos is a second-generation Cuban immigrant. As we're writing this, the combined market capitalisation of their companies exceeds $5.4 trillion. And of course, we should mention SpaceX founder and CEO, Tesla CEO, X Corp owner, and co-founder of OpenAI, Elon Musk, who immigrated to the US from South Africa. These significant economic giants represent only the top 1% of immigrant contributions to their adoptive home countries. The more than 280 million immigrants worldwide contribute additional billions in productivity and income taxes to their respective economies. A convincing case can be made that the global strength and vitality of countries like Australia, the United States, and Canada is in large part due to their historically open immigration policies.

A third fear that often attends immigration and cultural unfamiliarity relates to safety and security. This fear brings us back full circle to xenophobia. Recall that it means a "fear of foreigners." This fear taps into our fight or flight instincts, which both may trigger our fright instinct. Remember from earlier chapters that culture provides us with a measure of control over our environment. It serves as a coping mechanism for everything from relationships to work protocols. It is also true that the fear of things or people that don't resemble our thought communities fundamentally serves an evolutionary survival mechanism. Therefore, it helps to intentionally expose ourselves to new intercultural experiences and relationships so that we can cultivate empathy and open-mindedness as an antidote to our unfounded fears (more on this in Chapter 7).

Prejudice and Stereotypes

Technically a prejudice is simply a subjective, evaluative response to a given stimuli. That means it could be affectively positive or negative. It might seem intuitive to say that prejudice is bad, but prejudice wasn't always thought of as a negative characteristic (Gadamer, 1975). In fact, Gadamer argued that all understanding of the world inevitably involves some prejudice given that we are to some degree trapped inside our sociolinguistic conventions. Since the Enlightenment era, however, it has become common to think of prejudice as exclusively negative or unfavourable attitudes towards other people that are based on faulty and inflexible (stereotypical) attributions and assumptions (perhaps the exclusively negative connotation helps to explain our propensity for denying that we have any prejudices). Modern research has demonstrated that the experience of intergroup prejudice *is* harmful, and can lead to increased susceptibility of depression, psychological suffering, greater risk of negative health behaviours, and a lower satisfaction with one's life (Urbiola et al., 2023). Recent research has also shown that prejudice responses can present as ideas and attitudes (e.g., stereotypes), emotions (e.g., fear or hate), or behaviours (e.g., microaggressions, social distance, discrimination), and vary according to target population and context (Urbiola et al., 2023, p. 263).

A key example of an in-group marker that affects the personal and community life of approximately 87% of people around the globe is religion (Pew Research, 2022). Religion has been shown to motivate intergroup prejudice in a variety of ways (Rowatt & Al-Kire, 2021). Differentiation (exclusivity) is often at the core of social categorisation, and consequently a religious group's identity. Haidt (2012) argues that religion is a "team sport." It taps into social identity which possesses powerful group-level adaptation functions promoting cohesiveness, exclusive trust, and cooperation. Haidt refers to it as the *hive switch*, and to the extent that it binds people together for cooperation, it can also blind them from seeing the value of alternative perspectives and posture adherents for competition. Activation of religious identity has been shown to predict dehumanising attitudes towards immigrant populations and serve as an accelerant to prejudicial actions. Studies have also consistently shown a direct correlation between religiosity and unfavourable attitudes towards racial out-groups and non-dominant ethno-religious groups (Hall et al., 2010; Halperin et al., 2007). These kinds of prejudice often work hand-in-hand with stereotypes.

Stereotypes are often the cognitive precursor of prejudice. The word *stereotype* originates from the typesetting process found in the early printing industry of the late 18th century. It referred to the process of casting a mould based upon an original typography plate that duplicated the exact typesetting over and over again (viz., *stereo-type*). It wasn't until the early 1920s that public relations patriarch Walter Lippmann coined the psychological sense of the term as a selection process that is used to organise and simplify perceptions and attributions. As we discussed in Chapters 3 and 4, some of the mental schemata we inherit from our thought communities represent mental efficiencies, or shortcuts, and some of those shortcuts result in stereotypes.

It is worth drawing a distinction here between stereotypes and generalisations. A generalisation is a statistically valid observation based upon a sufficiently large sample size. We make generalisations all the time in social science and economic research. For example, the per capita income in the US for 2022 was $76,399 (based on GDP; see Figure 5.2). It is also true that US-American culture is individualistic (see Chapter 3). Those statements are generalisations, or etic observations, allowing us to conclude that people in the US behave more individualistically and are wealthier than many other people groups in the world. The generalisations can be true because they are based upon an average level of wealth and individualism across a large population. What we cannot do is apply those generalised conclusions to a specific individual from that population because any particular person may fall one, two, or even three standard deviations from the mean characteristic. To say that Joe Smith is rich and individualistic *because* he is a US American is a stereotype. In fact, Joe may come from a highly collectivistic family that lives in poverty. Attributing the generalised characteristics of a group back to specific individuals in a sample is a logical error called an *ecological fallacy*.

A great deal of what we know about cultural behaviour is based upon observing group characteristics and is very helpful in sensitising us to differences and adaptive responses. However, it is very important that we not inaccurately attribute those general cultural characteristics to individuals within the culture (Bennett, 2013).

The film *Crash* (Haggis, 2005) which won the 2006 Academy Award for Best Picture, is an interesting study in stereotypes, prejudice, and discrimination. It weaves a dozen characters into a nuanced narrative about their intersecting lives as they literally and metaphorically crash into one another in Los Angeles, CA. In one scene, two young male characters come out of a downtown LA diner and have the following conversation:

Anthony: "Did you see any White people in there waitin' an hour and thirty-two minutes for a plate of spaghetti?"

Peter: "No."

Anthony: "And how many cups of coffee did we get?"

Peter: "You don't drink coffee, and I didn't want any."

Anthony: "Man, that woman in there poured cup after cup to every single White person around us, but did she even ask you if you wanted any?"

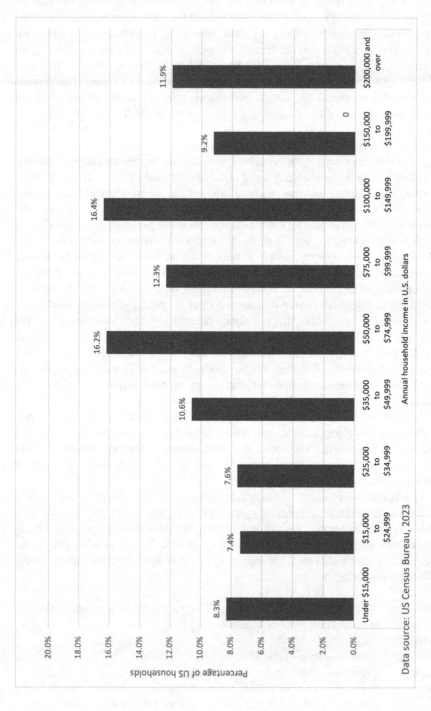

Data source: US Census Bureau, 2023

Figure 5.2 US Household Income Distribution.

Peter:	"We didn't get any coffee that you didn't want and I didn't order, and that's evidence of racial discrimination? Did you notice that our waitress was Black?"
Anthony:	"And Black women don't think in stereotypes? ... That waitress sized us up in two seconds; we're Black, and Black people don't tip. So she wasn't goin' to waste her time. Now somebody like that, there's nothin' you can do to change their mind."
Peter:	"So, uh, how much did you leave?"
Anthony:	"You expect me to pay for that kind of service?"

The entire film portrays various prejudices and stereotypes with a range of underlying motivations and functions from blatant, symbolic, tokenism, and aversive, to values-based and familiarity-based biases (Brislin, 2010; Katz, 1960). Some prejudices serve a utilitarian function because certain attitudes may lead to rewards or the avoidance of punishment within our thought communities. Other prejudices are ego-defensive, as illustrated by our earlier discussion of identity threat, in that they allow us to ignore certain personal attitudes under the guise of superiority. Lastly, some prejudices express strongly held values or sense-making shortcuts that shape how we see the world. As many of the *Crash* scenes make clear, stereotypic attributions are based upon an over application of limited and faulty observations and play into the dark side intergroup effects of denigration and disrespect. The scene above illustrates the extent to which everyone is prone to stereotyping given our inherent attachment to dominant sociolinguistic thought communities. Even Anthony's character stereotypes the server as "somebody like that... nothin' you can do to change their mind," all the while complaining about being stereotyped by the server herself.

Implicit Bias

Stereotypes and prejudices can serve as the cognitive and affective foundation of implicit biases. Implicit (unconscious) bias is a negative association that people unknowingly hold. Gadamer (1975) warned,

> we are led to ask with increasing urgency whether a primordial falsity may not be hidden in our relation to the world; whether, in our linguistically mediated experience, we may not be prey to prejudices or, worse still, to necessities which have their source in the linguistic structuring of our first experience of the world. (supplement II, para. 1)

He is restating a lesson from Chapter 4 where we first examined the hidden biases we inherit from our first language (L1). Beelmann and Lutterbach (2020) noted that these unconscious, learned attitudes and stereotypes affect our automatic cognitive processes (schemas) that are often derived from our thought communities and exert a visceral influence on behaviour. One form of those behavioural manifestations are *microaggressions*. Microaggressions are subtle verbal and nonverbal slights or insults that communicate disconfirming or negative messages to another person based solely on their marginalised or non-dominant group membership. Over time, the accumulation of these cultural messages contributes to an unwelcoming environment. Without mindful intervention, unconscious bias can result in unequal treatment of underrepresented groups and reinforce the use of stereotypes.

Racism

When we think about the dark side of intergroup relations, racism is often one of the first things that comes to mind. One of the most cited books on prejudice is Gordon Allport's (1954) *The Nature of Prejudice*. In his book, Allport regretted the fact that when we think about prejudice we often first think about interracial prejudice. However, as he observed, manifestations of prejudice have historically been more often about religion, ethnicity, culture, and language group. He noted that race, as a social category of thinking, is a fairly recent invention. Undoubtedly, the tendency to categorise others (even implicit associations) in terms of biological or physical traits (e.g., skin colour, hair colour, facial/eye type, etc.) has marked intergroup relations throughout time.

The earliest use of the word racism to describe interracial distinctions or motivate inequities is often traced back to a late 17th century classification scheme proposed by French physician François Bernier titled, *New Division of the Earth According to the Different Species or Races of Men Who Inhabit It*. It was an attempt to formulate a "scientific" theory of race predicated on biological features which could then be used to explain "meaningful" behavioural differences. Later advances in biology and genetics research would show that the relative DNA contributions to racial differences between human groups is fairly insignificant. Nonetheless, whether or not racial differences are biologically significant is really beside the point. The fact that the discourse of racial and ethnic categories has been used around the globe to structure and influence political, economic, and social realities requires that it be addressed at both personal and corporate levels.

Authors like Kendi (2019) define racism as "a marriage of racist policies and racist ideas that produces and normalizes racial inequities" (p. 17). Like Kendi, Cornel West (1993) highlighted power at the group level, claiming that it is responsible for systematic discrimination through institutional policies and practices. He noted that "racist discourses and actions have power functions beyond class/ economic exploitation… [we] need to understand the language mechanisms and structures that create and perpetuate racist systems" (p. 101). Power compounds the seriousness of race-based bias. This understanding of racism assumes a racialised worldview where race is a predictor of meaningful identity differences. When race becomes a distinguishing feature among groups, for example during eras of race-based slavery, then groups in power are able to embed those racial distinctions into institutions and policies that organise society in such a way as to perpetuate inequality and discrimination in access to opportunities, resources, and services.

We will discuss examples of this form of racism below when we discuss corporate expressions of bias.

Corporate-Oriented Bias Responses

Not only are there individually motivated and enacted dark side attitudes and behaviours, there are structural, systemic, and institutional dark side manifestations of bias, prejudice, and discrimination as well. When groups in power encode bias and discrimination into the operating systems of social, economic, and political institutions, it creates a cumulative inequality effect that can appear unintentional, or "natural." You might have noticed that we didn't define discrimination under the personal-oriented bias effects. The reason for that has to do with power.

Power in the hands of an individual can influence or control the behaviour of a limited number of people. It is true that an individual person can administer unequal treatment towards out-group members based on race, gender, social class, religion, and other categories (effectively prejudice in action). But the results will have a limited impact because there are legal protections against such behaviour in most societies. However, power that has acquired the appearance of institutional "authority" gains *prima facie* legitimacy. And discrimination carried out under the auspices of institutional authority is much more difficult to subvert, and much easier to deny in terms of culpability for harmful effects. While structural, systemic, and institutional racism are related concepts, it might be helpful to distinguish the nuances each term brings to an analysis of corporate racial bias.

Structural racism focuses on the often-unintended inequities that emerge in societal policies, practices and inter-organisational network effects that negatively influence certain racial or ethnic groups' access to resources and opportunities. For example, the connection between property taxes and funding for local public schools which disproportionately favours wealthier, majority community school districts over lower income districts that often have larger percentages of ethnic and racial minority groups. A similar phenomenon can be seen in the first- and second-degree network effects that impact hiring practices of many companies and organisations or the differential sentencing practices for similar crimes across ethnic and racial groups.

Systemic racism specifically refers to intentionally discriminatory policies and practices that were codified into legal, economic, political, or community systems that have perpetuated inequity, even if those original practices and policies have been rescinded. For example, the common post Second World War FHA practice of "red-lining" in US neighbourhoods that contributed to racially segregated suburban communities. An artefact of this practice is the Detroit Eight Mile Wall (also called the Birwood Wall), erected in 1941 so that the developer could get approved for FHA loans for homes built for middle income White families. The wall served as a separation line between the proposed White housing development and the adjacent primarily Black low-income neighbourhood which was characterised as "hazardous" for granting home loans. The systemic outcome of redlining continues to be reflected in average net worth disparities between White versus non-White Americans.

Other examples of systemic practices include biased policing practices and the vestiges of nearly a century of Jim Crow laws that deprived African Americans their due rights to vote, property ownership, employment, and education. One particularly pernicious form of systemic bias occurs in the form of media representation (Hall, 1994). Cultural studies theory describes how hegemonic media systems *re-present* symbols with preferred ideological meanings, including meanings related to racial, gender, class, and cultural identities. Those meanings can powerfully shape public understanding of people groups, issues, and events. Hall was particularly concerned about the role media play in shaping public perception of marginalised populations. When the media represent a given socio-cultural group, they select and emphasise particular characteristics that often caricature non-dominant groups. And in the case of indigenous groups, it sometimes has the effect of freezing those groups in a historical era. From advertising imagery to scripted characters and stereotypical behaviours, for some consumers the "diversity" they experience in life is largely built up from those vicarious mediated experiences. Hegemony is the influence one group has over another. And in the case of media, the dominant group that controls the production of content is able to constrain the identity construction choices. As with other dark side biases, media representation exists in what Hall (1997) called a theatre of struggle of competing ideologies. Each of these forms of bias reveals how systemic racism is built on the scaffolding of structural racism (Braveman et al., 2022).

Finally, *institutional* racism pertains to policies or behaviours embedded into specific organisations or institutions that perpetuate racial disparities. Institutional biases are covert in the sense that they appear to be "normal" operating procedures that have been in place for decades. For example, it has been argued that the format and knowledge items included on US university entrance exams like the ACT and SAT are biased in favour of White US students over non-White students (Elsesser, 2019). When discrimination is institutionalised it becomes self-perpetuating long after the original policies have disappeared from memory. It is this kind of racism that can be unintentionally engaged in, or the benefits of which can be enjoyed, without knowing consent of the original, ill-conceived practices. And it is this kind of racism which creates the controversial notion of bias-accrued "privilege" enjoyed by some segments of the population. The meaning of privilege in this sense is that institutional discrimination provides an unequal (dis)advantage to those that are affected by the institutional practice or policy. All three forms of racism are examples of corporate implicit bias, meaning that prejudicial and discriminatory attitudes and behaviours are baked into the substrata of society. These kinds of implicit bias have historically affected lending practices, access to healthcare, education, home ownership, accumulation of wealth, hiring practices, environmental injustice, biased policing, judicial sentencing, and voter suppression among other things.

It is important to point out once again that the ecological fallacy is just as true in its application to systemic and institutional bias as it was to the attribution of cultural behaviours. That is, just because someone is of a particular race does not mean that he or she has enjoyed a certain amount of privilege. Nor for that matter can we assume that just because someone is from a non-dominant race or socio-cultural group that he or she has been the direct recipient of discriminatory behaviour. But, on average across the broad populations of race and social class, we can identify disproportionate trends of inequality, injustice, discrimination, and historical representation of racial and ethnic stereotypes along group-based identities.

Intergroup Conflict

Our opening illustration of Bele and Lokai is reminiscent of intergroup conflicts that play out across the globe. In its more extreme forms, it looks like the re-emergence of violence in Gaza between Palestinians and Israelis in 2023, or the renewed flood of refugees into Thailand from the more than 70-year civil war in Burma between minority ethnic groups and ethnic Burmese. But it also can surface as mistrust or misunderstanding in a personal relationship between people from distinct cultural backgrounds. In either case, conflict is characterised by two or more interdependent parties that experience tension because of perceived differences in values, beliefs, behaviours, expectations, or access to desired resources. History bears witness to the fact that conflict is a natural outgrowth of the dark side of intercultural spaces (Landis & Albert, 2012). Learning to manage conflict in intercultural relationships is a key component of intercultural competence.

Our culture informs us of how to navigate conflict situations. In addition to cultural lenses like power distance and individualism-collectivism, our conflict style is influenced by our awareness of, or concern for, *face*. Ting-Toomey and Oetzel (2003)[1] defined face as "the claimed sense of favourable social self-worth and the estimated other-worth in an interpersonal situation" (p. 129). In other words, face is related to identity concepts like honour, dignity, reputation, shame, pride, and status. It operates on both group and individual levels depending on the nature of interaction and relationship between parties (Ting-Toomey & Kurogi, 1998). On the individual level, three motivating interpersonal needs drive our sense of face and efforts to save or restore face: 1) the need for control; 2) the need for approval; and 3) the need for admiration/respect (Giles, 2008; Spitzberg, 1991).

Our cultural patterns also shape the relative importance of personal self versus social, or public, self. For example, Ting-Toomey and Kurogi (1998) write that in some cultures "the 'social self' is expected to engage in optimal role performance, regardless of what the inner 'personal self' is experiencing at the moment" (p. 188). In other cultures, the attitudes and actions of the two levels of self are expected to be in sync. The alignment with either a personal versus social self is called *self-construal*, and is closely related to the idea of face (see Figure 5.3). Ting-Toomey (2015) reported that an independent versus interdependent self-construal has a significant effect on competent facework strategies. A person with an independent self-construal thinks of him or herself autonomously and separate from others. For the independent, stable self-face is their primary concern because they are personally responsible for their attitudes and actions and operate in a somewhat

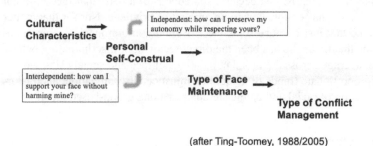

(after Ting-Toomey, 1988/2005)

Figure 5.3 Relationship Between Culture, Self-Construal, Face, and Conflict, adapted from Ting-Toomey (2015).

self-reliant fashion. In contrast, someone with an interdependent self-construal will see themselves with a more collectivistic lens and emphasise relational connectedness, solidarity, and focus on other-face or mutual-face needs.

When we are embroiled in an intercultural conflict like Bele and Lokai's, our preferred conflict style quickly emerges. We will outline common conflict styles below and discuss how they are related to self-construal and face.

Cultural Conflict Styles

When Ripley was a graduate student, he team-taught an intercultural workshop class with a fellow graduate student from Japan. They met weekly to prepare the lessons and activities for the class. When they met, Ripley would ask his colleague what she thought they should do for the lesson. She would defer and return the question without asserting much in terms of plan and structure for the session. So, Ripley would bring out his rough outline of notes as a place to start. His Japanese colleague would affirm the ideas, but when asked what she would like to modify or do instead, she would simply reaffirm the implied lesson from Ripley's notes. After several weeks of this, Ripley was unexpectedly called into his supervising faculty's office and chastised for not allowing his Japanese colleague to contribute to the planning sessions. Of course, this turn of events caught Ripley by surprise because his opening question was always "what do you think we should do?" In fact, he was beginning to feel like he had to do most of the work himself. Ripley and his colleague never discussed the situation face-to-face. The class continued, and the planning sessions subtly changed, with Ripley offering fewer ideas at a time and his Japanese colleague gently building on or adding to the lesson plan. It was only later that he realised he was caught up in a layered intercultural space in which individualistic versus collectivistic orientations, low context versus high context messages, and differing facework strategies were playing out.

Conflict styles and *facework* are symbiotic concepts (see Figure 5.4). Ting-Toomey and Oetzel (2003) think of facework as the actions we take to manage face needs during a conflict. Sometimes we are working to preserve harmony,

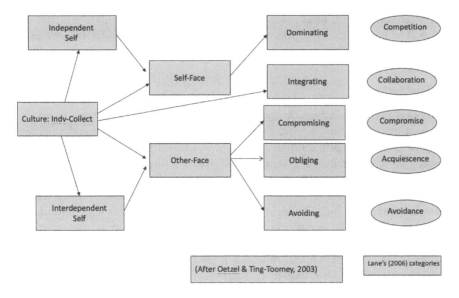

Figure 5.4 Facework and Conflict Style, adapted from Oetzel and Ting-Toomey (2003).

other times we are working to protect or restore self or other-face. And our cultural patterns, which influence our salient self-construal, impact the type of facework we will engage in. Facework involves behaviours that manage identity issues that are related to, but separate from, situation-specific conflict goals. Ripley and his colleague's conflict pertained to the course planning session goals. The way in which they approached the conflict, and its related self and other-image concerns, reflected their respective facework, or face management, strategies. Ripley's colleague employed a mediator in the form of the supervising faculty member instead of jeopardising the person-to-person relationship by introducing shame or dishonour to his face. It potentially allowed Ripley to allege his own private claims to the supervisor as well, while preserving the in-person harmonious working relationship. Research has shown that preferred cultural facework strategies align with specific traditional conflict styles.

In a common conflict styles inventory (e.g., Thomas & Kilmann, 1978) there are five primary conflict styles organised on two dimensions of assertiveness and cooperativeness. The styles include dominating/competing (assertive/uncooperative), avoiding (low assertive/uncooperative), compromising (somewhat assertive/ somewhat cooperative), obliging (low assertive/cooperative), and collaborating/ integrating (assertive/cooperative). Research on facework and conflict suggests that cultures emphasising self-face will prefer competing/dominating conflict styles that also correspond to low context, direct communication styles. On the other hand, cultures that emphasise other-face, or face-saving strategies, will prefer avoiding, obliging, and compromising conflict styles that correspond to high context, self-effacing communication styles (Oetzel & Ting-Toomey, 2003). If we are aware of these culturally influenced differences in conflict style preferences, we will be better situated to address conflict appropriately and effectively when it arises in our intercultural spaces.

Cancel Culture

The final dark side effect that we will examine is the 21st century phenomenon of cancel culture. Recent examples that have garnered national attention include students shouting down a US Supreme Court justice who was giving a speech on a university campus, and Hollywood actors getting their characters eliminated from a series due to private political statements expressed on social media. Cancel culture is a modern form of thought suppression or ostracism. Marginalising unpopular thought is not novel. Since the dawn of time dominant communities have attempted to silence new ideas that threatened majority positions and ideologies. For example, Copernicus challenged the geocentric nature of the universe with his radical heliocentric theory of the Earth revolving around the sun in 1543. It took more than 100 years before it was accepted by the broader scientific community, during which time some proponents were burned at the stake as heretics.

Cancel culture begs an epistemological question that we have bumped into throughout this book. That is, how do we come to know things? We have described how our thought communities shape us (Chapter 1), how culture affects our perceptions, beliefs, values, and norms (Chapter 3), how our inherited sociolinguistic frames influence our worldview (Chapter 4), and how our implicit biases operate unbeknownst to us (Chapter 5). In order to understand the corrosive effects of cancel culture on our intercultural and intergroup relationships, we need to briefly explore the three epistemic communicative postures.

Epistemology is the science of knowing. It was at the heart of mathematician René Descartes' quest to understand the relationship between reason and sense perception, resulting in his "I think, therefore I am" conclusion. In terms of its application to intergroup communication, there are three epistemic postures that can be adopted. The posture that receives the most attention in formal education is the third-person epistemic. Similar to logical positivism, a third-person posture relies on the application of appropriate methodologies to obtain valid and reliable observations that deserve our confidence. As discussed in this book, these are *etic* understandings from an outside, theoretically objective perspective. The third-person posture views knowledge and truth as stable, singular, and certain by controlling contextual and intervening variables. One of the benefits of the third-person perspective is the application of formal rules of logic that allow us to avoid fallacies in our reasoning. As might be clear, much of our scientific and practical understanding of the world operates on the basis of this empirical posture.

At the root of cancel culture is the dark side of empathy, or *antipathy*. Antipathy plays upon our social categorisation predisposition, which emphasises the first-person perspective. The first-person epistemic views knowledge as relative to social location and shaped by individual experience and cultural background. Rather than asking "what is the stable truth" of a situation, it focuses on how an individual experiences a situation. From a first-person vantage point, two people may come away from the exact same event with very different meanings depending on ingroup identity and personal history.

Certainly, an increased awareness of one's own socio-cultural biases can open up opportunities to engage alternative perspectives (more will be said about this in Chapter 7; cf., Gadamer, 1975). And the ability to communicate our personal perspectives is a fundamental human right. However, an exclusive emphasis on the validity of the first-person epistemic runs the risk of compartmentalising our understanding of the world. If each person's solipsistic perspective is equally valid, then truth becomes privatised, and intersubjective understanding virtually unattainable. Moreover, we become trapped in our own subjective universe and lose our capacity for empathy. If we are confined within our own biases, and ingroup perspectives dominate and foreground our understanding of virtually every issue, alternative ideas and explanations become irrelevant and uninteresting.

The missing ingredient in cancel culture is the second-person epistemic, or the power of perspective-taking. The second-person posture is the root of empathy and the ability to inhabit another person's position (Berthold et al., 2013). It subverts common social categorisation effects and makes room for grace and civility. The dark side of empathy has manifested in cancel culture in the form of hostility and incivility towards alternative perspectives, the marginalisation of opposition voices, and demonising of out-of-favour groups and ideologies. However, living harmoniously in a pluralistic society is dependent upon engaging in second person understanding. In our conclusion to this chapter, we offer several pathways out of the dark side that hinge on a second-person epistemic.

Pathways Out of the Dark Side

Standpoint Realities

We began our survey of dark side behaviours by noting that some groups have more symbolic power than others. That is, Commissioner Bele's ethnic group had more SES than Lokai's ethnic group, and therefore maintained hegemony (controlling influence) over them. When these kinds of situations exist, different groups often view the "same" reality from different standpoints. Standpoint Theory asserts that there are different viewpoints based on status, even if they derive from the same "reality" (Hartsock, 1997; Kinefuchi & Orbe, 2008). Underneath Standpoint Theory is the assumption that knowledge is inherently intertwined with power. The corollary of that assumption is that knowledge is always contingent on a social location and has implications for political relationships. Kinefuchi and Orbe (2008) asserted that "the racial locations that we occupy necessarily affect our ontological and epistemological orientations in the world" (p. 71). What that means is that no matter who we are, our apprehension of the world will be partial (e.g., flawed). The Apostle Paul made a similar observation in his first letter to the Corinthian church that "For now we see through a glass, darkly; but then face to face: now I know in part; but then shall I know even as also I am known" (I Cor. 13:12, KJVB).

Given the partiality of our perception, Standpoint Theory generated the concept of "strong objectivity." The idea is that the standpoints of those who are less powerful, non-dominant, or marginalised are less false perspectives than those from more powerful, dominant groups that often have more to protect by asserting their viewpoints. The recognition of partial perspectives in a pluralistic society is a critical first step towards finding the light in intercultural spaces.

We hope that it is plain to see that the central question is not, are we racist or not racist, are we sexist or not sexist, are we prejudiced or not prejudiced. If the concept of standpoints, or implicit biases, is valid, then the answer to many of these questions is yes, we are inherently biased.[2] That is a given. And as long as we dwell on the accusatory aspect of those questions, we will drive people into shameful silence, and the important conversations and self-change will never take place. The question should be, how can we align our conscious and unconscious attitudes and behaviours with our stated egalitarian and respect-endorsing values and beliefs (Hockett, 2017). In the following paragraphs we will offer two distinct methods for addressing the dark side.

Intergroup Contact Theory

In the biographical football film, *Remember the Titans* (Yakin, 2000), coach Herman Boone is hired in 1971 as the first African American head coach to lead the recently desegregated T. C. Williams High School football team in Alexandria, Virginia. Animosity, hostility, and racial division plague the team until Boone devises a way for the players to get to know each other more personally. The cultivation of friendships, together with the supportive coaching staff, shared goal of winning a state championship, and equal status communication eventually results in a high level of camaraderie and team cohesion. The film's opening and closing scenes portray White and Black teammates attending the funeral of their All-American captain, Gerry Bertier, ten years after their state championship, confirming the longitudinal effects of their relational bond. The film beautifully illustrated the positive outcomes postulated by intergroup contact theory.

Gordon Allport's (1954) *Contact Hypothesis* was developed in the context of post Second World War efforts to address prejudice amidst the desegregation of the US military and other public institutions. The reason why he engaged in his seminal study was because "No corner of the world is free from group scorn. Being fettered to our respective cultures, we... [all] are bundles of prejudice" (p. 4). Psychologists at the time hypothesised that most prejudice "against" others was a result of not having sufficient first-hand experience, or relationship, with the repudiated group. Their solution was to identify a set of intergroup contact conditions that would facilitate positive interaction, respect, and changed attitudes.

Allport's (1954) examination was extensive, including personality factors, institutional structures and systems, legal precedents, socialisation influences, desegregation of neighbourhoods, workplaces, and schools, and many other considerations. The primary intergroup contact conclusion was as follows:

> Prejudice (unless deeply rooted in the character structure of the individual) may be reduced by *equal status contact* between majority and minority groups in the pursuit of *common goals*. The effect is greatly enhanced if this contact is sanctioned by *institutional supports* (i.e., by law, custom or local atmosphere), and provided it is of a sort that leads to the *perception of common interests* and *common humanity* between members of the two groups. (p. 281. Emphasis added)

Subsequent research and practices have landed on the following four conditions: equal status communication, common purpose/goals, supportive social/authoritative climate, and cooperatively interdependent interaction. More than 700 contact hypothesis studies have demonstrated its effect on anxiety, individual and group threat, increased empathy, intergroup trust, perspective taking, and interpersonal liking (cf. Amir, 1969). Moreover, even absent optimal conditions, contact typically improves intergroup attitudes (Pettigrew & Tropp, 2006). This has been found for both direct, face-to-face forms of contact as well as for a variety of indirect forms of contact (i.e., contact that is not face-to-face, co-present, or in real time) including vicarious contact, extended contact, mediated contact, and imagined contact (Harwood, 2017; Kim & Harwood, 2019). The caveat to intergroup contact research is that contact must be of a certain quality. Even Allport (1954) noted that superficial contact would not produce the desired results:

> The nub of the matter seems to be that contact must reach below the surface in order to be effective in altering prejudice. Only the type of contact that leads people to do things together is likely to result in changed attitudes… It is the cooperative striving for the goal that engenders solidarity… common participation and common interests are more effective than the bare fact of equal-status contact. (p. 276)

Intergroup contact research has been criticised for not distinguishing between *illusory intergroup contact*, where interaction is more about optics, from legitimate, intimate intergroup interaction where in-group boundary modification has occurred (Hammack, 2010; Maoz, 2002). When contact conditions are met, new self-categorisations produce a high level of shared group identity.

The Dialogue Prerequisite

Another pathway out of the dark side towards reconciliation, peace building, and attitude change is intergroup dialogue (IGD; Carbaugh, 2013; Collier, 2016; Stephan & Stephan, 2001). IGD is viewed as a mechanism for reflexivity, inclusivity, perspective-taking, and contextualised action steps that incorporate personal, relational, and structural level issues and concerns. The intercultural practice is grounded in the constructivist philosophy of Martin Buber (1970) who emphasised open, direct, mutual, and present interactions with the intent to see how differences are interconnected. Dialogue is distinct from discussion and debate in that it is a co-creative, multi-vocal environment that involves listening as much as speaking while participants interrogate their attitudes, assumptions, and prejudices in light of the other's perspectives.

To understand IGD as a means for dismantling misattribution, stereotypes, and prejudice, we need to briefly explore its ethnographic aspects. In ethnographic research, we are mindful of the particularities of people, communities, and cultures. We are also mindful that forms of expression are unique to those groupings. In doing so, it quickly becomes obvious that there are many types of dialogue, and many different understandings of what it is and what it accomplishes. Buber (1970) envisioned his kind of dialogue as an "encounter," Bakhtin (1984) saw it as a "dialogic moment," and Gadamer (1975) described it as an intersubjective horizon. Common to all of these conceptualisations is a reciprocal reflexivity where authentic understanding of self and the other increases. In its many forms, dialogue has become part and parcel of most intercultural developmental theories and processes (e.g., Chapter 7).

Intergroup relations research soared following the US Supreme Court's 1954 Brown vs. Board of Education decision ending segregation in US schools (e.g., Henry Boone's opportunity to become the Williams High School Head Coach in this section's opening illustration). But research and theorising specifically in IGD arose in the 1970s in part because of the difficulty, and consequent short-term failure, of larger institutionalised movements like desegregation. While the primary emphasis of early programmes was prejudice reduction, more recent research has focused on current societal issues like political polarisation, social justice, xenophobia, and addressing group-based emotions that affect intergroup relations (Bobowik et al., 2018; Frantell et al., 2019; French et al., 2021). IGD has relied on theories like *realistic group conflict* (LeVine & Campbell, 1972), *social identity* (Tajfel & Turner, 1986), *social dominance* (Sidanius & Pratto, 1999), *intergroup emotions* (Mackie & Smith, 2002), and *integrated threat* (Stephan & Stephan, 2001), along with their corresponding concepts to overcome group-related hostilities and prejudice.

In this chapter we have seen that culture, social categorisation, and social class have the potential to produce dark side effects of ethnocentrism, prejudice, racism, and discrimination. We also suggested that there is both a personal and corporate responsibility to address dark side effects. We learned that approaches to navigating conflict vary according to known cultural variables. We concluded by discussing several pathways to improve empathy and engage stereotype change. *Stereotype change* is the process of altering one's fixed and faulty perceptions of particular groups. As we engage in intergroup contact and dialogue, we become more aware of our own over-application of shared characteristics to individuals within groups and gain the ability to acquire another person's perspective, which improves empathy. The contact hypothesis and IGD are but two strategies for developing intercultural communication competence. The bright side of these pathways is evidenced by the fact that Detroit's Birwood Wall, mentioned earlier, is no longer a barrier between social classes and racially distinct neighbourhoods. In fact, it stands as a testament to the resilience and determination of underrepresented groups to break down barriers and form integrated, welcoming communities.

In Conversation: Prejudice

Lily: We often think of discrimination or prejudice as occurring to people who look like me – brown, female, etc. But if I've learnt anything about the dark side of intercultural communication, prejudice cuts both ways. In other words, you don't have to be a member of the perceived majority in order to be prejudiced. I'm curious, have you ever experienced prejudice or discrimination overtly based on being a White male?

Ripley: If I have, it was probably a positive form of discrimination. You know, I imagine we have all experienced some degree of prejudice or discrimination based on socio-economic class, religion, region, or ethnicity. But as a young person, I can't say I was conscious of it on a routine basis. It wasn't until one of my African American friends told me that he was conscious of his being a Black male every day as he looked in the mirror while shaving that I realised the relationship between ethnoracial power and prejudice.

Lily: So, when you became aware of your "Whiteness" as such, did that affect the way you related to other people in any way?

Ripley: I definitely became more conscious of how I benefit from being Caucasian. I've always tried to interact with people respectfully regardless of their ethnicity or culture. But I think it made me more aware of how people can experience the same world in significantly different ways. What about you? Given your blended cultural identity, what has been your personal experience of prejudice?

Lily: You know, the funny thing is I often forget I'm not White because I think in Westernised ways for the most part and feel completely at ease with White people, as I'm married to one and most of my close friends are White. So, sometimes I'm startled when someone treats me as a non-White person. Like once when I was new in Australia, one of my colleagues said something like, "So, Lily, as a Black person, how would you..." I stared at him, because firstly I'd never been called Black before, and secondly, I didn't realise I was "different" to him enough to have a unique point of view on whatever we were talking about!

Ripley: So, you have never been mistreated or discriminated against because of your language status or ethnicity?

Lily: Yes, I have, as I've shared in some of the examples in this book. I guess the point I'm making is that often I forget I'm "different" until someone points it out, either with malice or in a completely guileless but obtuse way.

Ripley: Would you say that one of the pathways out of the dark side is a blended cultural identity? What I mean by that is you seem to have become so ethnorelative or reached an integrated identity such that you're able to interact with people in a very individuated way. Does that make sense?

Lily: I think that way of interacting with people in an individuated way, as you put it, is something I have had to learn because of my experiences as a sojourner; it's a process, and all of us are at different stages in that process, don't you think?

Questions for Reflection

1. Where do you think you are in the process of seeing people as inseparable from their ethnicity or race to seeing them as individuals? Is it even possible to separate our perception of people from their outward appearance?
2. What are the dangers or downsides of trying to see people independent of their ethno-cultural identities? Can it lead to denial and minimisation of culture? (See Chapter 7.)
3. Do prejudice and discrimination always have to be negative?

Notes

1 You can read John Oetzel's story in Chapter 8.
2 Framing issues in a simplistic binary opposition was a common tactic of the Sophists in Ancient Greek culture. Socrates repeatedly chastised the Sophists for their deceitful, simplistic, and harmful representations of ideas and issues. Oversimplified either/or constructions often create artificial arguments and conclusions based on logical fallacies.

References

Allport, G. W. (1954). *The nature of prejudice*. Macmillan.

Amir, Y. (1969). Contact hypothesis in ethnic relations. *Psychological Bulletin, 71*, 319–342.

Bakhtin, M. (1984). *Problems of Dostoevsky's poetics* (C. Emerson, Trans.). University of Minnesota Press.

Beelmann, A., & Lutterbach, S. (2020). Preventing prejudice and promoting intergroup relations. In L. T. Benuto, M. P. Duckworth, A. Masuda, & W. O'Donohue (Eds.), *Prejudice, stigma, privilege, and oppression: A behavioral health handbook* (pp. 309–326). Springer International Publishing. https://doi.org/10.1007/978-3-030-35517-3_16

Bennett, M. J. (2013). *Basic concepts of intercultural communication* (2nd ed.). Intercultural Press.

Berger, C. R., & Calabrese, R. J. (1975). Some explorations in initial interaction and beyond: Toward a developmental theory of interpersonal communication. *Human Communication Research, 1*(2), 99–112. https://doi.org/10.1111/j.1468-2958.1975.tb00258.x

Berthold, A., Leicht, C., Methner, N., & Gaum, P. (2013). Seeing the world with the eyes of the outgroup – The impact of perspective taking on the prototypicality of the ingroup relative to the outgroup. *Journal of Experimental Social Psychology*, *49*(6), 1034–1041. https://doi.org/10.1016/j.jesp.2013.07.007

Bobowik, M., Valentim, J. P., & Licata, L. (2018). Introduction to the special issue: Colonial past and intercultural relations. *International Journal of Intercultural Relations*, *62*, 1–12. https://doi.org/10.1016/j.ijintrel.2017.10.003

Braveman, P., Arkin, E., Proctor, D., Kauh, T., & Holm, N. (2022). Systemic and structural racism: Definitions, examples, health damages, and approaches to dismantling. *Health Affairs*, *41*(2), 171–178. https://doi.org/10.1377/hlthaff.2021.01394

Brislin, R. (2010). *The undreaded job: Learning to thrive in a less-than-perfect workplace*. Bloomsbury Publishing.

Buber, M. (1970). *I and thou* (W. Kaufmann, Trans.). Touchstone.

Carbaugh, D. (2013). On dialogue studies. *Journal of Dialogue Studies*, *1*(1), 9–28.

Cargile, A. C. (2017). Social dominance orientation: A root of resistance to intercultural dialogue? *International Journal of Intercultural Relations*, *61*, 40–53. https://doi.org/10.1016/j.ijintrel.2017.09.003

Chua, A. (2003). *World on fire: How exporting free market democracy breeds ethic hatred and global instability*. Random House.

Collier, M. J. (2016). An Intercultural peacebuilding framework: Extending the conversation through a focus on connections. In S. Roy & I. S. Shaw (Eds.), *Communicating differences culture, media, peace and conflict negotiation* (1st ed., pp. 15–28). Palgrave Macmillan. https://doi.org/10.1057/9781137499264

Corbett, S., & Fikkert, B. (2013). *When helping hurts: How to alleviate poverty without hurting the poor... and yourself*. Moody Publishers.

Cowling, M. M., Anderson, J. R., & Ferguson, R. (2019). Prejudice-relevant correlates of attitudes towards refugees: A meta-analysis. *Journal of Refugee Studies*, *32*(3), 502–524.

Dittmann, A. (2016). Understanding social class as culture. *Behavioral Scientist*. https://behavioralscientist.org/understanding-social-class-as-culture/

Eidlin, B., & McCarthy, M. A. (2020). Introducing rethinking class and social difference: A dynamic asymmetry approach. In B. Eidlin & M. A. McCarthy (Eds.), *Rethinking class and social difference* (Vol. 37, pp. 1–23). Emerald Publishing. https://doi.org/10.1108/S0198-871920200000037002

Elsesser, K. (2019). Lawsuit claims SAT and ACT are biased – Here's what research says. *Forbes*, 11 December. www.forbes.com/sites/kimelsesser/2019/12/11/lawsuit-claims-sat-and-act-are-biased-heres-what-research-says/?sh=4c3511ea3c42

Eskelinen, V., Pauha, T., Kunst, J., Räsänen, A., & Jasinskaja-Lahti, I. (2021). Exploring religiosity and attitudes towards Christians and non-believers among recent Muslim refugees to Finland. *International Journal of Intercultural Relations*, *80*, 206–216. https://doi.org/10.1016/j.ijintrel.2020.10.007

Fischer, R., Hanke, K., & Sibley, C. G. (2012). Cultural and institutional determinants of social dominance orientation: A cross-cultural meta-analysis of 27 societies. *Political Psychology*, *33*(4), 437–467.

Fiske, S. T., & Taylor, S. E. (1991). *Social cognition* (2nd ed.). McGraw-Hill.

Frantell, K. A., Miles, J. R., & Ruwe, A. M. (2019). Intergroup dialogue: A review of recent empirical research and its implications for research and practice. *Small Group Research*, *50*(5), 654–695. https://doi.org/10.1177/1046496419835923

French, P., James-Gallaway, C., & Bohonos, J. (2021). Examining intergroup dialogue's potential to promote social justice in adult education. *Journal of Transformative Education*, *20*(1), 44–61. https://doi.org/10.1177/15413446211000037

Gadamer, H. G. (1975). *Truth and method.* Seabury Press.

Giles, H. (2008). Communication accommodation theory. In L. A. Baxter & D. O. Braithwaite (Eds.), *Engaging theories in interpersonal communication* (pp. 161–174). Sage.

Gudykunst, W., & Hammer, M. (1988). Strangers and hosts: An uncertainty reduction based theory of intercultural adaptation. In Y. Y. Kim & W. B. Gudykunst (Eds.), *Cross-cultural adaptation: Current approaches* (Vol. XI, pp. 106–139). Sage.

Haggis, P. (Director). (2005). *Crash* [Film]. Lions Gate Home Entertainment.

Haidt, J. (2012). *The righteous mind: Why good people are divided by politics and religion.* Vintage Books.

Hall, D. L., Matz, D. C., & Wood, W. (2010). Why don't we practice what we preach? A meta-analytic review of religious racism. *Personality and Social Psychology Review, 14*(1), 126–139. https://doi.org/10.1177/1088868309352179

Hall, S. (1994). Cultural studies: Two paradigms. In N. B. Dirks, G. Eley, & S. B. Ortner (Eds.), *Culture/power/history: A reader in contemporary social theory* (pp. 57–72). Princeton University Press.

Hall, S. O. U. (1997). *Representation: Cultural representations and signifying practices.* Sage in association with the Open University.

Halperin, E., Canetti-Nisim, D., & Pedahzur, A. (2007). Threatened by the uncontrollable: Psychological and socio-economic antecedents of social distance towards labor migrants in Israel. *International Journal of Intercultural Relations, 31*(4), 459–478. https://doi.org/10.1016/j.ijintrel.2007.01.003

Hammack, P. L. (2010). Narrating hyphenated selves: Intergroup contact and configurations of identity among young Palestinian citizens of Israel. *International Journal of Intercultural Relations, 34*(4), 368–385. https://doi.org/10.1016/j.ijintrel.2010.03.002

Hartsock, N. C. M. (1997). Standpoint theories for the next century. *Women and Politics, 18*, 93–101.

Harwood, J. (2017). Indirect and mediated intergroup contact. In Y. Y. Kim (Ed.), *The international encyclopedia of intercultural communication* (pp. 1–9). Wiley Blackwell. https://doi.org/10.1002/9781118783665.ieicc0161

Henry, P. J. (2014). Culture and social class. In A. B. Cohen (Ed.), *Culture reexamined: Broadening our understanding of social and evolutionary influences.* (pp. 49–75). American Psychological Association. https://doi.org/10.1037/14274-003

Hewstone, M., Rubin, M., & Willis, H. (2002). Intergroup bias. *Annual Review of Psychology, 53*, 575–604. http://dx.doi.org/10.1146/annurev.psych.53.100901.135109

Hockett, D. (2017). *We all have implicit biases: So what can we do about it?* TEDx Talks, 18 September. www.youtube.com/watch?v=kKHSJHkPeLY

Hogg, M. A., & Reid, S. A. (2006). Social identity, self-categorization, and the communication of group norms. *Communication Theory, 16*(1), 7–30.

Huntington, S. P. (1993). The clash of civilizations. *Foreign Affairs, 72*(3), 22–49.

Jackson, J. (2024). The dark side of identity: Barriers to intercultural communication. In J. Jackson (Ed.), *Introducing language and intercultural communication* (3rd ed., Vol. 1, pp. 155–184). Routledge. https://doi.org/10.4324/9781003332442-6

James, W. (1893). *Psychology.* Henry Holt & Company.

Johnson, M. K., Rowatt, W. C., & LaBouff, J. P. (2012). Religiosity and prejudice revisited: In-group favoritism, out-group derogation, or both? *Psychology of Religion and Spirituality, 4*(2), 154–168. https://doi.org/10.1037/a0025107

Katz, D. (1960). The functional approach to the study of attitudes. *Public Opinion Quarterly, 24*(2), 163–204.

Kendi, I. X. (2019). *How to be an anitracist.* One World.

Kesebir, S. (2012). The superorganism account of human sociality: How and when human groups are like beehives. *Personality and Social Psychology Review*, *16*(3), 233–261. https://doi.org/10.1177/1088868311430834

Kim, C., & Harwood, J. (2019). What makes people imagine themselves in contact with out-group members: Exploring the relationship between vicarious media contact experiences and imagined contact. *Communication Studies*, *70*(5), 545–563. https://doi.org/10.1080/10510974.2019.1658612

Kinefuchi, E., & Orbe, M. (2008). Situating oneself in a racialized world: Understanding student reactions to crash through Standpoint Theory and context-positionality frames. *Journal of International & Intercultural Communication*, *1*(1), 70–90. https://doi.org/10.1080/17513050701742909

Kraus, M. W., Callaghan, B., & Ondish, P. (2019). Social class as culture. In D. Cohen & S. Kitayama (Eds.), *Handbook of cultural psychology* (2nd ed., pp. 721–747). The Guilford Press.

Landis, D., & Albert, R. D. (2012). *Handbook of ethnic conflict: International perspectives*. Springer.

LeVine, R. A., & Campbell, D. T. (1972). *Ethnocentrism: Theories of conflict, ethnic attitudes, and group behavior*. John Wiley and Sons.

Littler, M. (2020). Religion and intercultural communication. In G. Rings & S. Rasinger (Eds.), *The Cambridge handbook of intercultural communication* (pp. 446–459). Cambridge University Press. https://doi.org/10.1017/9781108555067.032

Mackie, D. M., & Smith, E. R. (2002). *From prejudice to intergroup emotions: Differentiated reactions to social groups*. Taylor & Francis Group.

Manstead, A. S. R. (2018). The psychology of social class: How socioeconomic status impacts thought, feelings, and behaviour. *British Journal of Social Psychology*, *57*(2), 267–291. https://doi.org/10.1111/bjso.12251

Maoz, I. (2002). Is there contact at all? Intergroup interaction in planned contact interventions between Jews and Arabs in Israel. *International Journal of Intercultural Relations*, *26*(2), 185–197. https://doi.org/10.1016/S0147-1767(01)00046-3

Neuliep, J. (2012). The relationship among intercultural communication apprehension, ethnocentrism, uncertainty reduction, and communication satisfaction during initial intercultural interaction: An extension of anxiety and uncertainty management (AUM) theory. *Journal of Intercultural Communication Research*, *41*(1), 1–16. https://doi.org/10.1080/17475759.2011.623239

Oetzel, J. G., & Ting-Toomey, S. (2003). Face concerns and facework during conflict: A test of the face-negotiation theory. *Communication Research*, *30*, 599–624.

Pettigrew, T. F., & Tropp, L. R. (2006). A meta-analytic test of intergroup contact theory. *Journal of Personality and Social Psychology*, *90*(5), 751–783. https://doi.org/10.1037/0022-3514.90.5.751

Pew Research. (2022). Key findings from the global religious futures project. www.pewresearch.org/religion/2022/12/21/key-findings-from-the-global-religious-futures-project/

Rowatt, W. C., & Al-Kire, R. L. (2021). Dimensions of religiousness and their connection to racial, ethnic, and atheist prejudices. *Current Opinion in Psychology*, *40*, 86–91. https://doi.org/10.1016/j.copsyc.2020.08.022

Rowatt, W. C., Carpenter, T., & Haggard, M. (2013). Religion, prejudice, and intergroup relations. In V. Saroglou (Ed.), *Religion, personality, and social behavior* (pp. 170–192). Taylor & Francis.

Schultze, Q. J. (2000). *Communicating for life*. Baker Book House.

Shaukat, A. (2020). Religious conflicts around the globe and a solution. *Modern Diplomacy*. https://moderndiplomacy.eu/2020/10/15/religious-conflicts-around-the-globe-and-a-solution/

Sherif, M., Harvey, O. J., White, B. J., Hood, W. R., & Sherif, C. W. (1988). *The Robbers Cave experiment: Intergroup conflict and cooperation*. Wesleyan University Press, University Press of New England.

Sidanius, J., & Pratto, F. (1999). *Social dominance: An intergroup theory of social hierarchy and oppression*. Cambridge University Press.

Somerville, W., Kapten, S. W., Miao, I. Y., Dunn, J. J., & Chang, D. F. (2020). Identifying and remediating personal prejudice: What does the evidence say? In I. T. Benuto, M. P. Duckworth, A. Masuda, & W. O'Donohue (Eds.), *Prejudice, stigma, privilege, and oppression: A behavioral health handbook* (pp. 179–200). Springer International Publishing. https://doi.org/10.1007/978-3-030-35517-3_1

Spitzberg, B. (1991). Intercultural communication competence. In L. S. R. Porter (Ed.), *Intercultural communication: A reader* (6th ed., pp. 353–365). Wadsworth.

Spitzberg, B. H., & Cupach, W. R. (Eds.). (2011a). *The dark side of interpersonal communication* (2nd ed.). Taylor and Francis. https://doi.org/10.4324/9780203936849.

Spitzberg, B. H., & Cupach, W. R. (2011b). Disentangling the dark side of interpersonal communication. In B. H. Spitzberg & W. R. Cupach (Eds.), *The dark side of interpersonal communication* (2nd ed., pp. 3–28). Taylor and Francis.

Stephan, W. G., & Stephan, C. W. (2001). *Improving intergroup relations*. Sage Publications.

Stephens, N. M., Markus, H. R., & Phillips, L. T. (2014). Social class culture cycles: How three gateway contexts shape selves and fuel inequality. *Annual Review of Psychology*, *65*(1), 611–634. https://doi.org/10.1146/annurev-psych-010213-115143

Tajfel, H., & Turner, J. C. (1979). An integrative theory of intergroup conflict. In W. G. Austin & S. Worchel (Eds.), *The social psychology of intergroup relations* (pp. 94–109). Brooks-Cole.

Tajfel, H., & Turner, J. C. (1986). The social identity theory of intergroup behavior. In S. Worchel & W. G. Austin (Eds.), *Psychology of intergroup relation* (pp. 7–24). Hall Publishers.

Thomas, K. W., & Kilmann, R. H. (1978). Comparison of four instruments measuring conflict behavior. *Psychological Reports*, *42*, 1139–1145.

Ting-Toomey, S. (2015). Facework/facework negotiation theory. In J. M. Bennett (Ed.), *The Sage encyclopedia of intercultural competence* (Vol. 2, pp. 325–330). Sage Publications. https://doi.org/10.4135/9781483346267

Ting-Toomey, S., & Kurogi, A. (1998). Facework competence in intercultural conflict: An updated face-negotiation theory. *International Journal of Intercultural Relations*, *22*(2), 187–225. https://doi.org/10.1016/S0147-1767(98)00004-2

Ting-Toomey, S., & Oetzel, J. G. (2003). Cross-cultural face concerns and conflict styles: Current status and future directions. In W. B. Gudykunst (Ed.), *Cross-cultural and Intercultural Communication* (pp. 127–147). Sage Publications.

Turner, J. C. (1985). Social categorization and the self-concept: A social cognitive theory of group behavior. In E. J. Lawler (Ed.), *Advances in group processes* (pp. 77–121). JAI Press.

Urbiola, A., Navas, M., Carmona, C., & Willis, G. B. (2023). Social class also matters: The effects of social class, ethnicity, and their interaction on prejudice and discrimination toward Roma. *Race and Social Problems*, *15*(3), 262–276. https://doi.org/10.1007/s12552-022-09368-1

West, C. (1993). *Prophetic reflections: Notes on race and power in America (beyond Eurocentrism and multiculturalism)*. Common Courage Press.

Wölfer, R., & Foroutan, N. (2022). Plurality resistance: Effects on intergroup relations and the mediating role of stereotypes. *International Journal of Intercultural Relations, 87*, 42–50. https://doi.org/10.1016/j.ijintrel.2022.01.005

Yakin, B. (Director). (2000). *Remember the Titans* [Film]. Walt Disney Company.

6   Cultural Transitions and Identity

The entire field of intercultural relations is motivated by the fact that when people from different backgrounds interact with each other, or when a person from one culture relocates to a different culture, there is an adjustment process that occurs during that transition. Proposition 7 of our intercultural spaces concept suggests that:

> In situations where a person ventures into a different cultural context, the possibility exists that they may enter into an intercultural space that is both conceptual and literal.

The phenomenon is illustrated by the experience of eminent Canadian acculturation scholar John Berry, whom we first met in Chapter 2:

> My engagement with intercultural relations started when I was growing up as a member of the only English-speaking family in a small village in the province of Quebec. My father, for whatever reason, when he moved our family from Ontario to Quebec in the 1940s decided that we should live in a French speaking village. In this setting, my developing knowledge of cultural differences became part of me, and eventually led me to study (through research), and to apply (through practice) this knowledge to issues of intercultural relations and acculturation. One vivid experience was an encounter with a Francophone boy of my own age who approached me on the road and told me that "The French are better than the English or Jews." I asked him how he knew this, and he replied that "The priest told us." I have pondered this encounter ever since, and have been determined to find the roots of such hostility and sense of superiority in intercultural relations.

Berry was confronted with the same kind of question that challenged First World War British intelligence officer T. E. Lawrence (aka, Lawrence of Arabia). Lawrence (1935) was an Arabic speaking archaeologist stationed at the Arab Bureau in Cairo, Egypt, who acquired renown for assisting with the Arab Revolt against the Ottoman Empire. In his wartime memoir, *Seven Pillars of Wisdom*, he asked a series of profound cultural transition questions: "How could I as me, meet

DOI: 10.4324/9781003318415-7

this new people? How would I have to change? What of me was superficial and might be sacrificed and what need I keep to remain myself?" These same questions are at the heart of Berry's (1997) acculturation model, as we shall see. Both Berry and Lawrence were running up against the natural human tendency of *homophily* (Kadushin, 2012). Homophily is the sociological principle that when people (as well as groups, organisations, countries, etc.) share common attributes, they are more likely to be drawn to each other.

Think about your own circle of family and friends, as well as the demographic distribution of your hometown, city, or village. It is very likely that your community is divided into ethnic or cultural enclaves, proving the sociological point of homophily regardless of where you live in the world. At this junction in our exploration of intercultural spaces we will interrogate our human tendency towards homophily and the key questions of what happens when we venture across cultural boundaries, and how we know when adjustment happens effectively. We will also explore what happens to a person's identity in the event of long-term interaction with other cultures. Over the years, much research has been conducted in this area, producing a number of models and distinctions in the cultural transition process. We will begin with the general concept of cultural adjustment and move towards specific outcomes as it relates to adaptation and identity formation.

Cultural Adjustment

At the centre of cultural adjustment is a transition change process, particularly change in personal psychological and social behaviour (Berry, 2005; Gudykunst & Kim, 1997; Sam & Berry, 2010). The issues surrounding that change process have been, and will continue to be, of paramount importance due to the increasingly interconnected nature of our global civilisation. Both intercultural and cross-cultural adjustment have received extensive treatment from both communication and psychological perspectives (Kim, 1987, 2019; Sam & Berry, 2010; Ward, 2022). Early studies tended to focus on *group-level* phenomena from an anthropological viewpoint as societies changed over time. Most of the recent research has examined *individual-level* change as a person socialised in one culture transitions into a second cultural environment (Kim, 2003). The subtle reason provoking the internal and external change is the recognition of someone, or someplace, else as "strange," and the moment that happens, we have entered an intercultural space. The idea of the cultural stranger was introduced by sociologist Georg Simmel, who felt that this type of specific experience of strangeness was a special category. It is distinct from simply being an "outsider" or a "wanderer" in the traditional sense; but instead his stranger was a member of the group or community while also remaining socially distant somehow because of his or her sociocultural origins. John Berry experienced this kind of strangeness throughout his upbringing and transition to adulthood, leading him to embark on a career studying the phenomenon:

My continuing involvement with people of other cultures was furthered by summer jobs during high school in bush camps with Indigenous peoples

(First Nations tribes in Canada), and by working as a deckhand and engineer on ships traveling to Africa and the Arctic. My last job was as the engineer on a biological research ship in Hudson's Bay, in daily contact with Inuit and Cree hunters and fishers. All the other people on board were either professors or graduate students. When I asked them how to get such a fun and satisfying life, they told me that I had to go to university. About the same time, my partner told me that I had to make a choice, saying that "It's the sea or me." So, I came ashore and started university classes at night, while working in a furniture factory. In both my job and in my classes, most of my colleagues were immigrants. At my university in Montreal, I was privileged to study with a professor who was both a psychologist and anthropologist. Later, I continued my studies at the University of Edinburgh with joint supervision in the psychology and anthropology departments, and carried out field studies in Sierra Leone and Arctic Canada. After earning my PhD, I emigrated to Australia to work with Aboriginal Peoples there and in New Guinea. My subsequent interests and research have all been informed by these early experiences. Consequently, a working assumption in my career has been that diversity is a fact of life; whether it is the "spice" or the "irritant" to people is the fundamental psychological, social, cultural and political issue of our times.

You might have noticed already that there are a number of different terms used to refer to the type of change an immigrant, expatriate or sojourner experiences during a cultural transition. Despite the attention in the literature, it is not always made clear, much less agreed upon, what exactly the expression "cultural adjustment" refers to. It will be beneficial at the outset to clarify what is meant by the various terms applied to the experience of cultural transition. It is not uncommon to see the terms adjustment, adaptation, and acculturation used synonymously, but there are important distinctions. Early in the study of cross-cultural research, Herskovits (1938) traced the history of several terms used synonymously to refer to the cultural adaptation process. He noted several inadequate definitions of terms like diffusion, assimilation, and acculturation, and concluded that:

> these terms merely represent phases of a single process by means of which either isolated traditions or considerable blocs of custom are passed on by one human group to another; by means of which a people adapt themselves to what has been newly introduced and to the consequent reshuffling of their traditions. (p. 14)

Herskovits later alluded to the notion of adaptation consisting of a series of options:

> where both original and foreign traits are combined so as to produce a smoothly functioning cultural whole which is actually an historic mosaic; with either a reworking of the two cultures into a harmonious, meaningful whole to the individuals concerned, or the retention of a series of more or less conflicting attitudes and points of view which are reconciled in everyday life as specific occasions arise. (p. 136)

Certainly, culture is adaptive by its very nature, as Kroeber and Kluckhohn (1952) also pointed out; cultural change is merely a process of "adjustment to newly perceived needs as presented by life's conditions" (p. 88). Two leading perspectives on cultural adjustment distinguish between acculturation as primarily concerning internal socio-psychological changes, and adaptation which pertains to behavioural changes people enact in response to new cultural environments (Berry, 1997; Ward, 2022). Much of the adaptation conversation revolves around understanding how people negotiate a "fit" with a new culture (Berry, 2005). Others see the ideas of adjustment, adaptation, and acculturation as hierarchical in their breadth on a spectrum from non-acceptance or avoidance to substitution, addition, synthesis, or even resynthesis/innovation (Gudykunst, 1977; Gudykunst & Hammer, 1988). Acculturation, on the other hand, while not ignoring external factors, tends to emphasise the importance of maintaining cultural identity during cultural transitions, resulting in a bi-dimensional continuum running from complete assimilation to complete separation (Berry, et al., 1987). Cultural adjustment, then, can be seen as an overarching term that refers to the actual change processes that occur in both psychological acculturation strategies and socio-cultural adaptation.[1]

In addition to the increasing conceptual clarity, the research surrounding cultural adjustment has evolved significantly over the years. Early research focused on behavioural attributions (Triandis, 1976), attitudes, traits and skills (Brislin, 1981; Gudykunst & Hammer, 1984; Hammer, 1987; Hammer et al., 1978; Harris, 1973), and performance (Klemp, 1979) consisting of personality and skill typologies that when acted out in specific cultural contexts would contribute to the potential for adaptation or effectiveness. Even at the time, these approaches to intercultural adjustment were criticised for being overly vague and contrived (Dinges, 1983). Fortunately, the scholarship around cultural adjustment has become much more nuanced and refined, thanks in good part to the work of John Berry, Colleen Ward, and Young Kim.

Acculturation

One of the most influential ways of thinking about cultural transition from a psychological perspective is Berry's (1997) acculturation orientation model (see Figure 6.1). Berry sets up his approach in the following paragraphs:

I have worked within the conceptual and methodological frameworks of both cross-cultural and intercultural psychology. By cross-cultural, I mean researching and making comparisons of findings between individuals who are living in disparate cultures that are not in contact with each other. By intercultural I mean researching individuals who are in contact and engaging with each other within culturally plural societies. I combine these two approaches by replicating intercultural studies in a number of plural societies, and then making comparisons across them. In this way, intercultural studies also become cross-cultural.

These two domains of research have been combined in my *eco-cultural* framework, which is guided by two principles and two sources of influence on culture and behaviour. These two principles are *universalism* and *adaptation*. The first proposes that all individual human behaviour is rooted in a set of common psychological and cultural processes and capacities; this allows for people of differing backgrounds to interact and to understand each other. Without such commonality, no communication nor mutual understanding would be possible.

The second principle is that all human behaviour is adaptive to the contexts in which they develop and are now expressed in daily actions. Of course, not all behaviours are adaptive, but most are; if this were not the case, our species could not have survived. In both cross-cultural and intercultural psychology, we have come to recognise the value of the adaptive character of human behaviours and have learned not to interpret or judge variations in observable behaviours according to any absolute external or imposed criteria.

In addition to those two principles, two related influences on human behavioural development and expression (in culture) have also shaped my perspective. *Ecological settings* (e.g., physical and social settings) shape the behaviours that are adaptive to them through the process of enculturation. Each ecological setting poses demands, opportunities, and constraints on how societies organise themselves, raise their children, and design their institutions. Secondly, the degree and strength of *intercultural contacts* with those of other cultural backgrounds alters the extant cultures and behaviours and creates the need for new adaptive structures and behaviours through the process of acculturation.

My career has been a long search for evidence for the validity of these four notions (universalism, adaptation, ecology, and intercultural contact) that underlies a psychology that is both cross-cultural and intercultural. This has led me to claim that there are some universals of acculturation and intercultural relations, and that these may be a valid and useful basis for many plural societies on which to begin to create functional policies and programmes in the interest of more positive intercultural relations. Intercultural relations can only take place if there are shared and universal underlying processes; and culturally sensitive intercultural relations can only take place if the cultural roots of the behaviours are understood and accepted by those in the interaction.

* * *

Berry et al. (1987) extended a longstanding anthropological definition of *acculturation* to refer to the dual process of cultural and psychological change that is a consequence of continuous, first-hand contact between distinct cultural groups. The dual nature of the process recognises both group-level changes to shared values and social structures as well as individual psychological processes involving the identification and internalisation of the significant symbol systems of the host society. Berry's (2015) model identifies four conceptually distinct acculturation orientations depending on the immigrant's response to two orthogonal dimensions: 1) the importance of maintaining their heritage culture and identity, and 2) the importance of developing relationships with members of the host culture. Figure 6.1 displays the four possible orientations that result from the coinciding answers to those two questions.

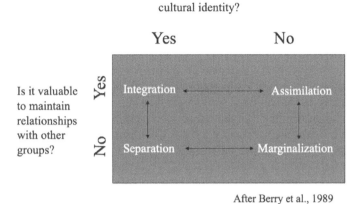

Is it valuable to maintain
cultural identity?

Yes   No

Is it valuable   Yes   Integration ←——————→ Assimilation
to maintain
relationships
with other
groups?   No   Separation ←——————→ Marginalization

After Berry et al., 1989

Figure 6.1 Berry Acculturation Strategies, adapted from Berry et al. (1989).

For example, consider a refugee family that was forced to flee their home country due to persecution and was eventually resettled to a new country. The members of the family will eventually reflect one of the four acculturation orientations (Smith, 2004). Some of the family members may experience the new host culture as unwelcoming for a variety of reasons, and at the same time they either choose, or are forced, to disengage from their heritage group. The result is a process of marginalisation. Occasionally study abroad students find themselves in this position. They may not have any same-culture students on campus to hang out with, and they sense a lack of receptivity from host culture students. Cliques of study abroad students from different cultural backgrounds will often form as a result, creating a bond over *third-culture* status. Immigrants with a marginalisation acculturation orientation will often experience the least amount of satisfaction in the host society, a sense of anomie, and inferior adaptation compared to alternative acculturation orientations (Berry, 2005; R. Bourhis et al., 1997, p. 377).

Immigrants that pursue an assimilation or separation orientation will achieve intermediate adaptation outcomes (Berry, 2005). Assimilation may be a choice on the part of the non-dominant group, or it may be an expectation of the dominant group in the host society, or some combination of the two motivations. In either case, the refugee family members that choose that path will relinquish their heritage culture and language and conform to the host society norms and values. Of course there are varying degrees of assimilation. Often, an immigrant will assimilate to economic or workplace norms, but will retain religious, familial, or other personal norms and values from their heritage culture. The opposite of assimilation is the separation strategy (or segregation if the strategy is imposed by the receiving society). If members of the refugee family pursue a separation orientation they will intentionally preserve their ethnic traditions, language, and beliefs, preferring to avoid interactions with the host culture when possible. Separation orientations often produce ethnic enclaves in various urban settings, for instance Chinatown in San Francisco, or Little Italy in New York City.

An integration orientation reflects a desire to maintain important heritage culture features like language, religious practices, and perhaps even culinary traditions while at the same time participating in the host society's educational, commerce, and political institutions and incorporating dominant group members into personal social networks. Berry (1997) noted that "the integration strategy can only be pursued in societies that are explicitly *multicultural*" (p. 11). Because integration implies adjustments on the part of the immigrant as well as the receiving cultural group(s), it is inherently mutual. In that sense, Berry observed that both the integration and separation strategies require a collective effort where an assimilation strategy can be pursued as an individual choice. Plural societies that are committed to positive multicultural policies and practice afford acculturation paths to immigrant groups that accommodate "the bidirectional change that takes place when two ethnocultural groups come into contact with one another" (R. Bourhis et al., 1997, p. 370).[2]

Integration acculturation orientations often go hand-in-hand with bicultural identities (Repke & Benet-Martínez, 2019; Ward et al., 2018). In the process of acculturating to a new environment, it is not uncommon to develop multiple cultural identifications (e.g., bicultural) that blend one's heritage culture and an acquired host culture in either a hybridised fusion of cultural features or alternate between compartmentalised cultural identities. A bicultural individual might find themselves *code-switching* back and forth between languages and identity features depending on the situation and the backgrounds of the people with whom they are interacting (alternating identity style) or manifesting a *third culture* entirely (hybridising style). The growing recognition of hybrid and mixed identities, like African-American, Hmong-American, or Mexican-American describe an increasingly complex story of cultural transition and composition. More will be said about cultural identity later in the chapter, but acculturation scholar Colleen Ward not only studied acculturation, she lives a hybridised identity as well.

How I Became an Acculturation Psychologist

Colleen Ward

My life changed when I had a junior year abroad. I went from the Deep South of the US to England. England was impactful enough to draw me back to Durham University to do a PhD on geder during the early era of feminism. My dissertation was about looking at the world from a different perspective, but this time it was a feminist perspective, because at that point in time, psychology was approached largely with a White male yardstick against which everything else was compared.

Then, at age 25 I thought, "Oh, I can do anything so now I'm going to switch fields and go to Trinidad and do a postdoc fellowship on religion;" specifically altered states of consciousness and mental health. I wanted to study spirit possession in the field. I had absolutely no training or skills to do that, but hey, I got the fellowship and off I went. It was a real eye opener, as much about living as an ethnic minority in a developing country, which I had never done before. It really altered the way I saw everything. I did my research and then I began looking for my first teaching appointment. I wanted to keep experiencing different places, so I think that really my first motivation was I wanted to travel. I wanted to see different parts of the world. So I got my first teaching appointment in Malaysia. And then, after that, Singapore. I really liked Southeast Asia; I was still doing bits and pieces with the altered states of consciousness, but the more conventional research I was doing pertained to cross-cultural psychology. It was still focused on gender as an integral issue, and then went on to attributions and other social psychological phenomena.

Eventually I moved to New Zealand in 1986. And not only did I move to New Zealand, I moved to Christchurch, which was very White and monocultural. They used to say back then that Christchurch was more English than England. I began to do some research with international students because at that time Malaysia was the country sending the largest number of international students to New Zealand. So that gave me my hook back to Southeast Asia where I had been at the beginning. At that point I started looking at the literature and it occurred to me that the topic of adaptation was a mess. There was lots going on, but there was very little agreement on theoretical frameworks or what adaptation meant. About that time, one of my MA students, Wendy Searle, wanted to do her research on international students' adjustment. That was the beginning of our distinction between psychological and socio-cultural adaptation. It was a simple idea, but it seemed to have struck a useful chord that people really picked up on. I eventually extended the research to include expatriates and immigrants.

As I reflect on my career trajectory, I can absolutely laugh at myself, because I was so naive about what adaptation meant in the real world when I started out. I mean, I had my research questions and I knew that there were cultural differences, obviously, but I hadn't figured out in the earliest years what that really meant in terms of how I should behave in a culturally appropriate manner. Which sounds ridiculous now, but I can't believe how much I see this in everyday life, even amongst my colleagues and peers. When I observed the lack of intercultural sensitivity as people communicated across cultural boundaries, I thought to myself, this is an academic question, this is what I'm going to do research on. Only later did it dawn on me that in my earliest days in Malaysia, when people said, "oh Colleen, that's the woman who speaks what's on her mind," that it was not a compliment! So I had to be really honest with myself as I started without a lot of practical insight about intercultural competence. I really did learn a lot being in the real world, the practical world of experience, how to become more interculturally sensitive and more interculturally competent. But it's a constant journey; it's a constant learning experience, it's never like you reach point X and you've got it all sorted out.

It may be obvious at this point that various *acculturation conditions* will impact an immigrant or refugee family's *acculturation orientation*, such as ethnic vitality of their heritage culture, second language proficiency, personal characteristics like closely held norms and values, religion, and the perceived or actual receptivity of the host society (Celenk & van de Vijver, 2014). Specifically, the influence of the receiving community in defining the immigrant's acculturation orientation cannot be overstated. Many early analyses of cultural adjustment assumed that the sojourner was an isolated, independent unit to be observed and measured. The contributions of Adler's (1975) "multicultural man," and Bochner's (1981) "mediating person" are characteristic of that approach and although they represented significant advances in our understanding of adjustment and the "third culture" phenomenon, they inevitably ignored the bi-directional, or social, aspects of the adjustment experience – viz., it takes place within a social network (Berry, 1997; Kim, 1987; Weimann, 1989).

Therefore, it is important to point out that numerous studies have shown that non-dominant groups and individuals do not always enjoy full agency in selecting their acculturation orientation due to reasons of exclusion, expectation, or discrimination (Berry, 2015; R. Y. Bourhis et al., 1997; Komisarof et al., 2020; Kosic & Phalet, 2006). Specifically, Berry (1997) as well as Bourhis et al. (1997) modified the original Berry model (see Figure 6.2) to better account for "the power the host society has in shaping strangers' acculturation experiences and outcomes especially through the development and enforcement of immigration policies... [placing] more emphasis on the social context and sociopolitical climate in which acculturation occurs" (Pitts, 2017, p. 5). The kinds of change and possible absence of agency experienced during cultural transitions leads to the observation that while to some extent acculturation is a practical matter of accessing resources in the new cultural environment, on a deeper psychological level, it strikes at the very

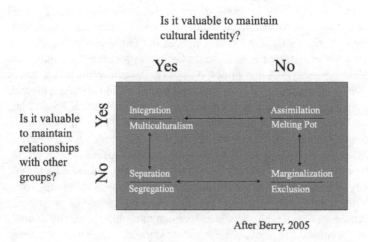

Figure 6.2 Societal Accommodation Strategies, adapted from Berry (2005).

core of personal identity. When intercultural spaces become overt, identity changes are woven into the acculturation process.

Cultural Transition and Identity

You may remember T. E. Lawrence's questions from the introduction, "How could I as me, meet this new people? How would I have to change? What of me was superficial and might be sacrificed and what need I keep to remain myself?" These are deeply personal questions about self, meaning, and identity. Recall from our conversation about Symbolic Interaction Theory in Chapter 3 that our personal identity is formed amidst interaction with others. When we transition into another culture, even if only for a short time, there are significant identity ramifications.

Identity as a general concept is quite complex and varied. At its base, it refers to affiliations and differentiation. Wolfe (1992), reviewing Zerubavel's book *The Fine Line*, observed that "To speak of identity is always to mark one thing off from another" (Wolfe, 1992, p. 375). We can have racial and ethnic identities, cultural identities, national identities, regional and tribal identities, sexual and gender identities, occupational identities, and religious or spiritual identities, just to name some of the more obvious categories.

Cultural and Ethnic Identity

Cultural identity is often used by scholars as an umbrella term to encompass a range of other identities, such as ethnicity, racial, gender, nationality, and even sexual identity. Klyukanov (2005) defines it communicatively as "membership in a group in which all people share the same symbolic meanings" (p. 12). Ethnic identity is commonly used synonymously with cultural identity because it is associated with a shared heritage, language, and oftentimes a common history or geographical origin. However, ethnicity is likewise a complex idea that is sometimes confused with a generalised sense of nationality. For example, if someone was born in Uganda, we might mistakenly assume they most closely identify with the political nation state. But that would gloss over the fact that there are an estimated 70 languages spoken in more than 56 distinct tribes within Uganda. The political boundaries of the country are a relatively recent phenomenon as a result of British colonisation in the late 19th and early 20th centuries. In truth, people born in a multilingual, tribal community are more likely to identify with their local region grounded in a common kinship heritage, cultural beliefs, faith traditions, and a shared language than to a broad political affiliation. From this example it is clear to see that ethnicity is a multi-faceted attachment to a people group that transcends national borders. The salience of your ethnic heritage can be affected by many outside factors like migration or immigration, vibrancy of your first language, and the intentional preservation of traditions.

Over time, the salience of our ethnic heritage can diminish due to loss of contact with our communities of origin, lack of opportunity to practice our first language, or marrying into other ethnic groups (Kim, 2015). In fact, research shows that by the third or fourth generation after immigration, the affiliation with a given national origin often fades (Kim, 2017). It is not uncommon to hear a person of Euro-American heritage refer to themselves as "just American" or perhaps use a metaphor like "Heinz 57" suggesting there are many ingredients in their ethno-linguistic past. Such a characterisation reveals two things about their self-understanding. First, it demonstrates that they fall into the dominant culture with Judeo-Christian traditions imported from Western Europe. And second, that they have a relatively unexamined cultural identity that influences them from an "out-of-awareness" position. People that have an unexamined cultural identity fail to see how culture influences our thoughts, attitudes, beliefs, and behaviour. As author Patty Lane states, "at no point in our human interactions do we take off our culture and set it aside. It is always with us in all of our relationships, in all of our thinking and our processing of the world around us" (Lane, 2002, p. 11).

For the remainder of this chapter, we will use the term "socio-cultural identity" to capture the intersection of your combined social and ethno-cultural identities and the sense of self that is derived from one's membership in a particular culture or group that has been shaped by a variety of factors, including language, religion, ethnicity, nationality, and social class.

A Communication Theory of Ethnic Identity

One of the first questions we encounter related to identity is, what is it comprised of, and how do we acquire it? Anthropologist Clifford Geertz (1966) wrote that humans are essentially born unfinished; "we all begin with the natural equipment to live a thousand kinds of lives and end having lived only one" (pp. 5–6). Geertz goes on to assert that human nature is completely dependent on cultural patterns for its substance, structure, and style. Hecht et al. (1993) provided an answer to our first question, namely that our ethno-cultural identities are shaped by individual, dyadic-role, communal, and performative elements; all of which are symbolic transactions that together constitute our identity (see Figure 6.3). The *personal frame* is the repository of our self-concept, and for some, the experience of a spiritual essence. From this individual level of identity spring notions of motivation, self-understanding and personal expectations. The *relational frame* leverages our earlier reference to the idea that all communication has both content and relationship dimensions as well as the concept of reflected appraisals (Cooley, 1922; Watzlawick et al., 1967). It is during our interactions with others that we begin to imagine how we appear to them, and by reflection how we appear to ourselves. These role relationships with parents, siblings, friends, and teachers contribute to our consensual sense of self in what Mead called reflected appraisals (Mead, 1934). That our identities are mutually constructed is made clear by the relational frame process.

The third component in Hecht et al.'s (1993) theory is the *communal frame*. Not only do we jointly negotiate our identities in one-on-one relationships, but we also find solidarity in collective thought communities. In the communal frame we see and experience the strongest ethno-cultural influence in that the identity features

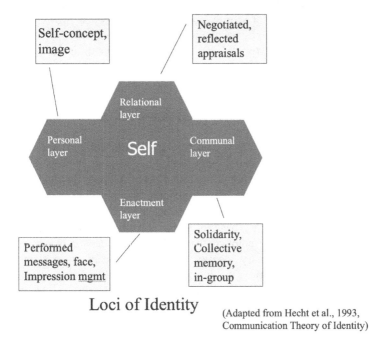

Loci of Identity   (Adapted from Hecht et al., 1993,
Communication Theory of Identity)

Figure 6.3 Communication Theory of Ethnic Identity, adapted from Hecht et al. (1993).

belong to the group, not the individual or the interaction. The communal frame is formed on the basis of interdependencies and shared bonds within a social network. Thus, identity is acquired, or understood, via the immersion into the signifying universe of the thought community where rules for membership are defined. Finally, the *performative frame* is where identity emerges within each of the other frames during interaction. As we enact roles within our relationships, affiliate with particular reference groups, and form a sense of who we are at our core, we express that combination of attributes in a coherent, yet dynamic self. All of the frames intersect with each other in the performative frame as we elevate one tile versus another within our identity mosaic during each particular interaction (Chao & Moon, 2005). Hecht et al. note that not all messages are about identity, but identity expresses itself in all of our messages.

Social Identity Complexity

In Chapter 1 we introduced the concept of social identity complexity as it relates to Proposition 4 and Chao and Moon's (2005) Cultural Mosaic Model.

Proposition 4: When in an intercultural space, there is usually discordance in one's internal cultural identities.

To further understand the dynamics in intercultural spaces, it will be helpful to understand the concept of social identity complexity. Roccas and Brewer (2002) describe social identity complexity as "the nature of the subjective representation of multiple in-group identities" (pp. 88–89). They present four structures in which multiple identities could be organised within a person, namely intersection, compartmentalisation, dominance, and merger.

Intersection is where a person's identity is organised as the intersection of multiple group identities or, using Zerubavel's framework, membership in multiple thought communities. Roccas and Brewer (2002) provide the example of a female lawyer's primary social identity as "the compound combination of both sex and profession, an identity shared only with other women lawyers" (p. 90). *Compartmentalisation* offers further insight into what happens in intercultural spaces, because it refers to social identities being organised in a context or situation-specific manner. Roccas and Brewer note, "in certain contexts one group membership becomes the primary basis of social identity, whereas other group identities become primary in different contexts" (pp. 90–91). *Dominance* is where one identity becomes the primary identity that supersedes all other identities. *Merger* is where "social identity is the sum of one's combined group identification" (p. 91). This structure allows for the most flexibility in identifying with others who share any of one's own identities. Acculturation scholar David Lackland Sam relates part of his journey as an immigrant grappling with his intersectional identity and how it led him into his area of research in the following narrative.

An Acculturation Story

David Lackland Sam

It was partly accidental that I found myself in the cross-cultural branch of psychology. I was doing a bachelor's degree in psychology back in Ghana, and my intention was to work in organisational psychology. I never thought of ending up in another country like Norway. However, I realised that if I wanted to go further within psychology, I needed to do postgraduate studies; the bachelor's degree was not enough. My goal was to do a graduate programme outside Ghana, preferably in an English-speaking country.

I come from a big family with eigt brothers and sisters. My oldest brother rose to be the headmaster of a secondary school, and he pushed me to study and further myself through academics. Being the youngest and the last to be consulted for anything, I wasn't going to rely on anyone else to take care of me. So, I started to look at programmes in the United States. But one of my professors whom I had asked to write a recommendation said "why don't you try the Scandinavian schools? They have good programmes, and if you can learn the language, and survive the weather, it's a good place to go." So just to please him, I sent two applications: one to Sweden and one to Norway. I gained admission to university in both countries. It was 1984, and at that time in Ghana there was a very unpredictable political climate, so a friend told me, "even if Norway is not the paradise that you're looking for, you are much better off starting there now and then moving to another programme if you want" (I had my eyes set on Canada).

My introduction to cross-cultural psychology was an interesting confluence of technical professional definitions in Norway, restrictive opinions about who could practice psychology, and a personal interaction with a friend at a party. My intention was to eventually practice organisational psychology, but an early meeting with a psychology professor made it clear that in order to be a psychologist in Norway, you had to be born and raised in Norway. Around the same time, I was asked at a party what it was like to be a foreign student in Norway. Surprisingly, I spent about one hour answering that question – basically talking about how difficult it is. The language is different, the food is different, and on and on. By the end of the conversation, I wondered if I was the only person who is experiencing Norway like this, or if this is something quite common. Those questions led to a semester research project on how international students adjust to the culture and, of course, I found that there were other people who were not very happy; they felt very isolated, they didn't feel they were part of Norwegian society. I went on to look at personality factors that contributed to positive adjustment, and eventually the mental health of international students.

Another turning point in my journey was a result of the increasing numbers of refugees arriving in Norway at the time and an internship at a school psychologist's office. I met a young Chilean boy who came into the office with a problem of not knowing who he is. He came to Norway around the age of five, he was then 18 years old; he spoke fluent Norwegian, but he didn't feel like he was a part of either culture. He was having an identity crisis. I could relate to this young man, as I eventually became a naturalised citizen in Norway. Between my experiences and this young boy's experience, I began thinking more about how important culture is, and the role it plays in immigration. As part of my PhD proposal process, I introduced myself to John Berry and spent a month with him in Canada. It's safe to say he opened an entirely new world for me. He started educating me about cross-cultural psychology and we ended up doing a large multinational comparative study together exploring acculturation and adaptation among immigrant youth.

That is my journey in a nutshell. You need to understand people's culture, and how culture makes them present themselves the way they do. My take on culture is that human beings created cultures for their survival. We are all trying to survive in this world, but we live in different ecological situations with different challenges. And so my society created a way of dealing with the environmental challenges and the ecological challenges that are unique to my region in Ghana. If you grow up in another part of the world, with different ecological challenges, your culture will have been designed to help you survive. I wouldn't want to pit cultures against each other, that one is better than the other, but rather based on the circumstances that we grow up in, our cultures develop in response to those challenges.

> Now comes the other aspect of intercultural relations. Until you get out of your culture, you really don't think about the other side, you don't even think about the fact that you have culture. I was an adult when I left Ghana for the first time. Up until that point, I took many things for granted. But from the moment you see that there are cultural differences and ethnocentrism, it opens up a whole new world of understanding. Until you interact with people from different backgrounds, you live within your stereotypes and prejudices. But by your openness and your willingness to interact with people, it has the potential of changing the whole dynamic. And that is what I'm interested in, a harmonious society.

Examples of the complexity of overlapping identities are plentiful within indigenous people groups. For example, while all Native Americans share a common global region and status, tribal identities cut across geographical and language bonds that might cause outsiders to categorise certain groups under the same label. For example, the White Earth Nation Band of Chippewa (Gaa-waabaabiganikaag) in northern Minnesota, USA, who speak Anishinaabe (meaning "the original people") are but one tribe who speak that language within the Band of Chippewa. The Jewish global diaspora that are affiliated by a common faith tradition despite having disparate national and language affiliations are another example of complex, intersecting identities.

Roccas and Brewer (2002) proposed that on a continuum of complexity from lowest to highest, the identity frameworks will fall in the order of intersection (least complex), dominance, compartmentalisation, and merger (most complex). The authors further proposed that those who have higher levels of social identity complexity are better able to relate to others who are "different" – or people from other cultures, in the context of the present discussion. This claim is supported by empirical results from Brewer and Pierce's (2005) research in which people with high social identity complexity were more tolerant and accepting of out-group members compared with people of low social identity complexity. Further, Knifsend and Juvonen (2014) found that social identity complexity facilitated cross-ethnic friendships in adolescents especially when adolescents had opportunities to form such friendships.

Integrative Theory of Adaptation

One of the key voices addressing identity and adaptation from a communication perspective is Young Yun Kim (2019). She provides some of her backstory on how she began studying these issues in the following paragraphs:

> It really is amazing how all of these things happen. I had completed my bachelor's degree in English back home at Seoul National University in South Korea and I got a job at a brand-new TV station; I had applied to become a producer-director of documentary programmes. I really don't know why I applied for that position, it just sounded interesting, and I got hired and was working on a

variety of documentary projects. I never even had an inclination of doing a PhD in communication or anything. And then, one day I read something about the East-West Center at the University of Hawaii – Manoa. They were accepting applications for graduate MA degree programmes in communication, and so, because I was working in TV broadcasting, I applied since it included mass communication. Prior to my graduate work, I had only travelled internationally to Japan for a few weeks. At the time I had no idea about intercultural or international communication, but general communication was interesting as it related to my job as a TV producer.

The East-West Center was formed by the US Congress in 1960 in order to promote mutual understanding and peaceful relationships between the United States, Asia, and the Pacific Islands. It was during my MA programme at the East-West Center that I met influential scholars like sociologist Daniel Lerner who was well known for his work in the Middle East in the area of development communication and Dick Brislin in cross-cultural psychology. As I neared the end of my programme, one of my mentors recommended I "go for my PhD," because he knew I was planning to return to the TV station. It was the fact that he saw the potential in me to be a scholar that shaped my decision to go to Northwestern University in Chicago.

The summer I visited Northwestern, I walked into the Communication Department and the building was empty except for one man typing away in an office. It turned out to be Charles Berger (one of the originators of Uncertainty Reduction Theory) – he was the only one working. I didn't know who he was or anything about him, but he turned toward me and started speaking to me in Korean! Apparently, he had served as an intelligence officer in Korea during the war, so he was very fluent. It was Berger who encouraged me to become interdisciplinary by taking courses in psychology, sociology, and anthropology; it really opened my eyes and contributed to my being a systems theorist today. Based upon my own personal experience of adapting to another culture, I realised that no one was looking at adaptation from a communication perspective, focusing on how people interact and communicate, so I proposed an interdisciplinary model in my dissertation.

The Role of Communication in Adaptation

As we have discussed, cultural adjustment may occur in the form of a positive identification with the host culture, or through a negative (lack of) identification with host conventions and people. In either case, communication theorists like Kim have suggested that communication functions as the primary means of coping and organising social reality (Albrecht & Adelman, 1987; Gudykunst & Hammer, 1988; Gudykunst & Kim, 1997; Kim, 2019). It operates on various levels from interpersonal to organisational, stabilising and modifying social life. In one of her earliest formulations, Kim (1978) articulated it this way:

> through communication [a person] acquires control over change in order to cope with the new environment... learning and acquiring new ways to face

problematic situations occur through communication, both verbal and non-verbal, and through interpersonal contact... (p. 199)

Others have indicated similar notions concerning communication as a social coping strategy, with the implication that if performed with host community members an individual acquires cultural patterns and social support resources through inter-action that allow positive identification with the host culture, and ultimately intercultural communication competence (Allport, 1954; Amir, 1969; Cook, 1957; Gudykunst & Kim, 1997; Hanvey, 1979; Smith, 1999, 2005). The theoretical train of thought can be summarised as follows: when examining a social process, such as adjustment to socio-cultural change, adapting to new groups and environments requires new knowledge and skills; and acquiring that knowledge and those skills requires interaction, which is facilitated by communication behaviours. However, neither the knowledge nor the skills necessarily have to come from host nationals, and the consequent form of adjustment does not necessarily have to reflect positive identification with the host culture. As we have seen from the Berry model, both positive and negative host culture identification still constitute adjustment along the spectrum of options.

Incorporating communication as a key coping mechanism in the adaptive process was the driving impetus behind Kim's (2001) Integrative Theory of Communication and Cross-Cultural Adaptation. She explains the motivation and uniqueness of her Integrative Theory as:

> There were certainly many theories about cultural adjustment at the time, and Berry's model was the dominant acculturation perspective, but no one was looking at it from a communication perspective, there was no communica-tive adaptation theory. I thought it was very important to look at the process of cultural change in personal transformation over time from a communication perspective. It allows you to look at the process as an interaction between the person and the environment – and there was no other theory that did that.
>
> In addition, my whole theory-building effort was grounded in a systems-theoretical approach and methodology, which is very different from a variable-analytic approach which emphasises linear causality. My theory does not do that. It looks at the holistic constellation of factors, what I call the "big picture." It takes into consideration the predisposing factors of the immigrant, the interior identity factors, the environmental factors, and the interaction communication variables – I put them all together in a sort of mapping of the phenomenon in an integrative fashion. I think this holistic approach appeals to people who think in a systems, or holistic way. It allows you to look at A + B + C, but then add D, E, and F as well. The model becomes quite complex, but it has enormous explanatory power when you add all the factors together because you're not just looking at the influence of one variable on another. It relies on structural equation modelling as opposed to regression analysis, which offers powerful insights into the process.
>
> Finally, my model is unique in that it views adaptation as a transformational process over time. The process of cultural adaptation, or acculturation, is not

static, it is not a one-time phenomenon, it takes a lifetime, it is a continuing process of change in which a person's interior condition becomes more fit with the other environment's immense challenges. The predicted outcomes of this transformational process are an increasing level of functional fitness, and psychological health; and eventually identity transformation toward a more intercultural identity as opposed to a mono-cultural identity. I think one of the unique aspects of my theory is that it is one of the only adaptation theories that actually explains *how* people change in this process, because it happens through a stress-encounter, adaptation, growth process. These are actually two separate models, the stress-adaptation dynamic is a process model, and the transformational-adaptation is a structural model, but of course they work together.

The Integrative Theory of Communication and Cross-Cultural Adaptation

To fully understand the trajectory of cultural transition, we need to identify the sequence of events, and isolate important variables at each of the stages. Kim (2003) thinks of *adaptation* comprehensively as "the dynamic process by which individuals, upon relocating to an unfamiliar cultural environment, establish (or re-establish) and maintain a relatively stable, reciprocal, and functional relationship with the environment" (p. 244). Her theory is integrative in that it acknowledges that cultural transition is an interpersonal process wherein one encounters variance in virtues, values transformation, language acquisition/loss, nonverbal signals, third culture formation, transition from collectivistic to individualistic, or low power distant to high power distant society, etc.

The first set of factors the model considers relate to what Kim calls *predispositions*, or antecedents of cultural adjustment (cf. Caligiuri, 2000). These factors include the similarity/dissimilarity between the heritage and host cultures (ethnic proximity), the immigrant's familiarity with the host culture and language (pre-departure training), personality traits that afford adaptiveness (e.g., openness/flexibility), previous experience with cultural transition, and demographic characteristics like age, education level, and family characteristics (see Figure 6.4). Most of these factors are normally under the control of the immigrant or sojourner, or at the very least can be addressed or mitigated. However, there are specific classes of immigration, refugee status for example, where the migrant loses a degree of influence over these factors, and in those situations, cultural adaptation can become much more complicated.

A second set of factors affecting the adaptation process derive from the *host environment conditions*. Previously, during our discussion of the Berry model, we mentioned that the receiving culture can present itself on a continuum from welcoming to hostile both in policy and interpersonally (Kunst et al., 2021). Similar to Kim's model, Kunst et al. (2021) have begun to highlight the role that majority, or dominant culture members play in the acculturative process of sojourners and immigrants (see Kunst's narrative in Chapter 1). Variables like host receptivity, conformity pressure, the size and strength of the local ethnic group(s), as well as the potential for interaction with the local host community can affect an individual's potential for positive adaptation.

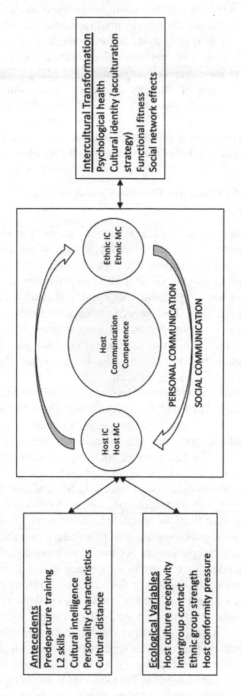

Figure 6.4 Kim's Structural Model, adapted from Kim (2001).

Adaptation and Interethnic Identity

The connection between socio-cultural identity and adaptation is complex. On the one hand, acculturation can lead to changes in socio-cultural identity that Kim (2006) attributes to the amazing plasticity of the human mind. For example, immigrants may adopt the language, customs, and values of their new country which can lead to new opportunities and experiences as well as a sense of loss of heritage culture identity. Kim (2006) suggested that a more *individuated* response to self and others that is "less constrained by the grips of conventional group categories" results in an *interethnic* identity and allows us to access greater ability to differentiate self and other and integrate with members of diverse groups (p. 293).

Kim's interethnic identity is consistent with the Mosaic Model of socio-cultural identity introduced in Chapter 1 which views the cultural person consisting of separate, distinguishable tiles that together constitute a coherent whole (Chao & Moon, 2005). Chao and Moon suggested that the tiles represent things like group affiliations, demographic characteristics, and geographic attributes. For example, Ripley is a White, middle-aged male from the western United States that plays soccer, rides a motorcycle, and attends church. Sometimes, in an international setting, national identity can become more salient in the perceptions of the out-group. But depending on the nature of the interaction, a combination of group affiliation and geographic region might be the initial reported identity affiliation. For example, when Ripley introduces himself at an international conference, he might say "I am a professor of intercultural communication at a university in St. Paul, MN in the USA." According to Chao and Moon (2005), people will draw upon the repertoire of their cultural mosaics in order to meet the relational demands of dynamic contexts in much the same manner as bicultural individuals code switch between sociolinguistic or ethnic cultures. In addition to our cultural identities being malleable and contextually constituted, the individual tiles can change over time based upon the weight or valence we attribute to them.

The Test of Cultural Transition

The actual path of cultural transition can be fraught with barriers and stressors. Imagine you have just landed at Narita Airport for your first trip to Tokyo, Japan. An early research characterisation of a sojourner's mental state described the anxiety that results from losing familiar signs and symbols of social interaction as *culture shock* (Oberg, 1954). Oberg described psycho-somatic symptoms ranging from irritability and paranoia to depression, loneliness, and physical illness. Subsequent research identified an approximate adjustment curve with discernible phases that sojourners and immigrants encountered as they acclimated to a new culture (Figure 6.5). Initially, the anticipation and fascination of the new experience fuels sojourners' emotions as excitement runs high. However, over time cultural differences begin to interfere with the ability to accomplish tasks, communicate, and get work done in the new setting and frustration can set in. The more one encounters those language, relationship, and functional task difficulties,

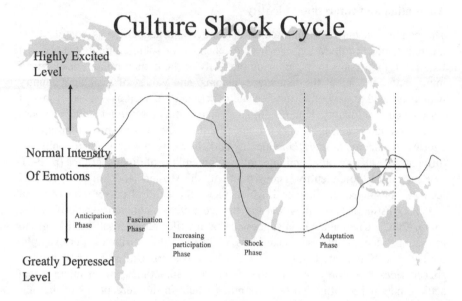

Figure 6.5 Culture Shock Cycle.

the deeper the frustration can be, until a form of depression manifests, or what scholars have termed the U-curve of culture shock (Church, 1982). Later the curve was extended to include reverse, or re-entry culture shock when the sojourner returned to his or her heritage culture (Gullahorn & Gullahorn, 1963). Eventually, the concept of acculturative stress replaced the less precise "shock" terminology in psychological literature (Berry & Annis, 1974), and the learning and growth benefits of cultural transition were increasingly acknowledged (Adler, 1975; Kim, 2001). Kim's (2001) stress-adaptation-growth model is an example of the positive, iterative change approach to cultural transition that has moved beyond simply problematising acculturative stress.

Both Kim and Berry recognise that there are competing ideologies surrounding cultural adaptation. From societal policymaking to personal expectations there are often underlying assumptions about what acculturation, or achieving optimal functional fitness with one's cultural environment, *ought* to look like. Most social scientists agree that cultural adaptation is a perfectly natural phenomenon and will take place on some level, and that successful adaptation leading to self-sufficiency and life satisfaction is a desired outcome (Kim, 2003, p. 252). The ideological differences arise in what *successful* adaptation looks like and how much agency the immigrant or sojourner has in the process. Berry's (2005) acculturation model assumes, ideally, that the immigrant has a great deal of agency within a pluralistic society in as much as he or she is able to make a conscious choice about accepting or rejecting the host and heritage cultures. The pluralistic ideology, reinforced by the growing influence of critical perspectives, construes cultural identity as fixed, and something that should be preserved in its original form, which results in problematising cultural adaptation as loss or even oppression.

Alternatively, models like Kim's (2019) Integrative Theory view cultural identity as dynamic and continuously evolving in the face of changing cultural landscapes. These kinds of perspectives are often grouped under an *assimilation* ideology label and attributed derogatory motives. And certainly there have been historical misuses of government power to strip people groups of their cultural identities. However, if assimilation is taken to mean adopting some of the host culture patterns in order to find a functional fit and satisfying quality of life, then it is resonant with any other species' common adaptive process. As Kim (2003) reflects, "few individuals in an unfamiliar environment can completely escape adaptation as long as they remain in, and are functionally dependent on, the mainstream culture. Conversely, few can attain complete assimilation no matter how hard or long they try" (p. 253). Cultural adaptation is not like an encounter with the Borg in *Star Trek: The Next Generation*, "resistance is futile, you will be assimilated!" Rather, it is an ongoing, dynamic, symbolic process, reminiscent of jazz or communication itself, finding the pocket in its ecological setting.

Conclusion

The stories of Berry, Kim, Ward, and Sam have illustrated the interrelationship between socio-cultural identity and acculturation. We have seen the sense of belonging that a strong socio-cultural identity can provide and the psychological and behavioural stress that acculturation can cause. It was also explained that positive psychological adaptation can be influenced by certain personality variables, environmental factors like host receptivity, and social support from host as well as co-ethnic communities. We have also learned that successful socio-cultural adaptation is predicted by cultural knowledge, relationships with host society members, and positive attitudes towards the host culture (Berry, 2005; Kim, 2019; Smith, 1999, 2005). It is clear that the relationship between socio-cultural identity and acculturation is complex and the path towards functional fitness can vary from person to person. The more we understand that relationship, the better positioned we will be to promote positive outcomes for immigrants and sojourners who are on that journey of cultural transition.

In Conversation: Acculturation

Ripley: There is a great deal of anxiety and tension in the world today over the topic of immigration. One of the tensions relates to cultural identity threat. Do you think an immigrant should be responsible for adjusting to the host culture? Or, should the host culture accommodate all of the cultural patterns of various immigrant communities?

Lily: I'm glad you asked this question because I feel quite strongly about it. I would say the responsibility for adjusting or acculturating into a host culture is entirely on the immigrant. But the responsibility of the

	host culture is to provide an environment in which immigrants do have opportunities and the freedom to acculturate.
Ripley:	That sounds a bit like an assimilationist policy. You don't strike me as such, so how is that different?
Lily:	Assimilationist policy implies a systemic view (from the host cultural perspective) that immigrants should simply become mainstreamed. What I'm saying is that we need to recognise that immigrants arrive into an established cultural context. To expect that context to adjust to the immigrants is unreasonable. But we can expect the context to be welcoming and not hostile.
Ripley:	Okay. How does the dynamic nature of culture factor into the immigration equation? That is, a graduate professor of mine once said, "cultures are not like ball-bearings, which when you shake them together in your hand, stay neatly apart." Don't all cultures change through the process of immigration?
Lily:	Of course. But just like how people change one another when they are in relationship, I see cultural change as a result of a mix of people as a relational and mutual process (or it should be!). In every society there is or will be a dominant cultural group due to geographical and historical factors. It is appropriate to expect dominant groups to be welcoming of others, but inappropriate to expect that group to force equal representation of every variation of diversity in that community.
Ripley:	That cultures are unique, and that each region is marked by wonderful cultural characteristics is part of the beauty of diversity to me. But striking the proper balance between preserving heritage cultures and welcoming new cultural neighbours can be tricky.

Questions for Reflection

1. To what extent is Ripley's final comment contingent on freedom of expression? Do you think specific political ideologies facilitate such freedoms more than others?
2. Have you personally experienced one of the acculturation orientations (integration, separation, marginalisation, assimilation)? If you haven't, do you think that affects your views on immigration?
3. How would you answer Ripley's first question if it was asked of you?

Notes

1 Some early research on cultural adjustment by Ruben and Kealey (1979) and Hawes and Kealey (1980) connected the notion of adjustment to intercultural effectiveness. Ruben and Kealey (1979) report findings that suggest "*adjustment* and *effectiveness* are functionally, if not conceptually related" (p. 38; emphasis in the original). Hawes and Kealey (1980) confirm the relationship between adjustment and effectiveness in that adjustment is a key indicator of overseas effectiveness.

2 There is no question that a great deal more research is conducted on the acculturation of non-dominant groups to the dominant society. Very little research has explored the effects of migrating populations on the host society (Domínguez & Maya-Jariego, 2008).

References

Adler, P. (1975). The transitional experience: An alternative view of culture shock. *Journal of Humanistic Psychology, 15*(4), 13–23.

Albrecht, T. L., & Adelman, M. B. (1987). *Communicating social support.* Sage.

Allport, G. W. (1954). *The nature of prejudice.* Macmillan.

Amir, Y. (1969). Contact hypothesis in ethnic relations. *Psychological Bulletin, 71*, 319–342.

Berry, J. W. (1997). Immigration, acculturation, and adaptation. *Applied Psychology: An International Review, 46*(1), 5–34. https://doi.org/10.1111/j.1464-0597.1997.tb01087.x

Berry, J. W. (2005). Acculturation: Living successfully in two cultures. *International Journal of Intercultural Relations, 29*(6), 697–712. http://dx.doi.org/10.1016/j.ijintrel.2005.07.013

Berry, J. W. (2015). Acculturation. In J. M. Bennett (Ed.), *The Sage encyclopedia of intercultural competence.* Sage Publications.

Berry, J. W., & Annis, R. C. (1974). Acculturative stress: The role of ecology, culture and differentiation. *Journal of Cross-Cultural Psychology, 5*(4), 382–406. https://doi.org/10.1177/002202217400500402

Berry, J. W., Kim, U., Minde, T., & Mok, D. (1987). Comparative studies of acculturative stress. *The International Migration Review, 21*(3), 491–511. https://doi.org/10.2307/2546607

Berry, J. W., Kim, U., Power, S., Young, M., & Bujaki, M. (1989). Acculturation attitudes in plural societies. *Applied Psychology: An International Review, 38*, 185–206. https://doi.org/10.1111/j.1464-0597.1989.tb01208.x

Bochner, S. (Ed.). (1981). *The mediating person.* Schenkman Pub. Co.

Bourhis, R. Y., Moise, L. C., Perreault, S., & Senecal, S. (1997). Towards an interactive acculturation model: A social psychological approach. *International Journal of Psychology, 32*(6), 369–386. https://doi.org/10.1080/002075997400629

Brewer, M. B., & Pierce, K. P. (2005). Social identity complexity and outgroup tolerance. *Personality and Social Psychology Bulletin, 31*(3), 428–437.

Brislin, R. (1981). *Cross-cultural encounters: Face to face interaction.* Pergamon.

Caligiuri, P. M. (2000). Selecting expatriates for personality characteristics: A moderating effect of personality on the relationship between host national contact and cross-cultural adjustment. *Management International Review, 40*, 61–80.

Celenk, O., & van de Vijver, F. J. R. (2014). Assessment of psychological acculturation and multiculturalism: An overview of measures in the public domain. In V. Benet-Martínez & Y. Hong (Eds.), *The Oxford handbook of multicultural identity* (pp. 205–213). Oxford University Press. https://doi.org/10.1093/oxfordhb/9780199796694.013.001

Chao, G. T., & Moon, H. (2005). The cultural mosaic: A metatheory for understanding the complexity of culture. *Journal of Applied Psychology, 90*, 1128–1140.

Church, A. (1982). Sojourner adjustment. *Psychological Bulletin, 91*, 540–575.

Cook, W. (1957). Desegregation: A psychological analysis. *American Psychologist, 12*, 1–13.

Cooley, C. H. (1922). *Human nature and the social order.* Scribner.

Dinges, N. (1983). Intercultural competence. In D. Landis & R. Brislin (Eds.), *Handbook of intercultural training* (Vol. 1, pp. 176–202). Pergamon.

Domínguez, S., & Maya-Jariego, I. (2008). Acculturation of host individuals: Immigrants and personal networks. *American Journal of Community Psychology*, *42*(3–4), 309. https://doi.org/10.1007/s10464-008-9209-5

Geertz, C. (1966). The impact of the concept of culture on the concept of man. *Bulletin of the Atomic Scientists*, *22*(4), 2–8. https://doi.org/10.1080/00963402.1966.11454918

Gudykunst, W. B. (1977). Intercultural contact and attitude change: A review of literature and suggestions for future research. In N. C. Jain (Ed.), *International and Intercultural Communication Annual* (Vol. 4, pp. 1–16). Speech Communication Association.

Gudykunst, W. B., & Hammer, M. R. (1984). Dimensions of intercultural effectiveness: Culture specific or culture-general? *International Journal of Intercultural Relations*, *8*(1), 1–10.

Gudykunst, W. B., & Hammer, M. (1988). Strangers and hosts: An uncertainty reduction based theory of intercultural adaptation. In Y. Y. Kim & W. B. Gudykunst (Eds.), *Cross-cultural adaptation: Current approaches* (Vol. XI, pp. 106–139). Sage.

Gudykunst, W. B., & Kim, Y. Y. (1997). *Communicating with strangers: An approach to intercultural communication* (3rd ed.). McGraw-Hill.

Gullahorn, J. E., & Gullahorn, J. T. (1963). An extension of the U-curve hypothesis. *Journal of Social Issues*, *19*, 33–47.

Hammer, M., Gudykunst, W., & Wiseman, R. (1978). Dimensions of intercultural effectiveness: An exploratory study. *International Journal of Intercultural Relations*, *2*(4), 382–393.

Hammer, M. R. (1987). Behavioral dimensions of intercultural effectiveness: A replication. *International Journal of Intercultural Relations*, *2*(1), 65–88.

Hanvey, R. (1979). *Cross-cultural awareness: An attainable global perspective*. Global Perspectives in Education.

Harris, J. (1973). A science of the South Pacific: Analysis of the character structure of the Peace Corps volunteer. *American Psychologist*, *28*, 232–247.

Hawes, F., & Kealey, D. J. (1980). *Canadians in development*. Canadian International Development Agency.

Hecht, M. L., Collier, M. J., & Ribeau, S. A. (1993). *African American communication: Ethnic identity and cultural interpretation*. Sage Publications.

Herskovits, M. (1938). *Acculturation*. Peter Smith.

Kadushin, C. (2012). *Understanding social networks: Theories, concepts, and findings*. Oxford University Press.

Kim, Y. Y. (1978). A communication approach to the acculturation process: A study of Korean immigrants in Chicago. *International Journal of Intercultural Relations*, *2*(2), 197–224.

Kim, Y. Y. (1987). Facilitating immigrant adaptation: The role of communication. In T. A. M. Adelman (Ed.), *Communicating social support* (pp. 192–211). Sage.

Kim, Y. Y. (2001). *Becoming intercultural: An integrative theory of communication and cross-cultural adaptation*. Sage Publications.

Kim, Y. Y. (2003). Adapting to an unfamiliar culture. In W. Gudykunst (Ed.), *Cross-cultural and intercultural communication* (pp. 243–257). Sage Publications.

Kim, Y. Y. (2006). From ethnic to interethnic: The case for identity adaptation and transformation. *Journal of Language and Social Psychology*, *25*(3), 283–300. https://doi.org/10.1177/0261927X06289429

Kim, Y. Y. (2015). Finding a "home" beyond culture: The emergence of intercultural personhood in the globalizing world. *International Journal of Intercultural Relations*, *46*, 3–12. http://dx.doi.org/10.1016/j.ijintrel.2015.03.018

Kim, Y. Y. (2017). Identity and intercultural communication. In Y. Y. Kim & K. McKay-Semmler (Eds.), *The International encyclopedia of intercultural communication* (pp. 1–9). John Wiley & Sons.

Kim, Y. Y. (2019). Integrative communication theory of cross-cultural adaptation. In C. Liberman, A. Rancer, & T. Avtgis (Eds.), *Casing communication theory* (pp. 105–116). Kendall Hunt.

Klemp, G. O. (1979). Identifying, measuring, and integrating competence. In P. Pottinger & J. Goldsmith (Eds.), *New directions in experiential learning: Defining and measuring competence* (pp. 41–52). Jossey-Bass.

Klyukanov, I. E. (2005). *Principles of intercultural communication*. Pearson Education.

Knifsend, C. A., & Juvonen, J. (2014). Social identity complexity, cross-ethnic friendships, and intergroup attitudes in urban middle schools. *Child Development, 85*(2), 709–721. https://doi.org/10.1111/cdev.12157

Komisarof, A., Leong, C. H., & Teng, E. (2020). Constructing who can be Japanese: A study of social markers of acceptance in Japan. *Asian Journal of Social Psychology, 23*(2), 238–250. https://doi.org/10.1111/ajsp. 12396

Kosic, A., & Phalet, K. (2006). Ethnic categorization of immigrants: The role of prejudice, perceived acculturation strategies and group size [Special Issue: Attitudes Towards Immigrants and immigration]. *International Journal of Intercultural Relations, 30*(6), 769–782.

Kroeber, A. L., & Kluckhohn, C. (1952). *Culture: A critical review of concepts and definitions*. Harvard University Press.

Kunst, J. R., Lefringhausen, K., Sam, D. L., Berry, J. W., & Dovidio, J. F. (2021). The missing side of acculturation: How majority-group members relate to immigrant and minority-group cultures. *Current Directions in Psychological Science, 30*(6), 485–494. https://doi.org/10.1177/09637214211040771

Lane, P. (2002). *A beginner's guide to crossing cultures: Making friends in a multi-cultural world*. InterVarsity Press.

Lawrence, T. E. (1935). *Seven pillars of wisdom: A triumph* (1st ed.). Doubleday.

Mead, G. H. (1934). *Mind, self & society from the standpoint of a social behaviorist*. University of Chicago Press.

Oberg, K. (1954). *Culture shock*. [Speech] Presented to the Women's Club of Rio de Janeiro, August 3, pp. 1–9.

Pitts, M. J. (2017). Acculturation strategies. In Y. Y. Kim & K. McKay-Semmler (Eds.), *The International encyclopedia of intercultural communication* (Vol. 1). Wiley-Blackwell & Sons. https://doi.org/10.1002/9781118783665.ieicc0006

Repke, L., & Benet-Martínez, V. (2019). The interplay between the one and the others: Multiple cultural identifications and social networks. *Journal of Social Issues, 75*(2), 436–459. https://doi.org/10.1111/josi.12323

Roccas, S., & Brewer, M. B. (2002). Social identity complexity. *Personality and Social Psychology Review, 6*(2), 88–106.

Ruben, B. D., & Kealey, D. J. (1979). Behavioral assessment of communication competency and the prediction of cross-cultural adaptation. *International Journal of Intercultural Relations, 3*(1), 15–47. https://doi.org/10.1016/0147-1767(79)90045-2

Sam, D., & Berry, J. (2010). Acculturation: When individuals and groups of different cultural backgrounds meet. *Perspectives on Psychological Science, 5*(4), 472–481.

Smith, L. R. (1999). Intercultural network theory: A cross-paradigmatic approach to acculturation. *International Journal of Intercultural Relations, 23*(4), 629–658.

Smith, L. R. (2004). *Refugee adjustment structures: Resettlement's effects on personal networks*. 2004 Biennial Meeting of the International Academy for Intercultural Research, Taipei, Taiwan, July.

Smith, L. R. (2005). The structural context of intercultural personhood: Identity re-formation. *International Journal of Communication, 15*(1 & 2), 89–112.

Triandis, H. C. (1976). *Variations of Black and white perceptions of the social environment.* University of Illinois Press.

Ward, C. (2022). Critical reflections on sociocultural adaptation. *International Journal of Intercultural Relations, 88*, 157–162. https://doi.org/10.1016/j.ijintrel.2022.03.010

Ward, C., Ng Tseung-Wong, C., Szabo, A., Qumseya, T., & Bhowon, U. (2018). Hybrid and alternating identity styles as strategies for managing multicultural identities. *Journal of Cross-Cultural Psychology, 49*(9), 1402–1439. https://doi.org/10.1177/002202211 8782641

Watzlawick, P., Beavin, J. H., & Jackson, D. (1967). *Pragmatics of human communication: A study of interactional patterns, pathologies and paradoxes*. Norton.

Weimann, G. (1989). Social networks and communication. In W. B. Gudykunst & M. K. Asante (Ed.), *Handbook of international and intercultural communication* (pp. 186–203). Sage.

Wolfe, A. (1992). Where (and whether) to draw the line [The Fine Line: Making Distinctions in Everyday Life, Eviatar Zerubavel]. *Sociological Forum, 7*(2), 375–380.

7 Intercultural Communication Competence

What makes someone good at communicating with someone from another culture? What does "good" communication mean? Who decides the communication was good? And does good communication look the same or similar in different cultures? As a graduate student, Lily pondered these questions ad nauseam. Being an international student living in a different culture, Lily was venturing in and out of intercultural spaces with sufficient frequency that she was motivated to navigate them competently. She was also intrigued by some of her experiences in the classroom. For instance, Lily encountered some well-travelled communication professors who didn't seem to know how to engage with the one or two international students in the class. This puzzled Lily because she would have expected a well-travelled expert in communication to navigate intercultural spaces with practised ease. But that was not the case. At the same time, Lily also encountered people in rural communities who had never seen a non-White person before, but they were able to converse with her with ease, with warmth and curiosity. Lily began to wonder what made such people distinct from the learned professors who didn't seem to know how to talk to her. This is not to say all professors couldn't navigate intercultural spaces or that all those who were new to intercultural communication were good at it – but Lily was curious to find out what people who navigated intercultural spaces with ease have in common.

Intercultural communication competence (ICC) or intercultural competence has a number of definitions. One of the commonly used ones is that ICC is effective and appropriate communication across cultural differences. Effective in that the communicators achieved the goal(s) of the communication, and appropriate in that they achieved said goals in a manner that was acceptable within that socio-cultural context. Context is an important consideration in competence because a person could be competent in one context and not another. For instance, a person who has worked and lived in one cultural context could be competent in that context but if she is reliant on her experiences and knowledge for her competence, she may not be competent in another cultural context with which she is unfamiliar. There are a number of models that conceptualise ICC (Meleady et al., 2021; for a full review see Spitzberg & Changnon, 2009), and there have been a number of attempts at measuring ICC over the years. Research shows that positive intercultural contact

DOI: 10.4324/9781003318415-8

or, in terms of the framework we have been talking about, positive experiences in intercultural spaces improve ICC. In turn, ICC facilitates minimising negative experiences in intercultural spaces. Although we don't want to delve into a comprehensive discussion of models and measures, we do want to highlight some of them for the purpose of identifying variables that contribute to ICC and discuss ways of cultivating these variables. We hope that doing so will help you navigate the intercultural spaces in which you may find yourselves.

Before we do that, it is helpful to share some of the historical background for research in ICC, at least early research in the United States. One of the earliest measures of ICC was formulated by Ruben and Kealey (1979). The events and thinking that led to the development of this early measure of ICC are recounted by Brent Ruben in his reflection of that time, which gives us a glimpse into the circumstances under which early research in ICC began.

Recognising Interculturality as a Foundational Concept for Communication Theory, Research, and Practice

Brent D. Ruben

Communication emerged as a social science discipline little over 75 years ago with the work of Harold Lasswell, Elihu Katz and Paul Lazersfeld, Claude Shannon and Warren Weaver, Wilbur Schramm, and David Berlo, and other scholars of the day. Initial efforts to explain this phenomenon focused on the mesage senders, content, and channels of transmission. This became the popular paradigm for communication. From these first efforts the challenges of *explaining* communication with this unidirectional flow model – and more so applications aimed at *predicting* or *controlling* communication outcomes – were vexing to researchers and practitioners alike. The essence of the problem was that *messages as interpreted by receivers* often didn't correspond all that well to the *messages senders were intending to convey*. Over time, variables associated with senders, messages, and channels received increasing attention, and receivers and the act of receiving messages became a more central focus of study, as researchers wrestled with the very fundamental anomaly that was an impediment to the usefulness of the classic paradigm.

For students of communication during this period, the quest for understanding unpredictable and uncontrollable dynamics and outcomes posed a significant challenge, one that was at once both frustrating and energising. For me, a major breakthrough came with Wilbur Schramm's introduction of the concept of "field of experience" as an enhancement to the linear view of communication. The concept of *field of experience* served to capture the full range of life events and learnings that shape individuals – learnings which individuals bring with them to every message creating and interpretive event. At a more macro level, this perspective suggests that our formative experiences relative to language, family, national identities, and other experiences shape us as people, simultaneously shape our verbal and nonverbal communication dynamics. The implications of these notions pointed to the simple and yet profound insight that it is through communication that "We shape our cultures and our cultures shape us."

My own interest in the field, like that of so many others, emerged at the intersection of theory and practice. As someone who was interested in both domains, I found myself being asked to serve in various settings where the goal was to design and implement programmes to help individuals from one country become effective communicators, leaders, and translators of knowledge to and from individuals in other cultures. Simple linear models of communication were not very helpful theoretically or in practice. Typically, the goal of the sponsors, organisations such as the Peace Corp, and US Agency for International Development, was to encourage the transfer of technical knowledge and expertise from "more knowledge rich" cultures to "less developed cultures" in order to elevate the wellbeing of recipients.

Those of us who worked in these programmes soon came to recognise that the value of these communication and knowledge-transfer efforts had a great many benefits for the "donors" as well as for intended recipients. At the same time, this work contributed significantly to more refined understandings of the way communication works. Working on government-sponsored overseas training programmes with psychologist Dan Kealey, I became personally involved in studying and facilitating the cultural transitions of individuals from Canada who were selected to posts in other "developing" cultures. The focus of our work was to identify factors that contributed to effective transitions, and to find ways to incorporate an emphasis on these topics in selection and cross-cultural pre-departure orientation.

There were suggestions in the literature and among professionals that particular problems were associated with persons who were prone to "culture shock." Discussions often focused on how to identify and engage individuals who would be less likely to experience culture shock for cross-cultural work, and how best to provide culture-specific knowledge training to offset challenges associated with cultural transition. Interestingly, as we studied this issue, we came to realise that adjustment problems were not necessarily the obstacle they were often thought to be. We observed that, often, individuals who experienced culture shock ultimately benefited from working through this personal turbulence. In some cases, the absence of adjustment struggles seemed more likely to occur for folks who were less aware of and attentive to culture and experiential differences they encountered. Our speculation, which was eventually reinforced by our research, was that it can be quite normal (and potentially beneficial) to take notice of and experience some turmoil adapting to cultural differences and then to reflect on these differences. Ideally, the process involves internalising the idea that each culture has its own patterns and valued practices, and eventually learning new ways to work with and through (and often appreciate) these differences.

We also found evidence for the idea that some behaviours – what we termed intercultural communication competencies – including *respect, interaction/*

response style, orientation to knowledge, empathy, role behaviour, conversation management, and *ambiguity tolerance* – seem often to be associated with interactional and organisational effectiveness in other cultures, and might ultimately be more important than culture-specific knowledge. With appropriate competencies, we believed, one could move through transitional strains, learn and grow from the process, and go on to have enhanced knowledge and skill to work with people and cultures very different from one's own.

We developed and advanced a tool we referred to as behavioural assessment of intercultural communication competencies and explored and refined these ideas in a number of follow-up writings (see Appendix B). Others build on this work. It has been gratifying to realise that this foundational research has been widely cited by a great many scholars and practitioners over the expanse of 50 years and has also spawned many follow-up studies leading to refinements on these earliest perspectives.

Through the aforementioned research and training efforts, I have come to recognise the value of what might be termed "interculturality" as a basic building block in understanding the nature and dynamics of communication in all settings. I see culture, broadly defined, is a foundational element in all communication. The term "interculturality" may be a good way to underscore this inherent characteristic of human communication. For me, this work has also been personally influential not only in my thinking about intercultural interactions of the traditional sort, but also in thinking about the challenges of diversity, equity, social justice, and inclusion, and in making sense of the cultural, organisational, and political schisms that permeate contemporary life.

I have come to recognise that confronting and reflecting upon differences is a good thing – something to actively promote for our students, our friends, and ourselves. As difficult as it sometimes is to deal with the emotional discomfort and cognitive disruption that can arise when we confront differences, these experiences also have the potential to result in personal growth and expanded flexibility and enhanced efficacy in social relations. The goal in pursuing these ends is to appreciate interculturality in its various manifestations and to avoid becoming too comfortably ensconced in one's own cultural, media-validated personal, political, and cultural communication echo chambers. The aim is to move beyond self-validating communication experiences, to engage with difference, to listen more carefully, to test one's ideas, and to be respectful of others' – ultimately applying the insights and guidance from classical Intercultural Communication Theory and practice to more fully understand and become effective in our own everyday experiences.

Conceptualising ICC

Our view is that ICC is a contextual process rather than a destination. In other words, people have the ability to improve their skills at navigating intercultural spaces over time, as they gain more experience and if they choose to reflect on those experiences to modify their behaviour for navigating intercultural spaces more effectively next time. While improving ICC has an individual element to it, ICC is also a shared process in that the intercultural spaces we occupy are occupied by others as well. For example, you may have an interaction with someone from another culture and come out of it thinking you did great. But the other person might walk away from that interaction thinking you were insensitive and difficult to talk to. Your self-perception says you were a competent communicator, whereas the other-perception says you were not. Given intercultural communication involves someone else, "other" perception matters!

Before delving further into ICC, it is necessary to mention a similar concept that is particularly prevalent in intercultural training work, which is cultural intelligence, or CQ. Earley and Ang (2003) define CQ as "A person's capability for successful adaptation to new cultural settings, that is, for unfamiliar settings attributable to cultural context" (p. 9). Van Dyne et al. (2012) delineate four factors of CQ, namely meta cognitive CQ, cognitive CQ, motivational CQ, and behavioural CQ. Meta cognitive CQ involves *planning* before an intercultural encounter, *awareness* of self and other during the encounter, and *checking* the information received during the actual intercultural encounter with known facts from previous experiences and adjusting accordingly. Cognitive CQ involves culture-general knowledge and context-specific knowledge. Motivational CQ involves intrinsic and extrinsic interest in people from other cultures as well as a sense of self-efficacy to be able to adjust to different cultural contexts. Finally, behavioural CQ involves verbal and nonverbal behaviour and the ability to adjust speech acts based on (cultural) context. CQ is a well-researched and measurable concept (Van Dyne et al., 2015). Yari et al. (2020) unpack the related concepts of CQ, global mindset, and cross-cultural competency by framing global mindset as a capacity for functioning effectively in culturally complex business situations. They frame cross-cultural competence as a person's effectiveness in drawing on their knowledge, skills, and attributes to work successfully with people from other cultures. As you can see, there is considerable conceptual overlap amongst these labels. Our intent in introducing you briefly to concepts similar to ICC such as CQ is not to create confusion, but rather to note that ICC is one of many approaches to defining and understanding "good" intercultural communication. That said, let's take a closer look at ICC.

In an attempt at identifying variables that contribute to ICC, Lily interviewed people from 15 countries and asked them to describe a competent intercultural communicator they have met. She asked probing questions about why the participants thought this person was competent, what sort of behaviours this person exhibited to be perceived as competent, and so forth. For example, when a participant said something like, "He is a good listener," Lily asked what that person did to convey to the participant that he was listening. In instances where that "competent" person was available, Lily interviewed them as well, and asked them the same questions. Her goal was to find out whether there were commonalities in what people described (perceived) as ICC, especially given the interviewees were from many different cultures. As it turned out, there were indeed commonalities in how the participants described a competent (intercultural) communicator. These common qualities that emerged from the analysis of all interviews were experience, empathy, positive

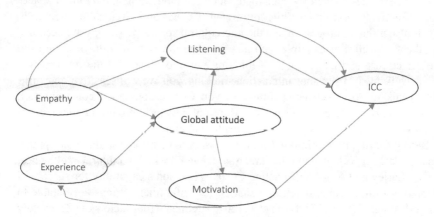

Figure 7.1 Integrated Model of Intercultural Communication Competence, adapted from Arasaratnam (2006).

attitude towards people of other cultures, active listening, and motivation to talk to people from other cultures (Arasaratnam & Doerfel, 2005). This study became part of Lily's doctoral work in which she went on to test the relationship between the five variables identified from the interviews, resulting in the Integrated Model of Intercultural Communication Competence (IMICC). The IMICC has been further developed over the years (Arasaratnam, 2006; Arasaratnam et al., 2010; Nadeem et al., 2020; Nadeem & Zabrodskaja, 2023).

IMICC (see Figure 7.1) accounts for instances where people without intercultural education and training may still be perceived as competent communicators if they are able to empathise with people of other cultures. In the opening paragraph of this chapter, we talked about Lily's contemplation of why some experienced and well-travelled people don't seem to be good at communicating interculturally, whereas others who have had no or limited exposure to cultural diversity are able to communicate across cultural differences with ease. IMICC provides insight into this question. Empathy, in other words, contributes to ICC even in the absence of formal intercultural training or exposure to other cultures. Someone who is able to connect to another person at a relational level by putting themselves into the other person's metaphorical shoes is likely to be perceived as a competent intercultural communicator, even in the absence of prior experience with intercultural communication. IMICC is one of the few models of ICC that was developed based on perceptual input of people from multiple cultures, commenting on actual behaviour of intercultural communicators.

Another well-known model of ICC is the Anxiety/Uncertainty Management (AUM) Model (Gudykunst, 1993, 1995). The AUM model is based on the premise that communicating with "strangers" (people from other cultures or people who are different from us) inherently involves an element of uncertainty, which in turn creates anxiety in us. The extent to which we manage this anxiety effectively determines the extent to which we are effective in our communication

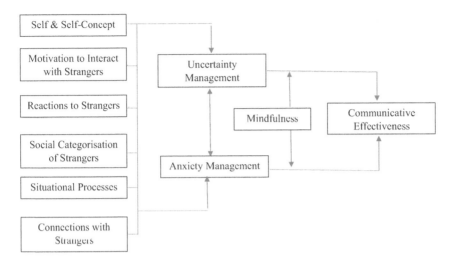

Figure 7.2 Anxiety/Uncertainty Management (AUM) Model of ICC, adapted from Gudykunst (2005).

with the "stranger." This path model identifies self-concept (our identities, self-esteem), motivation (need for predictability, group inclusion), reaction to strangers (empathy, tolerance to ambiguity, intergroup attitudes), social categorisation of strangers (positive expectations, perceived similarities, group differentiation), situational processes (ingroup influence, presence of ingroup members), connections with strangers (attraction, interdependence, quality/quantity of contact), and ethical interactions (dignity, inclusiveness, respect) as superficial causes.

According to AUM (see Figure 7.2), these variables inform the basic causes of uncertainty and anxiety management, which is mediated by mindfulness. The extent to which mindfulness does its job of mediating uncertainty and anxiety management determines the extent of effective communication, which is the outcome. Mindfulness, as conceptualised in AUM, relies on Langer's (1997) definition, which suggests that mindfulness involves, "(1) openness to novelty; (2) alertness to distinctions; (3) sensitivity to different contexts; (4) implicit, if not explicit awareness of multiple perspectives; and (5) orientation in the present" (p. 23). We will discuss mindfulness later on in this chapter.

While IMICC and AUM are causal or path models of ICC, other ways in which ICC has been conceptualised are in Deardorff's (2006) Process Model of ICC which is a compositional model and presents another conceptualisation that has also widely informed research in ICC. As we have been sharing stories of various intercultural scholars to give you insight into the people who have contributed to the theories and frameworks with which you are engaging in this book, here is a glimpse into Darla Deardorff's motivation for becoming an intercultural scholar, before we introduce her model. Speaking of her upbringing in a Church of the Brethren, she says:

This call, Jesus' call to be a peacemaker, and what does that look like, and what does that mean? I struggled with that, because often people aren't really paid vocationally to be a peacemaker. So, what does that look like vocationally? And I thought well, that means working for the United Nations. So when I was an undergraduate at Bridgewater College, I was able to arrange an internship with the Quaker United Nations office in Geneva Switzerland. So, an internship with an NGO, and that was during the Human Rights Commission meetings back during the first Iraq War. It was really interesting to kind of just observe what was going on in the deliberations and how wealthy countries got a lot more time on the floor to speak. To see the response of Iraq or China or other countries saying that it's an internal matter, it's not a human rights issue. It was very eye opening and it made me realise it (such deliberations) felt too far removed from the grassroots; and so it was that internship that kind of pushed me, I would say, into the field of international education.

And when my husband and I moved to North Carolina for graduate school, I literally looked in the phone book and found something called North Carolina Centre for Intercultural Understanding. And I thought well, that's it; that fits. That sounds like peacemaking, and I called them up and asked if they have any volunteer opportunities, but they didn't. I kept calling and kept asking, and finally they said fine, we'll find you something to volunteer for. So, I started volunteering now and then; finally, when they needed another staff person it was possible for me to become the fourth staff person at that centre. And so, most of my career I've been in the field of international higher education. (Deardorff, personal communication, 11/05/2022)

The Process Model of Intercultural Competence (see Figure 7.3) developed by Deardorff identifies *requisite attitudes* of respect, openness, and discovery, and curiosity, *knowledge comprehension* of cultural self-awareness, cultural knowledge, and sociolinguistic awareness, along with *skills* such as listening, observation, analysis, and interpretation, which lead to *external outcomes* such as ICC and *internal outcomes* such as adaptability, flexibility, empathy, and ethnorelativism.

There are other models which conceptualise ICC from a developmental perspective, such as the Developmental Model of Intercultural Sensitivity (DMIS; see Figure 7.4). The DMIS shows another way of looking at ICC as a linear progression from ethnocentrism to ethnorelativism (Bennett & Hammer, 2017).

The DMIS proposes that a person starts out with denial of the existence of valid alternative cultural perspectives ("my culture's way is the only right way"), then moves on to polarisation ("us" and "them" manifested as either defence or reversal), then minimisation ("we're all really the same, aren't we?"), and then acceptance ("my culture is one amongst many other valid cultures"), adaptation ("I'll adapt behaviours of other cultures when I'm interacting with someone from that culture, to be appropriate") and finally, integration ("I'll internalise some of the values I appreciate in other cultures because I also believe in those values"). However, Hammer's (2011, 2015) recent research has reclassified integration as relating to identity rather than a developmental competence predisposition, resulting in only five categories. The DMIS has been used in a number of studies, although some

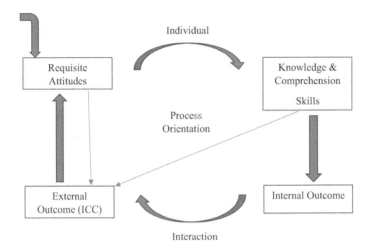

Figure 7.3 Process Model of Intercultural Competence, adapted from Deardorff (2006).

researchers argue that the development of ICC is not a linear process (e.g., Garrett-Rucks, 2014). However, DMIS researchers have noted that each of the stages identified in the model is a "predominant experience" rather than a rigid or predictive mode of operation, because intercultural behaviour varies by context (Bennett, 2013, loc 1275).

According to the DMIS, the progression from ethnocentrism to ethnorelativism happens as a person accumulates more intercultural knowledge and experience. This process involves forming more nuanced perceptual categories in our mind, with the accumulation of new information, such that we can experience complexity in other cultures or what we perceive as "other," through intercultural sensitivity. According to Bennett and Hammer, ICC is the ease with which a person translates intercultural sensitivity into behaviour across cultural differences. In other words, a competent intercultural communicator would navigate intercultural spaces with the same ease as she navigates spaces within her own culture. Below is the story of Milton Bennett and how he came to be an intercultural scholar.

Figure 7.4 Developmental Model of Intercultural Sensitivity, adapted from Bennett (1986).

The Intercultural Doors of Perception

Milton J. Bennett,[1]

In high school I had two loves. One of them was science, and the other, poetry. My two most consuming activities were preparing for science fairs and hanging out at the Down Under, which was a beat poetry coffeehouse under the Hawthorne Bridge in Portland, Oregon, complete with those candle-wax covered Chianti bottles and an open mic for aspiring authors. That scene was undeniably romantic, but I nevertheless followed my first love to Stanford, where I studied physics for two years. It was a wonderful experience, but it turned out what I really loved was the philosophy part of the science – not so much the calculus part. So, I turned to my other love and joined the creative writing programme at that same university. I haven't really given up physics, and the philosophy of science continues to influence my work a lot, but I was looking for some other threads to weave into my thinking.

Two other events at Stanford are important to this story line. One of them was my work with Professor Arthur Hastings, who was then the head of a small speech and theatre department there, but whose major interest was transpersonal psychology. After my MA work, Arthur invited me to come back to Stanford to do PhD work in consciousness studies, which was very appealing to me. And I would have done it had it not been for the likelihood that I would have been drafted to fight in Vietnam as part of that process.

The other was a less personal contact that was nevertheless significant. I took a cognitive psychology class taught by Albert Hastorf, who, besides being a brilliant professor that kindled in me an interest in cognitive and developmental psychology that persists to this day, was also was an early perceptual constructivist, notable for his study of the wildly discrepant perceptions of the movie footage of a controversial football game between Dartmouth College and Princeton University. Looking back on it now, his work was an early recognition of confirmation bias and the alternative facts that we now are encountering today.

The topics of philosophy of science, consciousness, and constructivist cognitive psychology were all percolating in my brain when an offer was made to all creative writing students to participate in one of the first, and as it turns out, last, legal studies of LSD. I got myself enrolled in the study and it was, as we used to say, mind blowing. I was able to make a few more of my own experiments (and we did indeed treat these as experiments – back in those days, we took the psychedelics seriously) and then wrote my final paper for Hastorf's class on the experience. Essentially, my explanation was that the substance destabilised perceptual category boundaries, generating both synaesthesia and unusual feelings of connectedness with an expanded context.

You notice that I'm avoiding the use of terms like enlightenment or spiritual experience. Nevertheless, the teaching assistant who read the paper apparently did not think that the topic was appropriate and gave it an F. At least I assume that was the case, because when I got the paper back, there was an F, but it was crossed out and replaced with an A with a little note from Professor Hastorf saying, "interesting speculation about this kind of unusual experience." While I certainly appreciated the passing grade and the comment, the really important thing about this confluence of events was that it generated the basic template for the next 40 years of my inquiry into the relationship of perception and experience. Unaided, I might add, by any further experimentation of that particular kind.

The next layer of this template occurred at San Francisco State University, where I went to get an MA in psycholinguistics. My rationale was to study how language guided perceptual processes. In addition to lots of perception theory, the programme included a heavy emphasis on general semantics and linguistic relativity. In the world of general semantics, the Whorf-Sapir Hypothesis fared much better than it did in psychology.

That time in San Francisco was close on the heels of the great controversy between Skinner's behaviourist explanation of language acquisition and Chomsky's idea of transformation based on an underlying universal grammar. Looking back, I see that my discomfort with both those positions was probably driven by my growing understanding of constructivist explanations of language, which these days would be represented by cognitive linguists such as George Lakoff. But then it was a lonely position to be supporting the idea of Whorfian linguistic relativity while it was being attacked by the Skinnerian behaviourists as being too humanistic, by Chomsky and universalists as being too deterministic, and by many psychologists as being too relativistic. Luckily, I came under the tutelage of Professor Dean Barnlund, an experimental psychologist who had migrated to communication studies, taught general semantics and brought an updated constructivist perspective. He was also an early proponent of intercultural communication. From his extensive travels and analysis, he would draw innumerable examples of the social construction of reality and made it normal to be thinking in terms of the Whorf-Sapir hypothesis.

My enduring insight from these days in San Francisco was that empathy is the exercise of perceptual plasticity. The idea that you can perceive the world and thus experience the world in particular ways means that you can reorganise your perception in such a way as to experience it in a different way, including one that is more the way someone else is experiencing it. That happens all the time; when we go to a movie, when we go to the theatre, when we go to a ballet performance. It's not an unusual thing that we do. It's just that it is unusual to think of empathy in terms of our everyday interaction with others.

During the middle of that MA programme, I took off for the Peace Corps – for the same reason as not going to the Stanford graduate programme – and spent two and a half years in Chuuk district, Micronesia. It was, in retrospect, really wonderful field work for testing the theories of language-related perception, altering perceptual boundaries for empathy and intercultural communication. Although the process that I went through was similar to that of most Peace

Corps volunteers and other long-term sojourners, I think I had the additional advantage of the conceptual frameworks that I'd been working on for analysing the experience.

Looking forward, I see some important directions for intercultural communication. As I've been arguing for some decades now, we need to become more aware of our constructivist roots and use developments in that approach to make our work more coherent and relevant. Minimally, this means getting past simplistic and reified definitions of culture that have too often been offered to clients who want simple solutions to their intercultural challenges.

Measuring ICC

Part of the consideration of testing the veracity of conceptual models involves identifying reliable measures for each one of the variables in the model, including ICC itself. As previously mentioned, one of the earliest measures of ICC was developed by Ruben and Kealey (1979). As you have read, Brent Ruben's story highlights the circumstances under which those initial variables that contribute to ICC were identified. The current version of Ruben's Intercultural Behavioural Scales is provided for you at the end of this chapter. While a number of attempts have been made since then to develop a measure of ICC, few such measures exist. One of the measures that has been tested in at least two languages is one developed by Lily after the conceptualisation of IMICC (Arasaratnam, 2009; Gonçalves et al., 2020). That measure identifies cognitive, behavioural, and emotional aspects of ICC. Despite existing measures, the need for robust, well-tested measures of ICC remains. You will note that much of the research in measuring ICC circles around those concepts of cognitive, behavioural, and affective or emotional variables because what we do know is that these interact to influence our effectiveness and appropriateness when we communicate interculturally.

While communication scholars were examining ICC from a communication perspective, cross-cultural psychologists were studying ICC from the perspective of personality traits. One of the widely used instruments to assess personality traits associated with ICC is the Multicultural Personality Questionnaire (MPQ) which identifies cultural empathy, open mindedness, emotional stability, flexibility, open-mindedness and social initiative as contributors to a multicultural personality (Van Oudenhoven & Van der Zee, 2002; Van der Zee et al., 2013). The MPQ has been widely used in research and demonstrated to be generalisable across cultures (Leone et al., 2005). Comparing dimensions of MPQ to the variables identified in the IMICC, for example, you can see conceptual overlaps such as (cultural) empathy, positive attitude towards people of other cultures/ open-mindedness, and social initiative/motivation. This overlap is encouraging because it highlights how researchers from different disciplines, using different methods, are still able to converge on the same variables associated with ICC. The MPQ also resonates with Ruben's scales on intercultural behaviour provided in Appendix B, as those scales also address knowledge, attitude, and behavioural aspects of intercultural interactions. Below is the story of the researchers who developed the MPQ, because their story also showcases how scholars' lived experiences influence their work.

In Search of Intercultural Competency

Karen I. Van der Zee
Jan Pieter van Oudenhoven

What makes some individuals interculturally effective, while others are not? This question has intrigued the both of us for most of our adult lives. All of us have friends or relatives who shy away from holidays to unknown places and revisit familiar places every year. Usually, thes individuals have a general preference for doing things in a repetitive way, feeling disturbed when the situation requires different behaviour.

Jan Pieter is certainly not one of them. "I grew up in the early 50s in a Catholic family with six children, five boys and a girl. My mother quite regularly invited people to stay in our house for a while. She usually met them via the church and wanted to help them because of their loneliness, mental problems, or lack of proper housing. We as boys had to make our room available for these guests. When one guest had left, it did not take long for the next one to come. Although they were not necessarily from different cultures, these temporary family members for sure did bring different customs and behaviours to the house."

Although in a very different way, the same sensibility for cultural perspectives was stimulated by the context in which Karen grew up. "I was born in the late 60s in Friesland, a province in the north of the Netherlands with its own culture and language. Although both my parents were of Frisian descent, I always felt that we were kind of outsiders. The 60s and 70s were the blossom period of the hippies in the Netherlands and most people in our village would consider my parents as hippies. This image was strengthened by the fact that my father worked as a journalist for the Dutch TV. They would regard us as 'Amsterdam-people.' At the same time, my father's colleagues at work would typically ask us whether we had left our wooden shoes in Friesland. Despite being with them, we would not fit in."

After obtaining his university degree, Jan Pieter was determined to find a job abroad. He decided to apply for a position at UNESCO in Michoacán, Mexico. The position was linked to a project aimed at educating illiterate farmers in farming techniques. One of the job requirements was fluency in Spanish. Although Jan Pieter hardly spoke any Spanish, he claimed fluency in the language. During three weeks, he practised all he could, taking whatever classes were available at the university and convincing fellow students with a Spanish background to speak with him as much as possible. Although the conclusion was that his Spanish needed refreshment, he performed successfully on the interview and got the job. This period allowed him to sense an entirely different cultural environment, oftentimes being the first blonde person ever seen in the Indigenous villages that he visited. "It was a period of enormous joy and learning. It made me really understand the nature of cultural differences. I became determined to commit my professional life to cross-cultural phenomena."

When we started to develop our intercultural competence framework in the late 90s, this Mexico experience was an important source of inspiration. Of course, we could build on Karen's background in personality psychology, her solid expertise in questionnaire development and Jan Pieter's background in cross-cultural psychology. However, Jan Pieter's feel for what it means to live and work in a different culture was crucial to formulate items that were really relevant to an intercultural context.

In the late 90s, Jan Pieter travelled to Mozambique where he was asked to help build up a social sciences faculty. Karen decided to join him during part of his trip. The first day she arrived in Maputo was a Sunday and Jan Pieter suggested taking a walk in the city centre. It was a beautiful sunny day, and the city was much quieter than during weekdays. On a desolated path that crossed a park, we started to feel a bit uncomfortable with no other people around. And yes, before we knew it, we were surrounded by a gang of eight young men. Jan Pieter was forced on the ground, the guys threatened him with a huge knife. Fortunately, we had left important documents and valuable possessions in the hotel. The guys took the money we had taken with us, enough to be satisfied. After Karen was also forced to hand over her watch, the gang disappeared. On the way back we tried to get help from guards outside houses that we passed, but we received no response. Apparently, the guards did not feel a moral obligation to help us, just doing the job they were paid for and that was it. The same appeared to be true at the police station, where officers seemed more interested in money than in protecting the law.

What happened had an impact on both of us, but particularly on Karen. We had planned a round trip to Swaziland and South Africa in a rental car. Usually we enjoy to travel guided by the Lonely Planet guidebook, trying to explore relatively undiscovered places. This time, Karen noticed that everything that was unfamiliar made her feel anxious. "One moment we arrived in a beautiful small village. The Lonely Planet advised a small romantic hotel. Jan Pieter entered the hotel while I waited for him in the car. Before I knew it, the car was surrounded by local men staring at me. The same faces appeared in front of the window where Jan Pieter was inspecting the room. This was too much, and I begged whether we could spend the night in a Hilton-like environment. It was not until we returned back home that I could open up to different cultures again. During the rest of our stay in Africa I was really shocked by my own sudden preference for everything that represented whiteness, Western culture."

Half a year later, we visited the yearly meeting of the Society of Social and Personality Psychology in Nashville. During this conference, Karen attended presentations by followers of Terror Management Theory. TMT claims that humans differ from animals because they are conscious of their own death.

This consciousness evokes paralysing fear. What protects humans from fear is their cultural worldview. TMT argues that when the perspective of dying becomes salient, individuals respond with stronger attachment to their cultural worldview. Mortality was made salient experimentally by asking judges to think about their own death. The results of these experiments reminded Karen of her experience in Maputo. "I suddenly understood much better what could have caused my strong attachment to my own culture. I hypothesised that part of the dimensions from our intercultural competence framework may promote intercultural effectiveness, *exactly because* they protect individuals from anxiety evoked by the threat that is inherent to intercultural situations. That could also explain why Jan Pieter was not affected in the same way."

Returning home, Karen performed two experiments in which she used the same mortality salience manipulation as in the TMT-experiment and examined responses to intercultural situations. The outcomes of these studies not only allowed us to replicate the assumptions of TMT, but also helped us to consolidate our theory behind the five dimensions of intercultural competence, namely, cultural empathy, open mindedness, social initiative, emotional stability, and flexibility.

We have devoted our professional lives to develop a deeper understanding of what is needed for that. We actively try to use our own experience and expertise in promoting competency development in others. To achieve intercultural competency, we believe that it is crucial to expose yourself as much as possible to intercultural situations and to reflect on what these situations evoke in you. That is how we keep learning. Living in the multicultural city of Amsterdam, opportunities are nearby.

Developing ICC

We mentioned earlier that we think of ICC as a process rather than a destination. One of the frameworks that has been used to describe communication competence describes four levels of competence that progressively build from the lowest level to highest, usually attributed to the work of William Howell (1982). At the start, there is *unconscious incompetence*, where a person (let's call him Sam) is neither effective, nor appropriate in his communication with someone from another culture, but at the same time is blissfully unaware of his incompetence. Sam thinks everything is fine, and he's doing just fine, whereas the other person finds Sam inappropriate or even offensive. Imagine if Sam happens to take Ripley's intercultural communication class, and starts to learn a few things about communicating across cultural differences. Sam reflects on his own experiences and begins to understand where he might have done better. Although he is now aware he needs to improve, he hasn't completed the course yet to know *how* he could improve. Sam is now *consciously incompetent*. In other words, while he may still be incompetent, he is at least aware of it. After successfully completing his intercultural communication course, Sam begins to try out what he learnt, whenever he has the opportunity to practise intercultural communication. He deliberately tries to see things from the other person's perspective, he intentionally listens, he tries to ask thoughtful questions, and he tries to withhold judgement on things he does not understand. Here, Sam is exhibiting *conscious competence*, wherein he intentionally adapts behaviour he knows to be effective and appropriate in communicating across cultural differences. Over time, effective and appropriate behaviours become so natural to Sam that he no longer has to deliberately adapt them. Like a seasoned driver, Sam exhibits *unconscious competence* as he seamlessly delves in and out of intercultural spaces. Although not everyone agrees with the veracity of this tiered approach to communication competence, and not everyone agrees that unconscious competence is superior to conscious competence, this model presents a helpful framework for understanding our own experiences of grappling with intercultural (in)competence.

As previously discussed, researchers have identified a number of variables or qualities that contribute to ICC. Developing proficiency in these qualities is one way to develop ICC. Although there are many variables that could be discussed in this section, we want to highlight a few that have not only been demonstrated as important for developing ICC but also are easy to practise even if you don't have many opportunities to interact with people from other cultures.

Firstly, (cultural) empathy is one of demonstrably significant contributors to ICC. Empathy involves cognitive and emotional role-taking (Calloway-Thomas et al., 2017). For example, when Feny meets a new international student – Jane – for the first time, Feny, who has never been away from her home, imagines what it would be like for Jane to be far away from her family, in a country where everything from the food to social customs are strange to her. Feny imagines how lonely it might be for Jane, and how challenging it might be to adapt to such a new environment. With that understanding, Feny introduces herself to Jane and invites her to a coffee after class so they could talk more. Feny's behaviour demonstrates empathy, where she puts herself in Jane's position and tries to understand what Jane must be experiencing. Jane too has the opportunity to exercise empathy in this scenario. Jane could put herself in Feny's position and imagine how comfortable it would be for Feny to hang out with her own established group of friends and not bother with the new student who clearly looked out of place. Perhaps it is strange in Jane's culture for a stranger to invite you over for a coffee at the first meeting. Perhaps "having coffee" is not a social activity with which Jane is familiar. But if Jane practises empathy, she might be inclined to agree to meet Feny for coffee because Jane understands the hand of friendship that is being extended, even if she does not understand the nuances of it. Practising mental and emotional perspective-taking, putting yourself in someone else's position to see things from their point of view is an exercise in empathy that we can all undertake regularly to build our empathetic muscles. We can do this when interacting with anyone, regardless of whether they are from a different culture or not.

Secondly, self-reflection is something in which we can all participate actively. Research shows that self-reflection is an essential component of learning from intercultural experiences (Lee, 2012). One way to define self-reflection is: "the inspection and evaluation of one's thoughts, feelings, and behavior and insight" (Grant et al., 2002, p. 821). Self-reflection can happen in a number of ways, from

purely mental activity to more tactile activity such as journaling. Noting the importance of journaling for better decision-making amongst professionals in applied
fields such as nursing, Dimitroff et al. (2017) observe that journaling is "a vehicle
for self-understanding, self-guidance, expanded creativity, and spiritual development" (p. 91). While self-reflection can be developed through formal mechanisms
such as assessments in intercultural communication courses, everyone can improve
their practice of self-reflection intentionally through activities such as journaling,
setting aside time at end of each day to reflect on the day, and working with a set of
questions to facilitate self-reflection after key conversations. For example, asking
ourselves questions like, what did I learn from my interactions today, how well did
I communicate today, if I had a chance to do-over today, how would I do things
differently, why did I react the way I did to situations today, etc. would be constructive. Writing our responses to such questions daily or weekly would be even
more constructive because we would then have access to our self-reflection later,
and be able to see how our thinking develops over time.

Thirdly, active listening is a skill that is worth developing in our efforts
to improve our ICC. The IMICC identifies active listening as a variable that
contributes to ICC. Jones et al. (2019) observe that active listening consists of cognitive components such as "attending, understanding, or interpreting messages,"
emotional components such as "being motivated and energized to attend to another
person" and behavioural components such as "verbally and nonverbally signalling
that a message has been received and understood" (p. 6). Active listening is therefore something we do deliberately, with intent to not only understand what the other
person is saying, but also be emotionally present and to ask clarifying questions
that communicate to the other person that we are listening. Active listening is a
skill that can be developed through practice, and there are exercises to facilitate
this. For example, Norkunas (2011) identifies a number of exercises to foster active
listening, one of which is to listen for what is not being said. To listen to a person's
story and then reflect on whether the person edited things out, why do you think
some of the story was unsaid, and for what reasons the person might have not
vocalised parts of the story.

Fourthly, developing mindfulness should be part of developing ICC. Gudykunst
(2005) described mindfulness as, "the readiness to shift one's frame of reference,
the motivation to use new categories to understand cultural or ethnic differences,
and the preparedness to experiment with creative avenues of decision making and
problem solving" (p. 226). As the description implies, to be mindful is to be actively
ready, motivated, and prepared, and it involves a willingness to look at things from
a different perspective and change one's existing ways of understanding things in
the face of new or different information. We noted in Proposition 6 in Chapter 1
that mindfulness is necessary for perceiving an intercultural space. Without mindfulness, we could venture in and out of an intercultural space without even realising
it. One study suggests that mindfulness can be developed if one practises mindfulness for at least ten minutes per day (Reitz et al., 2020). This may involve breathing
exercises, mindful movement, and mindfulness of thoughts, and active reflection
on how we are processing information at that present moment.

While empathy, self-reflection, active listening, and mindfulness are good things we should cultivate in our development of ICC, it is also important to acknowledge attitudes we should actively guard against. One such attitude is ethnocentrism, which was discussed in Chapter 5. Although ethnocentrism is, to an extent, inevitable because we are most familiar with our own culture and are inclined to evaluate other (cultural) perspectives from the perspective with which we are most familiar, extreme levels of ethnocentrism debilitates ICC. For example, in a test of a variation to the IMICC, Arasaratnam and Banerjee (2007) demonstrated that ethnocentrism weakens our motivation to interact with people from other cultures, thereby weakening our ability to develop ICC. Relatedly, Hosseini Fatemi et al. (2016) found a strong negative relationship between ethnocentrism and intercultural willingness to communicate. The researchers discovered that, in an Iranian context, students who studied English had lower levels of ethnocentrism, possibly due to the exposure to other cultural perspectives involved in studying a different language.

Unrelated to ethnocentrism but related to learning a different language, there is some evidence to suggest that the process of learning a second or third language itself facilitates the development of ICC (Arasaratnam-Smith, 2016). The reason for this could be because learning a new language facilitates the development of cognitive complexity (see Chapter 3). Additionally, learning a new language also helps us to understand cultural frameworks and values that shape that language, thereby extending our frame of reference (Imai et al., 2016; Jiang, 2000). Further, at least two models of ICC identify linguistic competence as an essential part of ICC (Byram, 1997; Fantini, 1995). In sum, learning a new language is another mechanism for developing ICC, not only because learning the language of a specific cultural context in which you wish to communicate competently has the obvious benefits, but also because learning a new language, regardless of what the language is, has inherent benefits for developing capacity for ICC.

Finally, we cannot overlook experience and intercultural training in this discussion of developing ICC. The IMICC identifies experience/training as one of the contributors to ICC. The DMIS also identifies experience and new (intercultural) knowledge as the catalysts for a person's development from ethnocentric views to ethnorelative ones. Those who live in culturally diverse cities have the opportunity to communicate in intercultural spaces on a daily basis. But those who live in relatively homogeneous communities have to be intentional in looking for intercultural contact. Fortunately, technological advancements have facilitated easier travel and access to different cultures through media for many people. Formal intercultural experiences through study abroad programmes are also available to many students. However, not everyone takes advantage of opportunities to learn from intercultural experiences, even if they have access to such opportunities; and not everyone necessarily learns from intercultural experiences. As we discussed before, growing from new (intercultural) experiences requires us to be mindful, to notice new things, self-reflective enough to process this new information in relation to what we know up to that point, and willing to change our attitudes and behaviours based on this new information.

There is some evidence to suggest that high sensation seekers, people who are attracted to novel and thrilling experiences such as skydiving or scaling mountains, are also likely to seek intercultural experiences or intercultural friendships because of the novelty and "risk" involved in intercultural spaces (Morgan & Arasaratnam, 2003; Nadeem, 2022). There is a relationship between sensation seeking and ICC because high sensation seekers are likely to seek out intercultural experiences, and intercultural experiences in turn facilitate the development of ICC, thereby reiterating the importance of intercultural experiences in developing ICC (Arasaratnam & Banerjee, 2011). Formal intercultural training and study is also beneficial, as is evident from the various stories of intercultural scholars showcased in this book. As you would have noticed, the stories show a pattern wherein people's intercultural experiences in their personal life leads them to be curious about understanding their experiences better by engaging in formal study or intercultural research. Intercultural experiences and training, especially paired with mindfulness and self-reflection, are another way of developing ICC.

Advancements in communication and learning technologies as well as the pervasive technology-mediated communication necessitated by the global pandemic that began in 2019 have made developing ICC through communication and education technologies a topic of relevance in a discussion of developing ICC. Based on a review of literature on enhancing teachers' ICC through technological tools, Jiang et al. (2021) observed that teachers should be appropriately equipped and trained to use contemporary technologies to facilitate ICC development in students. This observation had merit, considering the number of ways in which technological tools are being used to facilitate the development of ICC in students. For example, Shadiev et al. (2020) report of a study in which virtual reality (VR) was used to give students immersive experiences of intercultural spaces, interacting with other real students, resulting in improved ICC. Although VR technology might not be accessible to everyone, it is one possibility for immersive intercultural learning without travel (Liaw, 2019). Lindström and Pozo (2020) reported the use of images, films, and translation tools in helping health practitioners in multilingual contexts facilitate better communication across linguistic and cultural differences. Kampermann et al. (2021) pointed out that it is important to take into consideration cultural assumptions behind certain technological tools, for example individualistic values prevalent in the culture of the person or team that developed the tool, when using technologies to facilitate the development of ICC.

Developing ICC is a lifelong process. One way to describe the types of learnings that must happen in order to continue to develop ICC is represented in the Global Graduates Model (see Figure 7.5) developed by Lily (Arasaratnam-Smith, 2020).

This model identifies four types of understanding essential for preparing students for living and working in culturally diverse communities. Firstly, understanding of self, which involves not only understanding who we are through self-reflection and considered input from others, but also understanding ourselves as cultural beings whose worldview is influenced by the values and beliefs of the culture(s) in which we grow up. Secondly, understanding of others, which involves a number of variables which we have already discussed, such as empathy, active listening, and motivation to connect with others. Thirdly, understanding of self's responsibility to others, which involves recognising that because we live in communities, our individual decisions have impact on others. As such, we must consider the impact

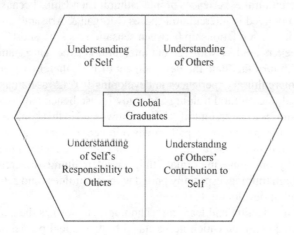

Figure 7.5 Developing Global Graduates, adapted from Arasaratnam-Smith (2020).

of our decisions on others even if we are well within our rights to make those decisions for ourselves. For example, you may have the right to speak on the phone while travelling on a train, but if the person next to you is asleep, you may consider not making that call at that time or speaking quietly so as to not disturb your fellow passenger. Fourthly, understanding of others' contribution to self, which involves recognising that we are all situated at a point in history wherein we are beneficiaries of the thinking, innovations, and sacrifices of those who have gone before us. For better or for worse, our predecessors' actions and decisions contribute to our present reality. This is a historical consideration of not only what we have inherited, but also what our successors will inherit from our choices and actions.

We hope this chapter has helped you gain a general understanding of ICC and strategies for cultivating it in your own lives. In the next chapter, we will pull everything we have talked about so far into a discussion of its relevance to us as people who live in diverse communities. Come along with us as we venture together into the intercultural spaces we inhabit.

In Conversation: Communicating Amidst Offence

Ripley: What kind of conversational space do we need to create in order to allow people the freedom to grow in ICC? What I mean is, some people are in the denial and/or defence stages, but spiral into silence because of political correctness.

Lily: Political correctness can really trip-up people sometimes to the extent that they can't even get beyond the perceived barriers of potential offence to have a conversation with someone different. Instead of focusing on talking to someone different, I think it is helpful to focus on forming a relationship with someone new – and use all the tools we use to engage in conversation with a new person.

Ripley: What do you have in mind when you talk about tools? Curiosity? Empathy?

Lily: Exactly. Curiosity, warmth, friendliness, interest... these things are applicable when we're trying to get to know someone new – their "difference" isn't a unique factor when applying these tools.

Ripley: Back to my initial question, how have you seen mindfulness used as a technique to overcome shame in talking about cultural sensitivity?

Lily: I think mindfulness is helpful in any conversation to read the situation and the person. So, if we're using the tools that we would use to get to know someone new, and if we are being mindful, we would gauge their reaction to what we ask and adjust our follow-up accordingly. We would read body language and perhaps nuance things.

Ripley: I see a connection between mindfulness and humility. In my faith tradition, we're told that it is a blessing to overlook an offence. So, as we extend grace to someone in conversation, we open up a space where they can become conscious of their incompetence without our having to point it out.

Lily: Assuming they're being mindful too! [laughs]. But yes, offence is taken, not given, as the saying goes. So, I think a posture of giving the other person the benefit of the doubt is constructive to ongoing conversation.

Questions for Reflection

1. Do you agree with Ripley's and Lily's last two comments about offence? Why or why not?
2. Have you ever experienced a situation where you avoided talking to someone different because you were afraid you might offend them? If you were to have a "do-over," would you make different choices?
3. What questions or topics about culture, ethnicity, or race have you avoided because you were worried you didn't share the majority opinion? How might you set up a conversational space to engage those topics?

Notes

1 Excerpted from Podcast 14: Milton Bennett, International Academy of Intercultural Research (Nov. 8, 2020).

References

Arasaratnam, L. A. (2006). Further testing of a new model of intercultural communication competence. *Communication Research Reports, 23*(2), 93–99.

Arasaratnam, L. A. (2009). The development of a new instrument of intercultural communication competence. *Journal of Intercultural Communication*, *20*(2), 5–16.

Arasaratnam, L. A., & Banerjee, S. C. (2007). Ethnocentrism and sensation seeking as variables that influence intercultural contact-seeking behavior: A path analysis. *Communication Research Reports*, *24*(4), 303–310.

Arasaratnam, L. A., & Banerjee, S. C. (2011). Sensation seeking and intercultural communication competence: A model test. *International Journal of Intercultural Relations*, *35*(2), 226–233.

Arasaratnam, L. A., Banerjee, S., & Dembek, K. (2010). The Integrated Model of Intercultural Communication Competence (IMICC). *Australian Journal of Communication*, *37*(3), 103–116.

Arasaratnam, L. A., & Doerfel, M. L. (2005). Intercultural communication competence: Identifying key components from multicultural perspectives. *International Journal of Intercultural Relations*, *29*(2), 137–163.

Arasaratnam-Smith, L. A. (2016). An exploration of the relationship between intercultural communication competence and bilingualism. *Communication Research Reports*, *33*(3), 231–238.

Arasaratnam-Smith, L. A. (2020). Developing Global Graduates: Essentials and possibilities. *Research in Comparative and International Education*, *15*(1), 20–26.

Bennett, M. J. (1986). A developmental approach to training for intercultural sensitivity. *International Journal of Intercultural Relations*, *10*(2), 179–196.

Bennett, M. J. (2013). *Basic concepts of intercultural communication* (2nd ed.). Intercultural Press.

Bennett, M. J., & Hammer, M. (2017). A developmental model of intercultural sensitivity. *The international encyclopedia of intercultural communication*. Wiley.

Byram, M. (1997). *Teaching and assessing intercultural communication competence*. Multilingual Matters.

Calloway-Thomas, C., Arasaratnam-Smith, L. A., & Deardorff, D. K. (2017). The role of empathy in fostering intercultural competence. In D. K. Deardorff and L. A. Arasaratnam-Smith (Eds.), *Intercultural competence in higher education* (pp. 32–42). Routledge.

Deardorff, D. K. (2006). Identification and assessment of intercultural competence as a student outcome of internationalization. *Journal of Studies in International Education*, *10*(3), 241–266.

Dimitroff, L. J., Sliwoski, L., O'Brien, S., & Nichols, L. W. (2017). Change your life through journaling – The benefits of journaling for registered nurses. *Journal of Nursing Education and Practice*, *7*(2), 90–98.

Earley, P. C., & Ang, S. (2003). *Cultural intelligence: Individual interactions across cultures*. Stanford University Press.

Fantini, A. E. (1995). Language, culture, and world view: Exploring the nexus. *International Journal of Intercultural Relations*, *19*(2), 143–153.

Garrett-Rucks, P. (2014). Measuring instructed language learners' IC development: Discrepancies between assessment models by Byram and Bennett. *International Journal of Intercultural Relations*, *41*, 181–191.

Gonçalves, G., Sousa, C., Arasaratnam-Smith, L. A., Rodrigues, N., & Carvalheiro, R. (2020). Intercultural communication competence scale: Invariance and construct validation in Portugal. *Journal of Intercultural Communication Research*, *49*(3), 242–262.

Grant, A. M., Franklin, J., & Langford, P. (2002). The self-reflection and insight scale: A new measure of private self-consciousness. *Social Behavior and Personality: An International Journal*, *30*(8), 821–835.

Gudykunst, W. B. (1993). Toward a theory of effective interpersonal and intergroup communication: An anxiety/uncertainty management (AUM) perspective. In R. L. Wiseman & J. Koester (Eds.), *Intercultural communication competence* (pp. 33–71). Sage Publications.

Gudykunst, W. B. (1995). Anxiety/Uncertainty Management (AUM) Theory: Current status. In R. L. Wiseman (Ed.), *Intercultural Communication Theory* (pp. 8–58). Sage Publications.

Gudykunst, W. B. (Ed.). (2005). *Theorizing about intercultural communication.* Sage.

Hammer, M. R. (2011). Additional cross-cultural validity testing of the Intercultural Development Inventory. *International Journal of Intercultural Relations, 35*(4), 474–487. https://doi.org/http://dx.doi.org/10.1016/j.ijintrel.2011.02.014

Hammer, M. R. (2015). The developmental paradigm for intercultural competence research. *International Journal of Intercultural Relations, 48,* 12–13. https://doi.org/https://doi.org/10.1016/j.ijintrel.2015.03.004

Hosseini Fatemi, A., Khajavy, G. H., & Choi, C. W. (2016). Testing a model of intercultural willingness to communicate based on ethnocentrism, ambiguity tolerance and sensation seeking: The role of learning English in Iran. *Journal of Intercultural Communication Research, 45*(4), 304–318.

Howell, W. S. (1982). *The empathic communicator.* Wadsworth Publishing.

Imai, M., Kanero, J., & Masuda, T. (2016). The relation between language, culture, and thought. *Current Opinion in Psychology, 8,* 70–77.

Jiang, Q., Soon, S., & Li, Y. (2021). Enhancing teachers' intercultural competence with online technology as cognitive tools: A literature review. *English Language Teaching, 14*(3), 1–11.

Jiang, W. (2000). The relationship between culture and language. *ELT Journal, 54*(4), 328–334.

Jones, S. M., Bodie, G. D., & Hughes, S. D. (2019). The impact of mindfulness on empathy, active listening, and perceived provisions of emotional support. *Communication Research, 46*(6), 838–865.

Kampermann, A., Opdenakker, R., Heijden, B. V. D., & Bücker, J. (2021). Intercultural competencies for fostering technology-mediated collaboration in developing countries. *Sustainability, 13*(14), 7790.

Langer, E. (1997). *The power of mindful learning.* Addison-Wesley.

Lee, L. (2012). Engaging study abroad students in intercultural learning through blogging and ethnographic interviews. *Foreign Language Annals, 45*(1), 7–21.

Leone, L., Van der Zee, K. I., van Oudenhoven, J. P., Perugini, M., & Ercolani, A. P. (2005). The cross-cultural generalizability and validity of the Multicultural Personality Questionnaire. *Personality and Individual Differences, 38*(6), 1449–1462.

Liaw, M. L. (2019). EFL learners' intercultural communication in an open social virtual environment. *Journal of Educational Technology & Society, 22*(2), 38–55.

Lindström, N. B., & Pozo, R. R. (2020). Perspectives of nurses and doulas on the use of information and communication technology in intercultural paediatric care: Qualitative pilot study. *JMIR Pediatrics and Parenting, 3*(1), e16545.

Meleady, R., Seger, C. R., & Vermue, M. (2021). Evidence of a dynamic association between intergroup contact and intercultural competence. *Group Processes & Intergroup Relations, 24*(8), 1427–1447.

Morgan, S., & Arasaratnam, L. A. (2003). *Intercultural friendships as social excitation: Sensation seeking as a predictor of intercultural friendship seeking behavior.* National Communication Association.

Nadeem, M. U. (2022). An extension of the Integrated Model of Intercultural Communication Competence (IMICC) with religiosity: An international students' perspective. *Sage Open, 12*(1), 21582440221082139.

Nadeem, M. U., Mohammed, R., & Dalib, S. (2020). Retesting Integrated Model of Intercultural Communication Competence (IMICC) on international students from the Asian context of Malaysia. *International Journal of Intercultural Relations, 74*, 17–29.

Nadeem, M. U., & Zabrodskaja, A. (2023). A comprehensive model of intercultural communication for international students living in culturally diverse societies: Evidence from China. *Frontiers in Communication, 8.* https://doi.org/10.3389/fcomm.2023.1332001

Norkunas, M. (2011). Teaching to listen: Listening exercises and self-reflexive journals. *The Oral History Review, 38*(1), 63–108.

Reitz, M., Waller, L., Chaskalson, M., Olivier, S., & Rupprecht, S. (2020). Developing leaders through mindfulness practice. *Journal of Management Development, 39*(2), 223–239.

Ruben, B. D., & Kealey, D. J. (1979). Behavioral assessment of communication competency and the prediction of cross-cultural adaptation. *International Journal of Intercultural Relations, 3*(1), 15–47.

Shadiev, R., Wang, X., & Huang, Y. M. (2020). Promoting intercultural competence in a learning activity supported by virtual reality technology. *International Review of Research in Open and Distributed Learning, 21*(3), 157–174.

Spitzberg, B. H., & Changnon, G. (2009). Conceptualizing intercultural competence. In D. K. Deardorff (Ed.), *The Sage handbook of intercultural competence* (pp. 2–52). Sage Publications.

Van der Zee, K., Van Oudenhoven, J. P., Ponterotto, J. G., & Fietzer, A. W. (2013). Multicultural Personality Questionnaire: Development of a short form. *Journal of Personality Assessment, 95*(1), 118–124.

Van Dyne, L., Ang, S., Ng, K. Y., Rockstuhl, T., Tan, M. L., & Koh, C. (2012). Sub-dimensions of the four factor model of cultural intelligence: Expanding the conceptualization and measurement of cultural intelligence. *Social and Personality Psychology Compass, 6*(4), 295–313.

Van Dyne, L., Ang, S., & Koh, C. (2015). Development and validation of the CQS: The cultural intelligence scale. In S. Ang & L. Van Dyne (Eds.), *Handbook of cultural intelligence* (pp. 34–56). Routledge.

Van Oudenhoven, J. P., & Van der Zee, K. I. (2002). Predicting multicultural effectiveness of international students: The Multicultural Personality Questionnaire. *International Journal of Intercultural Relations, 26*(6), 679–694.

Yari, N., Lankut, E., Alon, I., & Richter, N. F. (2020). Cultural intelligence, global mindset, and cross-cultural competencies: A systematic review using bibliometric methods. *European Journal of International Management, 14*(2), 210–250.

8 Learning and Living in a Culturally Diverse World

A little while ago, Lily and her husband had invited four of her colleagues and their spouses over for a meal. Most people had not met one another before. One of the guests kept making light-hearted comments such as, "Hey, I'm ethnic. That's how we do things," when talking about particular foods and such. As the ten people sat around the table talking and trying to get to know one another, someone asked the question of where each person was born. As answers started rolling in from South Africa to New Zealand, everyone was surprised that there was only one person at the table who was born in Australia, and that was the person who had kept identifying herself as "ethnic." This conversation is one illustration of the diversity that surrounds many of us even if we are not aware of the cultural roots of the most "normalised" of our neighbours. Regardless of whether we live amongst people who are distinctly different to us and stand out as "other" people, many of us interact regularly with people who were raised in different cultural traditions. In other words, many of us traverse amidst intercultural spaces daily. Hopefully, the topics we have discussed in this book will aid all of us to traverse these spaces more confidently and constructively.

We started this book by presenting the premise of intercultural spaces as a concept, framed by eight propositions which are worth revisiting as we delve into the final chapter.

Proposition 1: Intercultural spaces exist when differences in ethnic or cultural thought community are salient within a communicative context.

Proposition 2: Shared thought communities or cultural identities facilitate communication in intercultural spaces.

Proposition 3: The lack of shared thought communities or cultural identities debilitate communication in intercultural spaces.

Proposition 4: When in an intercultural space, there is usually discordance in one's internal cultural identities.

Proposition 5: An intercultural space can exist regardless of the participants' awareness of the salience of cultural differences.

Proposition 6: Mindfulness is necessary for perceiving an intercultural space.

DOI: 10.4324/9781003318415-9

Proposition 7: In situations where a person ventures into a different cultural context, that person exists in an intercultural space that is both conceptual and literal.

Proposition 8: The variables that contribute to ICC also contribute to successful navigation of intercultural spaces.

Framing intercultural communication as communication in intercultural spaces enables us to understand intercultural communication in an era where cultural diversity is not only prevalent in most urban communities but also as part of people's own sense of identity. We need a better way to understand when interpersonal communication becomes intercultural communication, in the diverse communities in which we live (Proposition 1). We need to understand ways in which we connect with others across differences (Propositions 2 and 3). We used Chao and Moon's (2005) idea of cultural mosaic to understand how different aspects of our cultural identities become relevant or come to the forefront under different circumstances (Proposition 4). We talked about instances where cultural misunderstandings can occur without our knowledge (Proposition 5). We talked about how to be alert to instances where we might find ourselves in an intercultural space (Proposition 6). We discussed the relevance of intercultural spaces when we travel to a different country or engage a new culture (Proposition 7). Finally, we explored ways in which we could successfully navigate intercultural spaces (Proposition 8).

If you have been reading this book, either because it was part of a reading list for an intercultural communication class or because you found the topic interesting, you already belong to a thought community of people who are interested in intercultural communication. You may have heard of the term, "interculturalist." Sometimes, this term is used to describe someone whose profession is in intercultural work, like a scholar or educator (e.g., Rasmussen, 2023); at other times the term is used to describe a state of mind that is actively open to and curious about cultural diversity (e.g., Holmes & MacDonald, 2020). For the purpose of our present discussion, we characterise an interculturalist as someone who is curious about intercultural spaces and committed to helping themselves and others navigate these spaces constructively. If you can identify with that definition, then welcome to the thought community of interculturalists! It is a diverse community indeed, consisting of people from every walk of life, various professions, and various cultures. You have heard many of their stories in this book. This chapter (and indeed this book!) about learning and living in a diverse world is written by interculturalists, for interculturalists – present and future. In this chapter, we will reflect on what it means to live amongst diverse people as an interculturalist.

Encountering Differences

As discussed in Chapter 5, one of the challenges of learning and living in a diverse world is that we are often in proximity to people who are "different" from us in ways that create intercultural spaces. That might, in turn, create conflict, or at the very least discomfort. For example, although this might be hard to do, imagine a time before social media and perhaps even before the internet – which, incidentally, was not very long ago in the grand scheme of things. People got their news from a newspaper that was delivered to their home or bought from a shop on the way to work. Or they watched the news at set times on the television or listened to it on the radio. This news was static all day, giving the reader time to process the information and think about how they want to react to it. "Regular" people did not have public personas or platforms from which to make their thoughts known. Those who did have a public platform were people who had to have some credential for holding that platform, like politicians, celebrities, or disciplinary experts, for example. And they voiced their opinions on the basis of those credentials, such as a professor commenting on a new breakthrough in biology or a politician commenting on policy. Opinions of regular people were shared in conversations, which were usually face to face or on the phone (of course, people conversed via letters for centuries, but we're focusing on the 20th and 21st centuries here). There was no written trail of these conversations to be revisited later or reposted out of context. And these conversations almost always happened on the basis of a relationship. People had to engage with verbal and nonverbal cues in such conversations (or letters) and think about what kind of (relational) impression they were making in communication.

Now, contrast such a time with today, where there is a constant flow of "news" on myriad channels of media that are accessible on myriad devices, anywhere, at any time. Every person with access to the relevant technologies has a platform from which to voice his or her thoughts. Anything from considered opinions to mere stream-of-consciousness, globally, instantly, and constantly. These publicly exposed thoughts can be appropriated and used by others in any way they choose. Anyone, without any sense of relational propriety or knowledge of relevant facts, can comment on these thoughts. As Jakob et al. (2023) observe, "Digital spaces provide an infrastructure for abusive discourse to spread more quickly and broadly than ever" (p. 509). The constant influx of news and opinions creates a relentless cacophony in which lines between facts and opinions are blurred (Hobbs, 2020). In fact, some algorithms in social media platforms are designed to limit exposure to diverse perspectives, creating echo chambers in which our own opinions are validated and biases confirmed (Choi et al., 2020).

This is the current social reality in which we navigate complex socio-cultural differences without the time or the headspace with which to engage in the nuances that such complexity demands. It is no wonder that some people are dealing with diversity by simply removing the dissenting voice from their social realm, in what has emerged as cancel culture, wherein a person whose view or value is contradictory to one's own is silenced through cyber shunning (Norris, 2023). Instead of engaging constructively and relationally with differences, people have begun to simply insulate themselves from confronting those differences or, worse, shouting down those dissenting voices through a flurry of emotionally charged and morally outraged public expressions (Clark, 2020; Rösner & Krämer, 2016).

The challenge with encountering differences in such a climate is that there is little to no room to employ strategies we discussed in Chapters 5 and 7 such as self-reflection, empathetic exchange of information, stereotype change, intergroup dialogue and further reflection based on such information gained – unless you are intentional in pausing to consider the situation and engage in constructive dialogue with the person who is "different." Jakob et al. (2023) identify a concept called toxic outrage, which they note as something that prevents open-mindedness. They characterise toxic outrage as a rhetorical strategy that promotes insensitivity towards others' points of view by "provoking negative emotional reactions" (p. 511). The authors further explain:

> Certain speech acts impede constructive democratic debate because they carry a disregard for the positions of fellow debaters based on the presumption that their experiences are irrelevant or untrustworthy... But we should expect an appreciation for both common ground and differences and, conversely, be interested in how certain forms of incivility and impoliteness, which we refer to as toxic outrage, prevent such open-mindedness. (p. 510)

Although Jakob et al.'s premise for the concept of toxic outrage is public debate, it has relevance for our current discussion on confronting differences. Learning and living in a diverse world requires us to navigate intercultural spaces on a regular basis; and navigating intercultural spaces involves encountering differences. If we cannot engage with a different point of view or different value system without getting outraged by its deviance from our own, or dismissing it as invalid in comparison to our own (which would be an ethnocentric thing to do!), then we are ill-equipped to confront differences. As we discussed in the previous chapters, and particularly in Chapters 5 and 7, navigating intercultural spaces requires us to not only attempt to understand a perspective that is different to our own, but also respect such a dissenting perspective as something of importance to the other person, regardless of whether we agree with it or not. This posture of understanding and respect of "difference" (with which we may or may not agree) is completely opposite to the toxic outrage brand of communication.

Intercultural scholar Nan Sussman makes this observation about the work of intercultural scholars:

> In a way, our field is swimming upstream from an evolutionary point of view. I mean humans socially evolved essentially to be xenophobic to protect themselves. To protect yourself, you needed to be with people who were similar, from your tribe. And so, in a way, I think phobia is baked into human nature. Our field is saying, no. You can work together, you can work with people who look different than you or have different values. It's a really significant task we have given ourselves. We need to translate our research and have more of an impact on global leaders and policymakers, to inform them of ways to improve intercultural relations. (Sussman, personal communication, 19/04/2022)

Communicating in thoughtful and respectful ways can be challenging, especially when confronted with differences that speak to deeply personal values, such as religious beliefs, and differences in ethical values. The good news, however, is that living and learning in a diverse world presents us with wonderful opportunities to expand our horizons, experience perspectives that are vastly different to ours, explore new ideas and possibilities that may never have occurred to us based on our limited point of view, and enrich one another with challenging and fulfilling relationships with a variety of people. We will dive into some of these possibilities a bit later as we examine considerations for living in a diverse world. Before we do that, let's talk about a couple more important topics that are relevant to learning and living in a culturally diverse world.

Ethics and Culture

One characterisation of ethics is that it is the systematic application of moral principles to tangible or concrete problems (Wines & Napier, 1992). The word ethic derives from a Greek root meaning "the art of character." The idea is that one's behaviour conforms to a standard of conduct for a given identity group based on a moral code (again, think *thought community*). In other words, ethical principles guide our behaviour both individually, and in groups. It stands to reason therefore that cultural differences in ethics will come into focus in many contexts, such as international business, international law, and intercultural relationships, to name a few. Evanoff (2020) differentiates cultural *conventions* from *mores* and *legal codes (laws)*. Conventions are "norms that are adopted by social groups to coordinate action among their members" (p. 188). They include things like table manners, business negotiation practices, and which side of the road to drive on. He defines *mores* as norms related to moral values, and religious beliefs that may inform moral values systems. Of course, a given society's legal codes are also often formed on the basis of sacred texts and conventions, but become codified into societal rights and responsibilities. Moral principles are often, although not always, derived from religious beliefs. There are many bases from which ethical standards may be derived, including religion, reason, social and natural law, or situational factors. Shweder et al. (1997) propose that humans across cultures speak three moral languages, namely an ethic of autonomy, an ethic of community, and an ethic of divinity. Ethic of autonomy bases morality on individual rights and justice for the individual; applied to groups, this ethic may result in antinomianism. An ethic of community bases morality on duty, respect, and other such concepts that preserve unity, resulting in either a deontological duty ethic or a utilitarian ethic. Finally, an ethic of divinity bases morality on concepts such as sin and purity as defined by a religious creed or set of virtues.

One of the questions that arises in intercultural spaces is whether there exists on some level a set of universal ethical principles. The fact that cultures are different refers to the idea of *cultural relativity*. For example, how we greet someone verbally and nonverbally will vary according to cultural context. But cultural *relativism* (sometimes referred to as cultural particularism) is the notion that value judgments from different cultures must be accepted as they are. Such a position makes it nearly impossible to negotiate and cooperate around complex global issues like pollution, global warming, natural disasters, dehumanisation, and responses to global conflicts and crises. If we run this position to its logical conclusion, all moral codes become context-specific and culture-bound, which means that no moral system is better than another (Samovar et al., 2017). It means that we would be forced to tacitly condone atrocities like Nazi concentration camps, sending in tanks to crush peaceful student protests, apartheid states and slavery, honour killings and genital mutilation of young women.

Relativism's binary opposite is *universalism*, which holds that there are standards for right and wrong which hold true irrespective of culture, people group, or time. For example, the United Nations' *Universal Declaration of Human Rights* Article 19 grants the following common right to all people:

> Everyone has the right to freedom of opinion and expression; this right includes freedom to hold opinions without interference and to seek, receive and impart information and ideas through any media and regardless of frontiers.

Clearly some nations do not adhere to Article 19 and censor the information people in their country are able to access, as well as restrict what they are allowed to express. But the point of Article 19 is that we often operate on the basis of certain universal principles like respect, honesty, freedom, kindness, and humane treatment that share widespread agreement. In turn, we hold to account those who do not endorse those standards. The downside of universalism is an uncritical application of ethnocentric moral standards that completely disregards the unique cultural contexts of other people groups.

Evanoff (2012) offered a middle-ground, relativity-based concept in *dialogic ethics* that recognises both the dynamic nature of culture and the need for communication and collaborative problem solving around international and humanitarian concerns. His premise is that all cultures evolve, and their systems of right and wrong adjust along with them.

> Cultural relativism seems progressive but is in fact conservative and tradition-bound because it obligates us to accept the values and norms of other cultures rather than giving us the opportunity to critically reflect on them... [and depicts] culture in "essentialist" terms... rather than in constructivist terms... and therefore susceptible to creative change... Such reflection results in greater objectivity, although never in pure, absolute objectivity – as humans we never have access to a "God's-eye" view of the world. (pp. 477–478)

If we accept Evanoff's proposition and enter into dialogue with a second-person epistemic, then there is room for negotiation, change, and agreement on moral codes that foster peace, harmony, and attainment of mutual goals.

Religion and Culture

While many Westernised cultures view faith as a private or personal matter and for example believe in separation of faith and state, faith is very much integrated into culture and identity in countless communities around the world. For example, as previously shared, Lily grew up in a multi-faith community in which Hindus celebrated their festivals and shared food with their neighbours of other faiths, Muslims did the same, and Christians also did the same with Christmas, which was only celebrated by Christians. There were no considerations of "offence" when publicly celebrating a faith-based festival because everyone understood it was a celebration for and by a specific group of people, and that all groups will get their turn to celebrate their own festivals. In other words, there was no public space that was devoid of or "protected from" religion. Religious expressions were very much part of cultural expressions in that community, in public and private spaces alike.

At the individual level, religious affiliation (or lack thereof) is arguably part of a person's sense of identity. As we mentioned earlier in the book, culture is expressed in values, beliefs, and norms. For example, a person who identifies as a Hindu may refrain from eating beef, a norm that is based on the value that cows are sacred, which in turn is based on the belief in the existence of a bovine goddess. Personal faith and religious affiliation very much shape values and behaviours such that it is impossible to discuss culture as norms, values, and behaviours without acknowledging the role of religion in shaping culture. The point to emphasise in this chapter of learning and living in a culturally diverse world is that freedom and acceptance of cultural expression go hand in hand with freedom and acceptance of religious practices as well. And, just as one does not have to agree with or adopt a cultural practice in order to accept its existence, the same goes for religious practices.

We think it is unhelpful to treat religious practices differently than cultural practices. More specifically, it is inconsistent if we accept that there is diversity of valid cultural practices while at the same time take offence or caution when it comes to accepting diversity of religious practices just because we do not subscribe to a particular religion. Our point is that living in diverse communities requires us to acknowledge the existence of diversity of cultures and religious practices, and understand that acknowledgement of one culture or religion isn't inherently an offence to, or dismissal of, another, as highlighted in Chapter 6.

Religious beliefs (or lack thereof) are indeed personal. But living in genuine relationship with diverse peoples means engaging with what is personal to us and them, regardless of whether our beliefs are the same. As Proposition 2 says, shared thought communities facilitate communication in intercultural spaces. And you will remember from Chapter 1 that thought communities describe the concept of shared beliefs, interests, ideologies, etc., such as all librarians, regardless of ethnic culture, could be considered as sharing a thought community in their identity as curators of knowledge. While differences in religious beliefs may seem deeply personal and often challenging to breach, those who are of one mind in the desire to engage with diverse people in constructive and relational ways are united into one thought community of people who value intercultural relationships. Ripley and Lily belong to such an international community. In other words, we may encounter people who belong to a different thought community in the category of religious beliefs, but we may all still belong to the same category of interculturalists!

Considerations for Living in a Diverse Word

In many parts of the world, although not in all, cultural diversity has increased dramatically in the past few decades due to global migration patterns and accessibility of global travel. Lily was travelling in a train recently and noticed she could not hear a single word of English being spoken in the din of conversations all around her. What was extraordinary about this observation was that Lily was in the city of London at that time, right in the heart of England, the country whose very name bears the name of the English language. As Van Oudenhoven and Benet-Martinez (2015) observed some years ago:

> As societies become even more multicultural, with fading majorities, the need for dealing with cultural diversity does not diminish. However, both immigrants and native inhabitants do no longer have a clear target group to which they should acculturate. The increasingly most likely group is the culturally heterogeneous society. An individualized approach for dealing with the cultural variety of groups and individuals from different cultures involves fostering intercultural competences. (p. 53)

When cultural diversity is pervasive, it can be challenging to navigate the complexities and nuances of what that diversity entails at political, social, and interpersonal levels. As Van Oudenhoven and Benet-Martinez note, an individual approach to dealing with cultural diversity is to foster intercultural competence. We discussed intercultural competence in Chapter 7. If individuals traverse through intercultural spaces constructively and with positive relational outcomes, the carryover effects on social and political realms are arguably optimistic. To that end, we offer some considerations for learning and living in a diverse world.

Considerations of Conflict

As we mentioned before, living in a diverse world means encountering diversity of people, values, beliefs, and opinions. This diversity has the potential to cause conflict at the interpersonal and international level. Unlike the time before the digital age of the internet and smartphones, conflict can be played out on a variety of platforms today, such as news, public opinion debates, forum threads, a plethora of social media, and of course, good old fashioned face-to-face communication. The challenge with engaging in conflict on multiple platforms is that many of these platforms do not lend themselves to constructive relational dialogue. In other words, if you have a disagreement with a friend in a face-to-face conversation, you have to look her in the face and present your point of view while watching her reactions to your words. You have to stay in the room to hear her response, and deal with the relational consequences with the words you've shared. You have to consider how this conflict would affect your friend's opinion of you and how much (or little) you value the friendship enough to invest in coming out on the other side of the conflict with your relationship intact.

These considerations are moot in an online thread where you can assume a pseudonym and verbally bash someone's view without ever facing them, ever worrying about your relationship with them, or worrying about saving face. You don't even have to stick around to defend your words if the person responds to your verbal bashing. You can simply "hit and run" to the next opinion you want to eviscerate. Conflicting views can simply be expressed loudly, repeatedly, with increasing vitriol, without any obligation to listen to the opposing view or even engage with the logic, such as it is, of an opposing view. Rösner and Krämer (2016), for example, note that, regardless of anonymity, users' aggressive language escalates when other users also use aggressive language. Lück and Nardi (2019) observe that incivility in online comments is detrimental to deliberative discussions. Similarly, Walsh (2020) argues that social media obstruct diversity and exposure to other points of view and exaggerate certain divisive issues, inducing anxiety and panic.

Living in a diverse (digital) world and effectively navigating intercultural spaces demands us to engage in more constructive means of conflict navigation when confronted with differences. We are circling back to this point we made in Chapter 5 to emphasise that confronting differences requires us to have a state of mind which is prepared to fully hear out an opposing point of view in a manner that validates the person, even if we completely disagree with their perspective – perhaps even if we think the other person's view is fundamentally immoral. For reasons that were described in Chapter 5, our instinct is to punish and demonise, which American revolutionary Thomas Paine (1795) noted "is always dangerous to liberty... He that would make his own liberty secure, must guard even his enemy from opposition; for if he violates this duty, he establishes a precedent that will reach to himself" (p. 37).

What we want to highlight here is that living in a pluralistic world requires us to suspend judgement while we hear each other out. It requires us to have intentionality in overcoming certain systemic barriers in the digital world to really listen to divergent views. Listening is neither conceding nor condoning, but rather hearing the other person out to understand where they are coming from. And with the choice to listen to differing points of view comes another choice, which is to live amicably with people with whose perspective we strongly disagree. Consideration of conflict (due to differences) from living in a diverse world involves engaging with those differences civilly. As Bardon et al. (2023) observe, "What civility as politeness demands is not the recognition of others' equal moral worth but merely the recognition of others' status as co-members of society with whom we must coexist" (p. 310). Living in a diverse world, we have opportunities, as never before, to exercise our civility and recognise people from various cultures as co-members of our communities with shared humanity.

Considerations of Language(s)

Living in a diverse world entails living in a world of many languages. Several countries have multiple official languages which are recognised as languages of the land. Other countries, like the United States, do not have any legally designated national language. But beyond such formal recognition of diversity of languages, most urban societies house not only people who speak different languages but also people who speak multiple languages. It is not uncommon for immigrants to speak one language at home and another at school or the workplace (Ramos Salazar et al., 2023). It is also not uncommon for migrants to be multilingual, with varying degrees of fluency. Code-switching, or the practice of alternating between languages in different settings, is a well-researched phenomenon (Mekheimr, 2023). Bi or multilingual people code-switch for a variety of reasons such as to reduce social difference between themselves and others who speak a particular language (Salleh et al., 2022), for educative purposes (Ali & Muhammad, 2023), due to lack of language competence (Umezi, 2023), or simply for convenience (Aorny et al., 2022).

It must be said that the ability to speak more than one language does not automatically translate into ease of living in a diverse world. As we discussed in Chapter 4, language plays a significant role in shaping our social reality, including our self-perception based on how our "native" language fits within the perceived hierarchy of languages in our local society (Kiramba & Oloo, 2020). For example, Lily grew up speaking Tamil in a country where Tamils were the minority numerically and in political and policy representation, such that Lily always saw herself as a "sub" citizen of the country. She saw herself that way despite the fact that she was a citizen by birthright and ethnicity, just as those who spoke the language of the majority. In a multilingual society, perceptions of a language hierarchy can influence perceptions of social identity in terms of where someone fits in that society. It is important to be aware of these dynamics when living in diverse communities. However, the ability to speak more than one language has far more advantages than disadvantages, including a predisposition to develop intercultural competence (Arasaratnam-Smith, 2016). There is evidence to suggest that code-switching between languages facilitates maintenance of language fluency in multiple languages as well as the ability to convey meaning in different ways (Beatty-Martínez et al., 2020).

Considerations of language when living in a diverse world also involves considering how language is used in digital spaces. Kelly-Holmes (2019) proposes that digital communication has evolved from monolingualism to what she calls idiolingualism. She observes that at the start of the digital age of the world wide web, communication was largely monolingual and in English. She characterises the second age of digital communication as consisting of multilingualism, or at least multiple languages in parallel use. The advent of the internet has witnessed the emergence of less visible language communities on the global stage, such as Chinese, Arabic, Portuguese, and German, to name a few, in addition to English. As Kelly-Holmes explains:

> The multilingualism era brought with it a lot of boundary work…, whereby countries and regions were increasingly separated from each other, with language being one of the main ways of doing this. As a result, the web, largely perceived as a global and boundaryless medium, instead became a place where

the essentialized links between language, territory, and national identity in fact became reinforced – for some, not all. (p. 31)

The boundaries fostered by multilingualism led to what Kelly-Holmes calls hyperlingualism, where there was a proliferation of language presence and differentiation of each of the spaces which these languages occupy. Kelly-Holmes concludes that hyperlingualism has developed in parallel to what is now idiolingualism, which is excessively personalised language that is behind algorithmic customisation. Ironically, the proliferation of languages in the digital space seems to have led to deeper separation in one sense, with individualisation and isolation of preferences.

While global migration patterns have introduced many cities to multilingual populations, there are still large groups of mono-lingual people, especially in Western English-speaking countries. From a communication perspective, we would suggest that learning another language or at the very least understanding social concepts and expressions in other languages is increasingly essential for living in diverse communities. As we discussed in Chapter 4, knowing a language reveals how a people-group interact with their world and the values they highlight by the presence (or absence) of words to name, describe, and communicate their lived reality. However, the point has to be made that with the advent of artificial intelligence (AI) capabilities, language barriers are not what they once were. AI is used to translate educational texts (Jiang et al., 2021), international trade (Brynjolfsson et al., 2019), and word compositions in a variety of scenarios (Tajik & Tajik, 2023). Tourists venture bravely into strange new lands armed with the translation app on their smartphones. Amidst such possibilities, one could ask whether the hard work of learning another language is worth it. The answer is, definitely yes! As Arasaratnam-Smith (2016) observes, the very process of learning a new language facilitates the development of new mental categories or schema, thereby predisposing the person to engage with (cultural) complexity in ways that a monolingual person cannot. It is exciting to contemplate that we live in a world where we literally hold in our hand technology that enables us to both understand a waiter who speaks another language *and* learn to properly speak the language of the waiter, if we so wish.

Intercultural researcher, John Oetzel, who is known for his work on intercultural conflict navigation, shares his story of moving to New Zealand with his family and using a range of behaviours that we have discussed so far, particularly understanding his new cultural context through understanding the language of the local people.

Building Relationships

John G. Oetzel

I moved from the United States to Aotearoa New Zealand with my family in 2011. My partner and I had made the choice to raise our boys in a different country and live in a different culture. My boys were 5 and 3 at the time and we were excited about our new adventure. We landed at the airport at 7 am and by 11 am I was at the Rauawaawa Kaumātua Charitable Trust for a pōwhiri (welcoming ceremony) to launch a new research project. I had met the CEO through one of my new colleagues and became involved in a project with kaumātua (Māori elders). The Rauawaawa is a social and health service provider for kaumātua. Māori are the Indigenous people of Aotearoa New Zealand (literally land of the long white cloud).

During the pōwhiri, another new colleague kindly explained what was happening and translated what was being said. After the ceremony, I met several kaumātua who taught me some "key" terms (e.g., wharepaku – toilet) and issued a wero (challenge) to me to learn te reo Māori (language) and tikanga (cultural practices). Early the next week, the kaumātua and organisational members took me and my family to the university, my new place of work, to formally present us. There was a second pōwhiri; this time the kaumātua were handing us over to the university. The kaumātua made sure to let me know that they cared for us and would look after us. I was greatly touched by this gesture, and this started a relationship that continues to this day.

Over the coming year, I worked on the project, and I began to learn about tikanga and about the colonial history in New Zealand. I went to seminars and talked to my research partners and the kaumātua to better learn about Māori culture and history. Near the end of our first year, our local primary school that my older boy attended invited students to join the rumaki unit (Māori language and cultural immersion programme). We talked to our boys about enrolling (our youngest wasn't old enough yet but would follow what his brother would do). We thought this was an amazing opportunity for them and they agreed.

After four years, I became conversational and yet never fluent; I did learn how to open and close meetings. We tried to speak Māori at home, but our boys resisted because we weren't good enough and it was easier for them to speak to us in English. I think they also liked falling back to their own comfort zone of speaking English because it was challenging for them to learn a new language although like most children they adjusted quickly.

During their early years at school, we worked hard to build relationships with other parents and the teachers. We went to many functions, volunteered at end-of-year school camps, and even attended several tangihanga (funerals) for community members and the parent of one of our sons' teachers. We wanted to be connected to our new community and make sure our boys were integrated into the school. They made some great friends and enjoyed their experience. We also had opportunities to learn about identity and self-awareness. At one event, it was announced that there was an opportunity for Māori and my son said loudly, "we can do that, we're Māori mum." Some of the teachers laughed, mostly they were really touched that he felt that way. It was an opportunity for us to talk about language, culture, and ethnicity. He didn't understand it completely that day, but eventually learned about the complexity of identity.

Our experiences in the kura were largely positive although not completely without challenges and disagreements. We had open dialogue with the teachers and followed tikanga to address concerns. It was interesting trying to live up to standards by which I preached in my research on managing intercultural conflict. We tried to follow tikanga in addressing these challenges and like with most relationships, these interactions strengthened some relationships and strained others. We continue to be good friends with one of the boys' teachers who greatly appreciated our commitment and willingness to have open discussion.

In more recent years, I often have a speaking role when we visit community partners, especially when we are starting new projects or building a new partnership. In the pōwhiri, the hosts welcome the guests and ideally a male speaker from the guests delivers a mihi and discusses why they have come. I find myself as the only male at many of these events, so I am honoured with the speaking role. I also get asked at work to serve as speaker to either welcome guests or serve as a speaker on behalf of guests. I have colleagues who are fluent speakers and very knowledgeable about tikanga who help me prepare and I'm grateful for their help. I have found my reo has gotten worse over the past few years as I haven't practised much except in these contexts. I memorise my presentations, work on proper pronunciation, and have learned some karakia (prayers) and mihi so that I can be respectful and follow tikanga. One area I haven't been as good at is waiata (songs). After a speaker presents, the group sings waiata to acknowledge the words and the speaker. I know a few waiata and participate when I know them, but there are such a range across different iwi (tribes) and regions that I often find myself unable to sing along. It is a beautiful aspect of tikanga.

When we moved to Aotearoa, we wanted to have experiences that we couldn't have in the USA and we certainly have had that. My friends, teachers, and research partners have been so kind to include us in their lives and share their beautiful culture with us. I feel privileged to have developed such strong relationships. One of my favourite whakataukī (proverbs) is "He Waka Eke Noa," which roughly translates to "We are all in this canoe together." It expresses the importance of building relationships and collaborating for common goals. My research focuses on the use of participatory/collaborative approaches to address health issues. My experiences have taught me that this can happen when we build respectful relationships and show a desire to learn about another's culture.

Considerations of Legacy

Living amongst diverse peoples means living amongst diverse histories. Just as our personal histories shape who we are today, cultural histories also have an impact on the collective psyche of a people-group. For example, the remnants of slavery still deeply impact Black–White relationships in the United States, some 150 plus years since the abolishment of slavery. Living in a diverse world means living in a world of diverse historical triumphs and scars. These can manifest in different contemporary expressions, such as celebrations of past victories like an Independence Day celebration, or the removal of symbols that are perceived as offensive reminders of past hurts, such as the removal of some confederate monuments in the United States (Benjamin et al., 2020). The surge in advocacy towards removing statues of people who symbolise oppression and abuse of power across many countries has scholars contemplating the pros and cons of such action. On the one hand, there are those like Younge (2021) who argue that no statue should be left standing:

> let us not burden future generations with the weight of our faulty memory and the lies of our partial mythology. Let us not put up the people we ostensibly cherish so that they can be forgotten and ignored. Let us elevate them, and others – in the curriculum, through scholarships and museums. Let us subject them to the critiques they deserve, which may convert them from inert models of their former selves to the complex, and often flawed, people that they were. Let us fight to embed the values of those we admire in our politics and our culture. Let's cover their anniversaries in the media and set them in tests. But the last thing we should do is cover their likeness in concrete and set them in stone. (p. 10)

While others, such as Eslin (2020) argue that statues representing painful historical persons and eras should remain for educational posterity. Two reasons undergird this perspective. First, remembrances of evil ward off the repetition of past sins. Secondly, in some cases we anachronistically apply a modern moral framework to an epoch that simply operated within a different set of circumstances. It is similar to our admonition of not judging another culture's behaviour by your ethnocentric understanding. At some future point every culture will be judged as barbaric in some respect. Regardless of whether they want statues to be destroyed or preserved as reminders of history, people on both sides of the argument seem to agree that statues in themselves are not history, but rather symbols of certain historic figures who, for social and political reasons of that time, were chosen to be immortalised in stone. Regardless of whether statues remain as reminders of historic events for educational purposes or whether they are removed as an act of protest against immortalising historic wrongdoers, it doesn't change the historical reality of the events all those decades, centuries, and millennia ago. The responsibility comes down to what artefacts, icons, and documents we leave for future generations to accurately convey the lessons of history. In other words, do we destroy sculpture from antiquity or remove the name of a government or military leader from a street or school because their reputations have been tarnished by modern sensibilities? What if events that seemed heroic and praiseworthy in the past are now considered atrocities against humanity? Or do we preserve historical artefacts as testaments of a time long before we were born? Is the offence the statue or the name itself, or its place of prominence in a public square? How is a statue different from a painting of a historical figure in a museum? What do we destroy and what do we preserve, and for what purpose? And how far back do we trace responsibility for past sins and grievances? As we noted in Chapter 2, the history of intercultural interaction is filled with more conquest than collaboration and co-existence. These are considerations of legacy with which we are faced as we live in a diverse world where the (historical) oppressor and the (historically) oppressed share a driveway.

We may not all agree on what historical symbols should be erased and what should be preserved. Perhaps a more important point is that the choices we make today will establish the legacy we leave for those who come after us. Our present actions shape future history. Just as our predecessors preserved or destroyed certain artefacts and narratives, affording or denying us the chance to engage them, living in a complex, diverse world demands our wise and compassionate consideration of the legacy we will leave for our successors.

Considerations of Co-Creation

When Ripley was in Uganda, a storyteller related a tale about a Ugandan fisherman that was relaxing in his lakefront hammock around midday with his fishing gear leaned against his shade tree. As he was enjoying the shade from the hot sun, a German businessman walked by and inquired why the fisherman was not out in his boat making use of the calm water and workday hours. The businessman wondered why the fisherman wasn't labouring to provide for his family.

"You aren't going to catch many fish resting in your hammock, are you?" inquired the businessman. "Why don't you make use of the time while the weather cooperates?"

The fisherman didn't open his eyes, but smiled and said, "And what will my reward be if I work that hard? I have what I need for my family."

"Well," the businessman replied, "if you catch more than you need, you could set up a store at the market and sell the extra fish and make a profit."

"And then what would my reward be?" asked the fisherman.

The businessman was starting to get annoyed; "You could buy another boat and hire some people to work for you – expand your business. You could build up a whole fleet of fishing vessels and create a fishing empire that sells fish across the country, even internationally!"

"Oh, yes," said the fisherman, "and then what will my reward be?"

At this the businessman was demonstrably upset, "You're not getting it!" he shouted at the fisherman, "you could become so rich that you would never have to work again; you could spend your days relaxing, going to the beach, without a care in the world!"

The fisherman just smiled again without opening his eyes and said, "And, what do you think I'm doing right now?"

Sometimes, seeing how someone else understands a situation provides an entirely different perspective that was previously inaccessible to us. It offers fresh insights into shared human experiences, and challenges existing stereotypes and culturally constrained thinking. When Ripley first heard this story, he immediately questioned his ingrained understanding of capitalism and Americans' orientation towards activity. In light of the job stress he occasionally feels, juxtaposed to the "quality of life" to which he aspires, the simple lesson struck a chord in Ripley.

Engaging with people who are different to us gives us this very opportunity because, as we discussed in Chapter 3, our cultural values, experiences, and beliefs shape the way we perceive the world around us. People who grew up in different socio-cultural contexts have different ways of seeing the same situation, or at the very least, different variations of interpretation. What is "obvious" to someone might be opaque to someone else. And what is "normal" to you could be completely revolutionary to someone else. Living in a diverse world gives us the opportunity to draw on the rich experiences of people in our neighbourhoods from corners of the world we may never see in our lifetime.

The idea of co-creating by drawing on input from different cultural perspectives is not new. For example, Nickerson and Goby (2018) report of a project where school children drew on the experience of different cultural perspectives in a project. Said Valbuena et al. (2020) speak of the concept of ludic co-creation, which they describe as, "the spontaneous emergence of socio-cultural Microsystems characterized by enjoyment and brought together by inter-epistemic dialogue" (p. 85). It is interesting that the element of enjoyment is captured in this definition, highlighting an important part of the experience of co-creating from diverse input. Think of ludic co-creation as cultural fusion cuisine. "Ludic" derives from the Latin word "ludus," meaning playful collaboration. When cultural perspectives collide, it carries the innovative potential of the Medici Effect that sparked the Renaissance era (Johansson, 2006).

So, what does intercultural co-creating look like? In the context of co-creating with people from different cultures, integration of resources could involve drawing on insights, experiences, and perspectives from different cultures. Insight into what those activities and interactions might look like is provided by another example of how to approach co-creation, by Murdoch-Kitt et al. (2020), who propose a framework of six dimensions of intercultural teamwork, particularly for intercultural (remote) teams that have to work together. Firstly, *discover work styles* as to whether team members prefer an independent or interdependent style of working, by engaging in self-reflection and activities that enable people to identify their preferred work style. Secondly, *understanding core beliefs*, which refers to whether team members have an individualistic or collectivistic orientation when relating to the team. Thirdly, *enabling trust*, which has to do with matters of substantiated and relational trust where team members need to be able to share about themselves, learn about others, and collaborate to achieve common outcomes. Fourthly, *assessing information*, which is about objective and subjective sources from which information is gathered to analyse situations and engage with co-creation of ideas. Fifthly, decoding *communication styles*, which involves understanding direct and indirect communication style orientation of team members. Finally, *designing shared goals*, which is about exploring to what extent team members find the goals attainable or challenging in the co-creation process. The authors propose using collaborative activities to explore each of these dimensions together, to learn and grow together in the process of co-creating.

Based on an experiment in co-creation using a simulated dystopian virtual environment in which participants were asked to build a city, Raybourn (2000) reported that the limitations presented by the dystopian environment created a common need for participants to work collaboratively with one another. Further, she notes that enabling participants to co-create their own story in the virtual environment resulted in a level playing field that facilitated "more equitable interactional communication behaviors" (p. 29), as the commonality in the co-creation of their story served to minimise any perceived power differences. This too gives a glimpse into what intercultural co-creation might look like, highlighting the importance of sharing personal narratives, "enabling trust" and building a common narrative for what you are trying to accomplish together (Murdoch-Kitt et al., 2020).

Everyday Interculturalists

You may be familiar with the phrase "global citizen" or "global citizenship," which is often used to refer to the idea of being aware of our roles and responsibilities as members of a global village, considering matters of advocacy and duties with a global outlook rather than a parochial one. There is a whole body of literature that engages with this idea of global citizenship (e.g., Cabrera, 2010; Carter, 2013; Seo et al., 2023). Considerations of global citizenship are important. However, sometimes the idea of being "global" can be daunting when the dynamics and challenges of our local environment may seem sufficient for us to handle without having to think about what we can contribute to the entire globe, especially when global issues have layered complexities of political, social, and economic variables over which we have little control. Perhaps it is more constructive to think of our contribution on a smaller scale by reframing our role as everyday interculturalists.

We have been talking about communicating in intercultural spaces throughout this book. Our intent, of course, is to understand intercultural spaces better so we can communicate better in those spaces. To foster positive relationships across cultural differences, thereby fostering communities that flourish amidst cultural diversity not despite the diversity, but *because of* it. We have talked about the possibilities and opportunities that living in a diverse world presents, such as co-creating drawing on rich diversity. While all of us may not be powerful politicians or people of national or global influence, all of us do have a realm of influence in our immediate relational circles within our workplaces, classrooms, communities, families, social groups, etc. It is in this realm of relational influence that we have the opportunity to exercise our role as everyday interculturalists.

We said earlier that we characterise an interculturalist as someone who is curious about intercultural spaces and committed to helping themselves and others navigate these spaces positively. Unpacking that definition, curiosity about intercultural spaces implies not only an interest in understanding intercultural spaces better, but also an active engagement with intercultural spaces as a researcher would, to observe, analyse, and reflect on each experience of an intercultural space, learning from it and expanding one's frame of reference based on new understanding. A commitment to help yourself and others positively navigate intercultural spaces refers to an active orientation towards developing your own intercultural communication competence (ICC) as well as helping others understand what's going on in an intercultural space and helping them develop their ICC. In superhero terms, we as interculturalists can use our superpowers in our areas of influence, no matter how large or small they are! We may not have high-tech gadgets, high security facilities for secret meetings, or even a cape for our superhero activities, but we do have some super-P-O-W-E-R-S that are worth discussing. We have talked about variables that hinder intercultural communication in Chapter 5, we talked about variables that contribute to ICC in Chapter 7, and we have explored many concepts that have hopefully helped you understand intercultural spaces better. Putting that knowledge into action as an interculturalist, you are called to wield these P-O-W-E-R-S that you already possess.

Prudence

Prudence refers to a measure of cautiousness or careful consideration of a situation before action. Kronman (1985) defines prudence as "a trait or characteristic that is at once an intellectual capacity and a temperamental disposition" (p. 1569). Hariman (2003) further proposes that "A strong sense of prudence must be one that is true to the peculiar conditions of thinking within human affairs and is capable of working with problems that have not yet fully revealed themselves" (p. 288). Reflecting on prudence as a concept could take us down long and interesting philosophical corridors into which, alas, we mustn't venture at present for the sake of staying on topic. The point is, an interculturalist who is curious about intercultural spaces and committed to helping oneself and others navigate these spaces positively is prudent because they understand that there is a cultural gap between description and interpretation in intercultural spaces (see Chapter 3). Things are not always as they appear at first glance, and we must not jump to conclusions. An interculturalist knows they must be mindful in intercultural spaces, staying alert for new information that might help them anticipate things that are not immediately evident. An interculturalist exercises prudence when they prioritise listening over acting precipitously.

Each of us, in our own realms of influence, can exercise prudence in intercultural spaces, being mindful, listening carefully to what's going on, considering all the facts before reacting emotionally to a perceived insult, for example. We can exercise prudence by putting ourselves in the other person's shoes to try to understand their perspective, and helping others to do the same in the hope that they too will seek understanding before reacting.

Optimism

Optimism is a personality trait that is linked to motivation and a myriad of positive mental and physical health benefits (Carver & Scheier, 2014). According to Scheier et al. (2001), optimists are "people who expect to have positive outcomes, even when things are difficult" (p. 191). Interculturalists are aware that difficulties and challenges are normal in intercultural communication because of the inherent cultural differences. Yet, we actively venture into intercultural spaces anyway, because we are curious about them and recognise the value they offer. By the earlier definition of an interculturalist, we as interculturalist are committed to helping ourselves and others navigate intercultural spaces positively. Implied in that commitment is an optimistic outlook that navigating intercultural spaces positively is possible, despite the many challenges that cultural differences present.

An optimistic outlook helps us to examine a deeply divided relationship or a volatile misunderstanding and pursue understanding with hope of reconciliation and restoration. Interculturalists can bring an optimistic perspective on (intercultural) challenges that daunt others. Because optimism is associated with motivation, and motivation in turn is a contributor to ICC, as we discussed in Chapter 7, optimism is a potent superpower of an interculturalist. It is easy to listen to the barrage of bad news in the media and feel pessimistic about the state of our world. But we have the choice to help facilitate better communication in our diverse social groups and neighbourhoods by highlighting our common hopes and using the tools we discussed in this book to help others find a way through challenging relationship dynamics or understand cultural variables that may be contributing to a negative situation.

Wisdom

Wisdom is good judgement, erudition, insight. Proverbs 19:8 says, "The one who gets wisdom loves life; the one who cherishes understanding will soon prosper" (New International Version). Many scholars have attempted to grapple with wisdom (Bangen et al., 2013; Grimm, 2015). Wisdom is another one of those richly philosophical topics that could swiftly lead us down roads paved by the likes of Socrates, Aquinas, and many others. But for the purposes of our discussion of wisdom as a superpower of an interculturalist, a helpful framing is provided by Ardelt (2004) who says:

> I suggest wisdom-related knowledge has to be *realized* by an individual through reflection on personal experiences to be called wisdom and that the wisdom-related knowledge that is written down in texts remains theoretical or intellectual knowledge until a person re-transforms it into wisdom. From this perspective, wisdom is a characteristic of people and not of texts. (p. 305)

You may have heard the adage "knowledge is power." The very fact that you are reading this book indicates not only that you are educated enough to be able to read, but also that you are able to acquire more knowledge using that education. That makes you some of the most powerful people in a world where even at the time of this writing over 15% of adults across the world are illiterate. While that might not seem like a large number, literacy is not education. Literacy is often a precondition to formal education which is accessible to even fewer people. As an educated person with knowledge of intercultural spaces, and understanding of cultural differences that influence communication, you have great agency to not only share your understanding with friends and family but also continue to educate yourself further. By reading this book, you have gained (hopefully new!) know-ledge about communicating in intercultural spaces. But it is the reflection in which you now engage, using that knowledge to understand yours and others' experiences better, that you gain agency to improve communication in intercultural spaces. Your agency translates into insights and wisdom about intercultural spaces that you can share with others. For example, a perceived offence or insult to one's cultural identity could elicit a defensive reaction. However, using the knowledge and understanding you have gained in journeying through this book, you have the option of exercising wisdom, to check whether you fully understand the situation before you react in a manner that could hinder further dialogue. Wisdom is a rare superpower that is always valuable.

Equanimity

Equanimity refers to calmness or psychological stability, a disposition of composure regardless of the situation. It is closely related to the concept of mindfulness which we discussed in Chapter 7. Rogers et al. (2021) explain further:

> In its behavioral conceptualization, equanimity has been considered to be the central mechanism of change in mindfulness practice because it is the non-reactive stance that prevents attachment (craving) and avoidance (aversion) while exposed to an internal or external trigger, thereby producing an extinction response during unwanted experiences. (p. 108)

Equanimity is seen as both an even-mind state of mind as well as intentional separation between what we perceive (both positive and negative) and our first or instinctual reaction to that perception (Juneau et al., 2020). In other words, there is an element of suspending judgement when one engages with a situation with equanimity. Van Der Zee and Van Oudenhoven (2000) found that this type of emotional stability is a cornerstone of developing a multicultural personality.

Although equanimity is often discussed in relation to meditation and other spiritual practices (e.g., Astin & Keen, 2006), we refer to equanimity as a superpower that is useful for gathering information and understanding what the other person is trying to communicate before reacting in haste, especially in intercultural spaces where cultural differences could create misunderstanding that can be taken personally. Seeking positive experiences and avoiding negative ones is psychologically normal behaviour. As such, it is understandable that the inherent uncertainty in intercultural spaces may be perceived negatively by some people. There's some evidence in research, however, that deliberate cultivation of equanimity through breathing exercises and mindful meditation moderate our natural reactions to situations (Juneau et al., 2021). The relevance of equanimity to communicating in intercultural spaces was further emphasised by Jijina and Biswas (2021):

> With the cultivation of equanimity, one is more open to a range of experiences, and the capacity for tolerating distress increases. Impulsive habitual emotional reactivity decreases and the individual may respond more adaptively. The experts emphasised that equanimity also includes an even-minded disposition extended

towards all beings in which there are reduced prejudices, bias, and preconceived notions. The experts emphasised that equanimity may seem deceptively similar to apathy, indifference, or passivity. However, in states of equanimity, there is a high level of compassion and a sense of inter-connectedness. (pp. 11–12)

As observed above, equanimity is a superpower that will enable you to enter intercultural spaces with an openness to discovering what these spaces have to offer and the relationships in which you can invest.

Respect

Respect is a term that has become ubiquitous in a world where everyone seems to be clamouring to be heard, to be recognised as a unique individual, and to be given the choice to define what that looks like. In an early work, Darwall (1977) made the distinction between appraisal respect, which he characterised as a positive appraisal of a person, and exclusively reserved for people, and recognition respect. He proposed that recognition respect can be directed at any number of things, such as respect for the law, or respect for someone's feelings, or indeed respect for a person because the person is human. Darwell went on to say:

> The distinction between appraisal respect and recognition respect for persons enables us to see that there is no puzzle at all in thinking both that all persons are entitled to respect by virtue of their being persons and that persons are deserving of more or less respect by virtue of their personal characteristics. (p. 46)

This distinction is helpful because what many seem to be demanding is recognition respect. But it can be confused with appraisal respect if the behaviour they want to see as a show of respect is something that acknowledges their talents or virtues rather than the dignity that should be afforded to them as a human. But once more, we are in danger of straying off into an enticing philosophical alleyway when the point that needs to be made in the present discussion is that showing (recognition) respect to others in intercultural spaces by listening, empathising, or engaging in constructive dialogue, is another superpower at our disposal. We can exercise this superpower at will, in whatever circles we operate, with whomever we interact. We also have the superpower to model respectful behaviour to others around us, hopefully encouraging reciprocity. Although there are certainly cultural differences in how respect is shown, received, and perceived (e.g., Sung, 2004), recognition respect gives us a starting point from which to communicate.

Solidarity

Solidarity is unity in agreement, shared ground, or an understanding of being "in it" together. Making reference to the walls separating the notion of self from other, Arnsperger and Varoufakis (2003) explain solidarity as follows:

> Solidarity… refers to a phenomenon made possible because these walls are more porous than rational choice theory would permit; it alludes to a series of human interactions unfolding in the space *between these walls*, in a kind of no man's land where the plight of the others inspires us to experiment with violations of our current "preferences"… throw away the masks of self-sufficiency, reach out for one another, … and, at rate moments, believe that there is more to us than some weighted sum of desires. Those of a romantic disposition may even conclude that solidarity-with-others is a prerequisite for throwing out a bridge over to our "better" self. (p. 181)

We discussed in Chapter 7 that empathy is a key variable in ICC and a key tool in any interculturalist's toolkit. Empathy is a precursor to solidarity (Woods, 2020). That means an interculturalist is ideally suited to build solidarity. As Arnsperger and Varoufakis observe, solidarity helps us to set aside our personal preferences and reach out to one another. Solidarity is a superpower that can facilitate unity amongst diverse people. With your knowledge from Chapter 3 on how we perceive diversity, with your understanding from Chapter 5 of the potential for toxic perceptions of diversity, and with the tools you have acquired from Chapter 7 on ICC, you are well-equipped to facilitate solidarity in your circles of influence.

Conclusion

At the start of this book, we issued an invitation to a journey of self-discovery and unexplored horizons:

> We invite you on a quest of self-reflection and discovery that we hope will facilitate life-affirming intercultural dialogues and relationships in your communities. This question requires courage and humility. Along the way, your core assumptions may be challenged, and your very worldview may be questioned. While confronting some assumptions and views on the one hand, this quest may also reward you with allies in places you least expected and offer transformative insights. In this book, we offer you an opportunity and a challenge: an opportunity for discovery, and a challenge to do something about what you discover. If we are successful, our hope is that you will return to your spheres of influence as beacons who guide others through intercultural spaces.

Now that we have neared the end of this journey, we hope your experience has met the expectations of the invitation. We hope you have had a transformative experience during your journey. Some of you may have seen the movie *Freedom Writers* (LaGravenese, 2007). There is a scene in which the students from a class meet with Miep Gies, the lady who supported Anne Frank's family when they were hiding from the Nazis. When the students express that she was a hero, she corrects them and says no, she was just an ordinary person who did what she could. She goes on to add that every person can turn on a small light in a dark room. She paints a powerful visual image to point out that all of us, no matter our social position in society, have the ability to do the right thing, to "be a beacon who guides others through intercultural spaces," as we said earlier in this book.

But you are not any ordinary person. As an interculturalist who is curious about intercultural spaces and committed to helping yourself and others navigate these spaces positively, you have super P-O-W-E-R-S at your disposal that you can start wielding immediately! We hope you feel not only inspired but also empowered to use what you have learned in this book, both from our reflections as well as the stories of the many intercultural scholars shared in these pages. They are stories of men and women who have chosen to be interculturalists through various circumstances of their lives. Their work has not only transformed disciplines, but also shaped future generations of interculturalists, such as yourselves. While we have had the privilege of interacting with them and learning from them, we hope you too have enjoyed gaining insight into their lives in a manner that helps you appreciate their work even better.

Regardless of whether your neighbourhood is culturally diverse or not, we live in a vastly diverse and interconnected world. Your expertise and your agency to effect positive change are much needed everywhere. You have the ability to effect positive change wherever you live. Engaging with cultural diversity is a complex and courageous business! Nevertheless, engage with it we must. The choice we have is whether to engage destructively, spreading mistrust and fear, or constructively, spreading hope. Our hope is that you will be compelled by the desire to contribute to positive intercultural communication in your communities and propelled by the knowledge and understanding you have gained in journeying with us through this book. Thank you for the privilege of letting us accompany you along a journey that is deeply personal to both of us.

Conversation: Hope

Lily: So, Ripley, now that we're at the end of the book, what do you hope the students or readers will do with what we have shared in this book?

Ripley: My hope for the readers of our book is that they will experience the transformative power of cultural intersections. In my own intercultural journey, I have been changed by the interactions I've experienced with so many people from different backgrounds. To the extent that we can open those doors for our readers, I will feel successful. What about you, what do you hope they will take away?

Lily: I hope our readers have been informed, challenged, inspired, and empowered – I know it's a lot to hope for! But my own journey of working on this project with you and listening to the wonderfully vibrant narratives of the intercultural scholars, whose work has shaped my own thinking, has been indelibly transformative and enriching. I have learned so much just in the conversations you and I have had. I hope for the same for our readers.

Ripley: We've covered a lot of ground in this book, and have tackled some pretty difficult issues within the dark side of intercultural relations. What gives you hope that our efforts are not in vain?

Lily: Yes, there are many dark things in this world. But there's light too – and I am convinced there is enough light to make a difference! I believe there's an innate sense of purpose in each one of us, even if we don't always pursue it. I am convinced education is one of the most powerful vehicles for developing the tools that enable us to contemplate, to self-reflect, to act constructively and with compassion. To the extent that our book serves to enhance relational and purposeful intercultural communication, this work is a contribution to the overall "hope" project!

Ripley: We mentioned in our conclusion to Chapter 1 that improving our ability to communicate interculturally is at the centre of solving a host of other local, regional, and international problems. We said that in order to collaborate and cooperate across various barriers and boundaries, we have to learn how to interact respectfully. I wholeheartedly agree that our project here has the potential to move our readers forward towards that goal. And if we're right, that global solutions are worked out at the dyadic level, then there is hope indeed!

Questions for Reflection

1. How do you think you've grown in journeying through this book?
2. In what ways has your intercultural communication competence developed?
3. What are one or two practical next steps you can take to use your intercultural super P-O-W-E-R-S to positively impact your relationships and community?

References

Ali, Z., & Muhammad, N. (2023). Code-switching between Lasi and Urdu among teachers at secondary level high school in Bela. *Southern Journal of Arts & Humanities, 1*(2), 12–23.

Aorny, K. A., Haque, M. N., & Hossain, M. M. (2022). Code-switching and social media in Bangladesh: Emergence of a new English. *Linguistics Initiative, 2*(2), 93–106.

Arasaratnam-Smith, L. A. (2016). An exploration of the relationship between intercultural communication competence and bilingualism. *Communication Research Reports, 33*(3), 231–238.

Ardelt, M. (2004). Where can wisdom be found? *Human Development, 47*(5), 304–307.

Arnsperger, C., & Varoufakis, Y. (2003). Toward a theory of solidarity. *Erkenntnis, 59*, 157–188.

Astin, A. W., & Keen, J. P. (2006). Equanimity and spirituality. *Religion and Education, 33*(2), 39–46.

Bangen, K. J., Meeks, T. W., & Jeste, D. V. (2013). Defining and assessing wisdom: A review of the literature. *The American Journal of Geriatric Psychiatry, 21*(12), 1254–1266.

Bardon, A., Bonotti, M., Zech, S. T., & Ridge, W. (2023). Disaggregating civility: Politeness, public-mindedness and their connection. *British Journal of Political Science, 53*(1), 308–325.

Beatty-Martínez, A. L., Navarro-Torres, C. A., & Dussias, P. E. (2020). Codeswitching: A bilingual toolkit for opportunistic speech planning. *Frontiers in Psychology*, *11*, 1699.

Benjamin, A., Block, R., Clemons, J., Laird, C., & Wamble, J. (2020). Set in stone? Predicting confederate monument removal. *PS: Political Science & Politics*, *53*(2), 237–242.

Brynjolfsson, E., Hui, X., & Liu, M. (2019). Does machine translation affect international trade? Evidence from a large digital platform. *Management Science*, *65*(12), 5449–5460.

Cabrera, L. (2010). *The practice of global citizenship*. Cambridge University Press.

Carter, A. (2013). *The political theory of global citizenship*. Routledge.

Carver, C. S., & Scheier, M. F. (2014). Dispositional optimism. *Trends in Cognitive Sciences*, *18*(6), 293–299.

Chao, G. T., & Moon, H. (2005). The cultural mosaic: A metatheory for understanding the complexity of culture. *Journal of Applied Psychology*, *90*(6), 1128–1140.

Choi, D., Chun, S., Oh, H., Han, J., & Kwon, T. T. (2020). Rumor propagation is amplified by echo chambers in social media. *Scientific Reports*, *10*(1), 310. https://doi.org/10.1038/s41598-019-57272-3

Clark, M. (2020). DRAG THEM: A brief etymology of so-called "cancel culture." *Communication and the Public*, *5*(3–4), 88–92.

Darwall, S. L. (1977). Two kinds of respect. *Ethics*, *88*(1), 36–49.

Eslin, P. (2020). Monuments after empire? The educational value of imperial statues. *Journal of Philosophy of Education*, *54*(5), 1333–1345.

Evanoff, R. (2012). A communicative approach to intercultural dialogue on ethics. In L. Samovar, R. Porter, & E. McDaniel (Eds.), *Intercultural communication: A reader* (13th ed., pp. 476–480). Wadsworth.

Evanoff, R. (2020). Introducing intercultural ethics. In G. Rings & S. Rasinger (Eds.), *The Cambridge handbook of intercultural communication* (pp. 187–202). Cambridge University Press.

Grimm, S. R. (2015). Wisdom. *Australasian Journal of Philosophy*, *93*(1), 139–154.

Hariman, R. (Ed.). (2003). *Prudence: Classical virtue, postmodern practice*. Penn State Press.

Hobbs, R. (2020). *Mind over media: Propaganda education for a digital age*. W.W. Norton & Company.

Holmes, P., & MacDonald, M. N. (2020). The "good" interculturalist yesterday, today and tomorrow: Everyday life-theory-research-policy-practice. *Language and Intercultural Communication*, *20*(1), 1–5.

Jakob, J., Dobbrick, T., Freudenthaler, R., Haffner, P., & Wessler, H. (2023). Is constructive engagement online a lost cause? Toxic outrage in online user comments across democratic political systems and discussion arenas. *Communication Research*, *50*(4), 508–531.

Jiang, T., Li, W., Wang, J., & Wang, X. (2021). Using artificial intelligence-based online translation website to improve the health education in international students. In *2021 2nd International Conference on Artificial Intelligence and Education (ICAIE)* (pp. 25–28). IEEE.

Jijina, P., & Biswas, U. N. (2021). Understanding equanimity from a psychological perspective: Implications for holistic well-being during a global pandemic. *Mental Health, Religion & Culture*, *24*(9), 873–886.

Johansson, F. (2006). *The Medici effect: What elephants & epidemics can teach us about innovation*. Harvard Business School Press.

Juneau, C., Shankland, R., & Dambrun, M. (2020). Trait and state equanimity: The effect of mindfulness-based meditation practice. *Mindfulness*, *11*(7), 1802–1812.

Juneau, C., Shankland, R., Knäuper, B., & Dambrun, M. (2021). Mindfulness and equanimity moderate approach/avoidance motor responses. *Cognition and Emotion, 35*(6), 1085–1098.

Kelly-Holmes, H. (2019). Multilingualism and technology: A review of developments in digital communication from monolingualism to idiolingualism. *Annual Review of Applied Linguistics, 39,* 24–39.

Kiramba, L., & Oloo, J. (2020). Identity negotiation in multilingual contexts: A narrative inquiry into experiences of an African immigrant high school student. *Teachers College Record, 122*(13), 1–24.

Kronman, A. T. (1985). Alexander Bickel's philosophy of prudence. *The Yale Law Journal, 94*(7), 1567–1616.

LaGravenese, R. (2007). *Freedom writers.* Paramount Pictures.

Lück, J., & Nardi, C. (2019). Incivility in user comments on online news articles: Investigating the role of opinion dissonance for the effects of incivility on attitudes, emotions and the willingness to participate. *SCM Studies in Communication and Media, 8*(3), 311–337.

Mekheimr, M. A. (2023). Pedagogical functions of code-switching in EFL college settings: Perceptions and perspectives of students' attitudes and motivations. *BSU – Journal of Pedagogy and Curriculum, 2*(3), 11–42.

Murdoch-Kitt, K., Emans, D., & Oewel, B. (2020). Designing six dimensions of intercultural teamwork: A next-gen challenge in co-creation processes. In S. Boess, M. Cheung & R. Cain (eds.), *Synergy – DRS international conference 2020, 11–14 August.* https://doi.org/10.21606/drs.2020.398

Nickerson, C., & Goby, V. P. (2018). Convergence and collaboration: Co-creating meaning within culturally diverse workforces. *International Journal of Organizational Analysis, 26*(5), 941–952.

Norris, P. (2023). Cancel culture: Myth or reality? *Political Studies, 71*(1), 145–174.

Paine, T. (1795). *Dissertation on first-principles of government.* D. I. Eaton.

Ramos Salazar, L., Diego-Medrano, E., García, N., & Castillo, Y. (2023). An examination of family cohesion and self-esteem as mediators of bilingualism and reading achievement among second-generation immigrant students. *Journal of Latinos and Education, 22*(4), 1660–1675.

Rasmussen, A. (2023). Imagining and building the nation through citizenship education: An interculturalist perspective on the case of Denmark. *Language and Intercultural Communication, 23*(3), 268–279.

Raybourn, E. M. (2000). Designing an emergent culture of negotiation in collaborative virtual communities: The case of the domecitymoo. *ACM SIGGROUP Bulletin, 21*(1), 28–29.

Rogers, H. T., Shires, A. G., & Cayoun, B. A. (2021). Development and validation of the equanimity scale-16. *Mindfulness, 12,* 107–120.

Rösner, L., & Krämer, N. C. (2016). Verbal venting in the social web: Effects of anonymity and group norms on aggressive language use in online comments. *Social Media+ Society, 2*(3), 2056305116664220.

Said Valbuena, B. W., Montoya Carvajal, A., & Fernanda Pinzon, L. (2020). From a ludic loom of ideas to the spiral of intercultural co-creation. In *Proceedings of the 16th participatory design conference 2020 – Participation(s) otherwise – Volume 1* (pp. 85–95).

Salleh, N., Ramli, R., Zakaria, N. S., & Fiah, A. F. M. (2022). Code-switching among the indigenous people of Sarawak. *International Journal of Law, Government and Communication (IJLGC), 7*(29), 448–465.

Samovar, L. A., Porter, R. E., McDaniel, E. R., & Roy, C. S. (2017). *Communication between cultures* (9th ed.). Cengage Learning.

Scheier, M. F., Carver, C. S., & Bridges, M. W. (2001). Optimism, pessimism, and psychological well-being. In E. C. Chang (Ed.), *Optimism & pessimism: Implications for theory, research, and practice* (pp. 189–216). American Psychological Association.

Seo, M., Yang, S., & Laurent, S. M. (2023). No one is an island: Awe encourages global citizenship identification. *Emotion, 23*(3), 601.

Shweder, R. A., Much, N. C., Mahapatra, M., & Park, L. (1997). The "big three" of morality (autonomy, community, and divinity), and the "big three" explanations of suffering. In A. Brandt, & P. Rozin (Eds.), *Morality and health* (pp. 119–169). Routledge.

Sung, K. T. (2004). Elder respect among young adults: A cross-cultural study of Americans and Koreans. *Journal of Aging Studies, 18*(2), 215–230.

Tajik, E., & Tajik, F. (2023). A comprehensive examination of the potential application of Chat GPT in higher education institutions. *TechRxiv.* doi:10.36227/techrxiv.22589497.v1.

Umezi, P. I. (2023). Code-switching among university students in Anambra state: Evidence of poor Igbo linguistic competence and performance among Igbo youths. *IGIRIGI: A Multi-Disciplinary Journal of African Studies, 3*(1), 22–33.

Van Der Zee, K. I., & Van Oudenhoven, J. P. (2000). The multicultural personality questionnaire: A multidimensional instrument of multicultural effectiveness. *European Journal of Personality, 14*(4), 291–309.

Van Oudenhoven, J. P., & Benet-Martinez, V. (2015). In search of a cultural home: From acculturation to frame-switching and intercultural competencies. *International Journal of Intercultural Relations, 46*, 47–54. https://doi.org/10.1016/j.ijintrel.2015.03.022

Walsh, J. P. (2020). Social media and moral panics: Assessing the effects of technological change on societal reaction. *International Journal of Cultural Studies, 23*(6), 840–859.

Wines, W. A., & Napier, N. K. (1992). Toward an understanding of cross-cultural ethics: A tentative model. *Journal of Business Ethics, 11*, 831–841.

Woods, K. (2020). Refugees' stories: Empathy, agency, and solidarity. *Journal of Social Philosophy, 51*(4), 507–525.

Younge, G. (2021). Why every single statue should come down. *The Guardian, 1*, 6–21.

Appendix A
Conversation between Ripley and Lily on Intercultural Spaces

Ripley: Intercultural spaces is a really interesting idea in the sense that it's a space or horizon that we enter into. The interesting thing about a horizon is that you and I, from different vantage points, can look at this place, and we're both looking at the same place but we're looking at it from different vantage points, right? And we share this horizon... and philosophers like Heidegger use horizons as in between or median spaces. And so, these philosophers talk about horizons being the spaces where the interesting conversations might be happening; where it's an in between space. And so that really interests me about this idea of an intercultural space, but what I think is problematic about that is when that space occurs. The example you give in Chapter 1 about you and this friend having an intercultural space when you're watching this film and not understanding it the same... it's that *you* were in an intercultural space well before she was. She didn't see a problem, right? She's watching this and she is not in an intercultural space. And I immediately think about some of my students' experience. A student who is from the non-dominant group at a university, they often feel like they are... or maybe they *always* feel like they're in an intercultural space and the others aren't. If intercultural communication only happens in these spaces... one person feels like they're always in that space and the other person hardly ever feels like they're in that space, when does intercultural communication happen – or not happen?

Lily: For me the premise of that concept of intercultural space is my own contemplation of when does interpersonal communication become intercultural. And I contemplate that because... you and I are having a conversation just now. We're from very different cultural backgrounds, but we are, for the most part, having a perfectly *interpersonal* conversation in that we're communicating on a common basis of understanding and our cultural vantage points, points of view, are not necessarily altering the meaning of our communication in a substantial manner in which it leads to... not miscommunication but misalignment of meaning or misappropriation of meaning, maybe. But, we could be having the same conversation and suddenly, we're talking about a topic where our cultural values are very much at the forefront of what we are communicating or how we see this issue… and suddenly, it becomes… to me, it becomes an intercultural communication because culture has indelibly altered or shaped the meaning of the communication. It's a very conceptual thing rather than a literal thing, obviously, this space. But I think there is a literal sense to it as well because when you described your student who is from a different culture or different skin tone… feels like they're always in an intercultural space literally because they're surrounded by White people, for instance, and they feel like they're the outsider and they have to be on high alert every time. That is quite different to… that's part of it, I'm sure. But that's quite different to what I'm trying to capture in the first place. Does that make sense?

Ripley: Yeah, so you're saying that when culture becomes the salient factor in understanding each other then all of a sudden we're in this intercultural space…

Lily: That's it!

Ripley: …when it becomes problematic, right?

Lily: Yes.

Ripley: And so, I think… a couple of things. On the one hand intercultural spaces by definition problematise culture. That it only becomes relevant when it becomes an issue. That's something that we should probably unpack. Secondly, it seems like… how do we tell… like, your standard approaches to when is something *inter*-cultural, right? You mentioned the contextual definition of we're in a different country, we expect that we will experience culture that's different to our own. Then another definition of that is identity based. So, Mary Jane Collier, Milton Thomas, suggest that we only enter into intercultural interaction when it becomes a significant *identity* disconnect. I think the fact that you and I can have conversations even though you were born and raised on the other side of the world from me, in a different country, in a different language community, with different cultural values and patterns… but we share certain things, for instance, faith alignment, academic interests…

Lily: We were both trained in the West, in the same discipline.

Ripley: Exactly. So, there are these points of alignment that supersede those other things so we don't feel like we're talking across cultures often… but when you introduce this idea of intercultural spaces, it does help to explain… sometimes you say things in a way that I don't quite understand, and I'm going, okay, explain that, because that sounds like an Australianism, right? And so, then it's kind of at a linguistic level that I don't quite catch you. So, I think that's depending on how we define what "inter" is in intercultural… but then that space concept of when people enter in… that's what's intriguing to me because if intercultural only occurs in these spaces, that suggests that both people are in those spaces… and so, my ultimate question on this thing is… but wait, some people are in that space before the other person gets there…

Lily: My premise is that they're both in it, but they're not necessarily cognisant of it. One or both may not be cognisant of it until after the fact. And that's when I think you asked the question about intentionality and construction of messages. How can you construct messages intentionally without being cognisant of it? And then we talked a little bit about that. These (intercultural spaces) explain situations where you have a conversation about something with somebody, and then later life experiences teach you more… and you reflect on that conversation or interaction and you understand it and you're like, ah, I didn't get it at that time, but it was a cultural difference that was going on that caused the misunderstanding… at that time I thought we were good, but, it's in hindsight that I reflect on that and realise it was an intercultural space.

Ripley: Let me get that scenario, because I think that might be interesting. So, the example I include in Chapter 5 of me co-teaching a class with a Japanese grad student…

Lily: Yes, I think that's a great example of how in hindsight you looked at that situation… I was just thinking of another example. Another example would be, this is a Sri Lankan going to the UK for the first time and staying with an English family and he was hungry from the travel and it was lunchtime or whatever and the host said, you must be hungry, do you want a sandwich, and he said, oh no, don't trouble yourself and she said okay that's fine.

Ripley: Even though he was hungry?

Lily: He was very hungry. And he said that's fine, and that was it. The offer was withdrawn, and he went hungry. And in his mind the expectation was that she would say, no, no, it's no trouble at all, let me fix you a sandwich and he says no, truly I'm okay; (and she says) no, I insist, it will make *me* feel better if I feed you, let me fix it; (and he says) okay… and that's the interaction!

Ripley: That's what he wanted.

Lily: That's what he wanted; that's what he was used to. But… he went with the first no, and she said okay, that's fine, and she let it go.

[Both laugh]

Ripley: No more offers forthcoming.

Lily: Yes. So, I thought that's a good example of intercultural spaces where one person was aware of it. In your case your colleague was aware of it while she was in that space; you weren't. And in this other example the guy was aware of it and the host wasn't… oh actually, I wonder whether he was aware of it. He might've not been…

Ripley: They both could've been unaware of it.

Lily: Yes, exactly. But clearly culture had played a role in that miscommunication, misalignment of meaning – to me that's an intercultural space.

Ripley: So, intercultural spaces... it's almost like a wormhole in space... they exist, people just aren't there yet or aware of them, right?

Lily: No.

[Both laugh]

Ripley: So these spaces exist... they pre-exist...

Lily: No, they cannot!

Ripley: Like other dimensions like time exist, we're just not in them yet.

Lily: They cannot pre-exist though. If communication is about co-creating meaning, and an intercultural space is a conceptual space that is co-created by the participants, they (intercultural spaces) cannot pre-exist.

Ripley: So, you're saying that one person can spin up the cultural space, the other person is in it but they don't realise it.

Lily: Or neither realises it. Although they have co-created it, they haven't done it consciously.

Ripley: We can create intercultural spaces together without realising...

Lily: Yes.

Ripley: So, the minute the space becomes recognisable... we become aware of it, then we have to deal with it. But we actually could be in an intercultural space... we've co-created it obliviously.

Lily: Yeah.

Ripley: And so, that oblivious occupation of intercultural spaces really is the source of miscommunication, right?

Lily: Yes.

Ripley: It *can* be a source of miscommunication...

Lily: Or, if one person is aware and the other person isn't, that's also potential for miscommunication... and even if both people are aware, there could still be a miscommunication if they don't have the tools with which to overcome the...

Ripley: Process it.

Lily: Yeah, so they're not like wormholes that pre-exist.

Ripley: But from a communication standpoint it's co-created; it's an entering into... because there's a perceptual component, then there's a communicative component. This is my distinction between, "one cannot not communicate" and actual communication. I think we're all existing and interacting with one another and not always necessarily communicating. Because to me communication is an entering into by both participants so you're co-mmuning, sharing together...

Lily: So, there's an intentionality?

Ripley: There's an intentionality to that. We have to enter into communication. But, on the same hand, we are always sending out signals, right? And other people are *perceiving* us... by the choice of my clothing or the way I style my hair, or whatever. So, I think other people are perceiving us, but to co-mmunicate I believe we have to enter in together; and so, I think you're saying that in an intercultural space, to co-create that, we're both entering in together.

Lily: Yes.

Ripley: For some people culture doesn't become salient to them, and for other people it becomes salient... and so we don't simultaneously become aware of culture as problematic in that space, even though we're in an intercultural space.

Lily: Or both of us may recognise culture is salient here, but that's not problematic. I think the distinction maybe I need to make is that in an intercultural space, miscommunication is not a given.

Ripley: So, culture is not always problematic in an intercultural space?

Lily: It's not problematic, but it's salient. It (culture) changes meaning in a manner that would be absent if culture wasn't salient.

Ripley: So, I think this changes how we're going to define how an intercultural space occurs. So, when you and I interact, given that you're a Sri Lankan Australian... bilingual, trilingual, multilingual... and I'm a barely multilingual Euro-American... isn't culture then always salient? We're always in an intercultural space – even just moments ago we said we're not really in an intercultural space.

Lily: Is that always the case? So, for instance, I say to you, hey Ripley, are you looking forward to dinner tonight? And you say, yeah, sure, and I say why, and you say, well, I've been looking forward to catching up with friends, and it'll be a nice time to catch-up... that's not really intercultural communication! Because... where's culture's salience in that one?

Ripley: It could come into play in your definition of friends, it could come into play in your definition of dinner...

Lily: It *could*, but it doesn't in this case because of our common basis already... we have some commonality, don't you think? As we said before, I studied in the US, so I understand the cultural context and we're talking about these mutual acquaintances...

Ripley: Would that have been the case without you adjusting and accommodating you knowing what the norms are in Western cultures? So, in that sense, you're in the intercultural space and you're accommodating.

Lily: No, I would say it's not an intercultural space at all for me because these are common elements where, to me, differences in culture aren't salient... because there are no cultural differences in that conversation... they're not salient.

Ripley: Wouldn't there have been cultural differences had you not studied in the West?

Lily: Sure.

Ripley: Okay. So, what I'm saying is, it is a cultural space, but you're simply accommodating and adapting. I don't have to adapt. You're using my native language, you're using my understanding of dinner and friendship. But if I had to accommodate to you, and your Sri Lankan understanding of friendship and dinner, how would the conversation sound different?

Lily: If I were a fresh-off-the-plane Sri Lankan woman having a conversation with you, regardless of the physicality of the context?

Ripley: Yeah.

Lily: I think it would be a very different conversation... actually, will it be a different conversation? It may or may not be a different conversation... okay, I got it! So, let's say we don't have anything in common...

Ripley: That you didn't study in the West, you don't know what American mealtimes look like...

Lily: That's it. And if we happen to meet at a conference; we're at a conference, in Malaysia, somewhere, in a third country that's not our home country, we're having a conversation and you say, I'm going out for dinner with some of the colleagues from the conference, and I say, oh, that's nice, and are you looking forward to it, and you say, yes, I'm looking forward to catching up with my friends, etc. Are there cultural differences there that are salient to that exchange of meaning?

Ripley: Well, you tell me. What does dinner mean to an average Sri Lankan? What time of day, what're you eating?

Lily: In that conversation I think that doesn't matter, because we understand each other perfectly.

Ripley: Does dinner mean the same thing as it does in the States?

Lily: Sure, yeah, it's the evening meal.

Ripley: If I tell you I'm eating with friends, who does that include? How do I know these people?

Lily: It doesn't matter. You consider them friends, so I would interpret them as friends.

Ripley: I know, but what does friendship mean? You see what I'm saying? So, in Sri Lanka if you say, hey, I'm meeting friends, how long have you known those people?

Lily: I totally get what you're saying. But for me, in that particular example that difference doesn't matter. Because it's a very superficial exchange where you say I'm looking forward to having dinner with friends, and I say, ah, okay, that's nice. I don't have to take any more meaning from that... whether they're acquaintances or friends... it doesn't matter to me because I conceptually understand that you're sharing a meal with people whom you consider friends.

Ripley: An evening meal.

Lily: Yes, an evening meal.

Ripley: Okay, so let me give you a regional cultural difference in the US, this happened to me the first time I went to the Midwest. So, growing up in the west, dinner was the evening meal and you ate it from, you know, 5 to 6:30 at night on average. But when I went to the Midwest, and

I was doing some farmwork one summer... people said oh, it's dinner time, and I think to myself, it's only noon! Because in that setting, rural Midwestern culture... dinner was the noon meal, supper was the evening meal. And so if I told you, oh, I'm having dinner with friends, somebody would've thought, oh, you're getting together at noon, does that mean you're not working this afternoon? Right? Because you're going to go have dinner.

Lily: Well, let's work with the same scenario then. Dinner is an evening meal in Sri Lankan culture as well, as it is in your understanding of what dinner is. However, if you had invited me to come along, and said, why don't you come along, at dinner time? You wouldn't have said at dinner time, because you're American. You would've been precise and said we're eating at 7:15 at this place. But if it's a Sri Lankan, let's say if the roles were reversed, and I'm the one having dinner and we have this conversation, and I say to you, you're very welcome to join us at dinner time – then there's a cultural difference there. Because you don't know what dinner time is or what I mean by dinner time. You could ask, of course.

Ripley: Like, what time should I get there?

Lily: Yeah, exactly. So, in Sri Lanka it would be about 8, 8:30. And if I assumed you know what dinner time is, then culture becomes salient. But if that second part didn't happen, culture is not salient to us understanding each other. Even if I thought you were having dinner at 8:30, it doesn't matter because I understand you're eating a meal with friends, it doesn't affect me either way.

Ripley: Until you're invited, right?

Lily: Yes.

Ripley: Even though, I would argue that... so, we were in an intercultural space in the first scenario because we're talking about having dinner with friends, and we had different understandings of what dinner was and when it was. So, there's this intercultural space... yeah, it didn't complicate that particular interaction, but the difference was there. We walked away with different ideas.

Lily: I agree. Maybe we would've walked away without being cognisant that we were in an intercultural space.

Ripley: Right.

Lily: But for me that's not a negative thing necessarily because, what I'm saying is, it doesn't necessarily cause acrimonious misunderstanding. So, intercultural space isn't a space where misunderstandings occur (by definition).

Ripley: Yeah. And I think that's helpful to make sure that it's not just problematising... although... I enjoy listening to John Durham Peters, and he talks about all communication being communication at a distance. Like, if you think about the physics of communication, we're always communicating... like, put your hand up [holding palm out to touch Lily's palm]. We wouldn't think of that as being at a distance, but he thinks of even that as at a distance. Because physically our atoms are not touching, even though we feel like they're touching. There's always space. So, I'm fascinated by that concept that we are always communicating at a distance. But how much distance. So, as applied to an intercultural space, that's where I would say... and part of what we're trying to tease out here are the boundary conditions for interculturality. Because the boundaries for identity, the boundaries of cultures... that when we have these intersections... that's part of what I'm trying to tease out in this conversation. The boundaries of the intercultural space.

Lily: Do you think we need to then think about a threshold or a liminality where it could become an intercultural space but the communication doesn't cross that threshold or it's in a liminal space before we cross... Just like that conversation we had, until an invitation is issued for dinner, we're still liminal on the threshold. We haven't crossed into that space...

Ripley: Is there a warning track around an intercultural space [laughs] to let you know if you're moving into it. That's interesting... those boundaries are positionalities within our cultural frameworks. Not only does it (cultural framework) change the way we see the boundary, it affects our gaze to one another... almost like Standpoint Theory, right? That your positionality affects your gaze, and I think within an intercultural space those concepts are somewhat related that when we enter that space and our positionalities affect... you know, gaze is about interpretation, right?

Lily: Yes – because I'm wondering whether those who are experienced... you know how in competence literature, the variables that contribute to intercultural competence are experience, training, all these other factors. Do you think those who are experienced and trained or aware of cultural differences have an elevated perspective – not elevated as in superior, elevated as in...

Ripley: Awareness

Lily: Awareness – such that they're able to see the threshold when you're approaching it?

Ripley: Yes.

Lily: Rather than if you aren't experienced...

Ripley: Yes.

Lily: Ah, I like that!

Ripley: It's like conscious verses unconscious competence.[1]

Lily: Yes, yes. I wonder if we should add that.

Ripley: So, the conscious in competence or conscious competence – yeah, those are higher levels of awareness because you're conscious or mindful. Absolutely. I think they will be more attuned to the intercultural space...

Lily: Yeah, or the thresholds that define the space.

Ripley: Yeah. So, in a sense, as we train students or others about cultural differences and intercultural communication, part of becoming more competent is becoming more attuned to those spaces.

Lily: Yes.

Ripley: Right. And what is a predictor of when those spaces could occur... and some of them are pretty basic and logical and you know, we could say, oh, we speak different languages, that space will occur...

Lily: I like that.

Ripley: I'm not sure what to do with that. Where to go with that [laughs].

Lily: Well, I think we could articulate it in terms of perspective, using that analogy of... what did you say? Positionality!

Ripley: Yeah.

Note

1 See Chapter 7.

Appendix B
Intercultural Communication
Behaviour Scales[1]

Behavioural Observation Guide A: Respect

Instructions: Individuals vary in the extent to which they express respect and regard for others' thoughts, opinions, or feelings. Their actions may take many forms ranging from verbal and nonverbal expressions of minimal regard to statements, gestures, and tones that are extremely respectful and indicative of very positive regard. Please indicate on a 1 to 5 continuum the pattern of expression that was most characteristic during the period of observation.

Description

The verbal and nonverbal expressions of the individual suggest a *clear lack of respect and negative regard* for others around him or her. By his or her actions, the individual indicates that the feelings and experiences of others are not worthy of attention or consideration. Examples include a condescending tone, lack of eye contact, and general lack of attention or interest.

1. The individual responds to others in a way that communicates *little respect* for others' feelings, experiences, or potential. The individual may respond mechanically or passively or may appear to ignore many of the thoughts and feelings of others.
2. The individual indicates some respect for others' situations and *some concern* for their feelings, experiences, and potential. They may indicate some attentiveness to others' efforts to express themselves.
3. The individual indicates (through eye contact, general attentiveness, and tone) a *concern* for the thoughts, opinions, or feelings of others. The individual's verbal and nonverbal behaviour encourages others to feel worthy of interaction and provides a sense that others' thoughts, opinions, and feelings are of interest and valued.
4. The individual indicates a *deep respect* for the worth of others' thoughts, opinions, and feelings. The individual indicates (through eye contact, general attentiveness, and tone of voice) a clear respect and valuing of the thoughts and feelings of others and encourages continuing interaction.

Rating

Circle the number that best describes the individual's behaviour.

1	2	3	4	5
Low Respect				High Respect

Behavioural Observation Guide B: Interaction/Response Style

Instructions: Responses to another person or persons in an interpersonal or group situation range from *descriptive, nonvaluing* to *highly evaluative*. Indicate on a 1 to 4 continuum which interaction pattern was most characteristic during observation.

Description

1. *Highly evaluative.* The individual reacts immediately to others' verbal and non-verbal contributions in a highly judgmental and evaluative manner. The individual appears to measure the contributions of others in terms of a highly structured, predetermined, and rigid framework of thoughts, beliefs, attitudes, and values. Responses, therefore, communicate clearly and quickly whether the individual believes others to be "right" or "wrong." Reactions are made in declarative, often dogmatic fashion and will closely follow the comments of others, indicating little or no effort to digest what has been said before judging it.
2. *Evaluative.* The individual responds to others verbally and nonverbally in an evaluative and judgmental manner and measures the comments of others using a predetermined framework of thoughts, beliefs, attitudes, and values. The frame-work is not totally rigid but does imply a clear basis for determining whether others' contributions are "right" or "wrong" and they are visibly impatient and interrupt others. Responses tend to follow fairly closely on the heels of ter-mination of discussion by others, but there is some break, indicating a min-imal attempt to digest and consider others' ideas before responding positively or negatively.
3. *Evaluative-descriptive.* The individual appears to measure the responses of others in terms of a framework based partly on information, thoughts, attitudes, and feelings gathered from the particular interaction and the individuals involved. They offer evaluative responses, but they appear to be less-than-rigidly held and subject to negotiation and modification. The time lapse between others' comments and the individuals' response suggests an effort to digest and consider input before reacting either positively or negatively.
4. *Descriptive.* The individual responds to others in a manner that draws out infor-mation, thoughts, and feelings, but only after gathering sufficient input so that the evaluative framework and responses relate to the individual(s) with whom they are interacting. The individual asks questions, restates others' ideas, and appears to gather information prior to responding with their opinions.

Rating

Circle the number that best describes the individual's behaviour.

1	*2*	*3*	*4*
Highly Evaluative			Descriptive

Behavioural Observation Guide C: Orientation to Knowledge

Instructions: People explain themselves and the world around them in varying ways. Some personalise their explanations, knowledge, and understandings, prefacing their statements with phrases such as, "*I* feel…" or "It seems to *me*…" Others tend to generalise their explanations, understandings, and feelings, implying that there is only one way to make sense of the people and events around them, and that others will see things in this same way. An example of this orientation is embodied in a statement such as "Mexican food *is* too spicy." This phrase suggests that the food itself is cause of a particular response, rather than acknowledging that their personally subjective tastes are the source of their reaction – and that others might have a different view – as would be indicated by a statement such as "Mexican food is too spicy for me." Indicate on a 1 to 4 continuum which expression was most characteristic during the period of observation.

Description

1. *Physical orientation.* The individual treats perceptions, knowledge, feelings, and insights as inherent in the people and objects being perceived and assumes other people will always share the individual's perceptions, attitudes, and feelings if they are mature, knowledgeable, or insightful. Thus, differences with others' perceptions imply that the others are "wrong" or lack insight or knowledge. This orientation might lead to a statement such as, "Mexican food is too hot." An individual with this orientation might use phrases such as, "We're all familiar with the way X's act in such a situation," "It's inevitable that…," "What else would you expect from…," and so on.

2. *Cultural orientation.* The individual treats perceptions, knowledge, feelings, and insights as highly generalizable from one individual to another within a culture and assumes that other persons of similar cultural heritage will tend to share common views and perceptions. A representative statement might be, "North Americans find Mexican food far too hot for their tastes." They may also use phrases such as, "In this country…," "Canadians are typically…," "In American cities, people are…," or "In that culture…"

3. *Interpersonal orientation.* The individual treats perceptions, knowledge, and feelings as personal, but also potentially generalizable to others to some extent and tends to assume that others in an immediate group share the individual's perceptions, feelings, or thoughts (as with friends, colleagues, family, other

members of a group). An individual whose orientation to knowledge is of this sort might say, "No one in my family would like these tacos," or may use phrases such as, "We feel...," "My husband and I believe...," "Most of you in the group know that...," "Many people in my department...," and so on.

4. *Intrapersonal orientation.* The individual treats perceptions, knowledge, feelings, and insights as personally based, as shown by a statement such as, "I don't like Mexican food," which makes clear that the mismatch between the food and the individual is a consequence of that individual's particular tastes, perceptions, likes, and so on, and may have nothing necessarily to do with Mexican food. He or she does not regard differences in perception as inherently right or wrong. Examples of phrases that may be characteristic of this orientation are "I feel that...," "It is my view that...," "I believe...," and so on.

Rating

Circle the number that best describes the individual's behaviour.

1	*2*	*3*	*4*
Physical Orientation		Intrapersonal Orientation	

Behavioural Observation Guide D: Empathy

Instructions: Individuals vary in their ability to convey the sense that they understand things from another person's point of view. Some individuals seem to communicate a fairly complete awareness of another person's thoughts, feelings, and experiences; others seem unable to display any awareness of another's thoughts, feelings, or state of affairs. Indicate on a 1 to 5 continuum which pattern of behaviour was most characteristic during your observations.

Description

1. *Low-level empathy.* The individual indicates little or no awareness of even the most obvious, surface feelings and thoughts of others. The individual appears to be bored or disinterested or simply operating from a preconceived frame of reference that totally excludes others' experiences.
2. *Medium-low empathy.* The individual may display some awareness of obvious feelings and thoughts of others. They may attempt to respond based on this awareness; often the responses seem only superficially matched to the thoughts and feelings of others involved in the interaction.
3. *Medium empathy.* The individual responds to others with reasonably accurate understandings of the surface feelings of others around but may not respond to, or may misinterpret, less obvious feelings and thoughts.
4. *Medium-high empathy.* The individual displays an understanding of responses of others at a deeper-than-surface level and thus enables others involved in the

interaction to express thoughts or feelings they may have been unwilling or unable to discuss around less empathic persons.

5. *High empathy.* The individual appears to respond with great accuracy to apparent and less apparent expressions of feeling and thought by others. They convey a sense of interest in others and provide verbal and nonverbal cues that they can relate to their experiences.

Rating

Circle the number that best describes the individual's behaviour.

1	2	3	4	5
Low Empathy				High Empathy

Behavioural Observation Guide E: Role Behaviour

Instructions: Indicate how often participants exhibited each pattern of role behaviour during the time periods observed.

Description

For each of the following categories, circle the number on the continuum that best describes the frequency of the behaviour. Use the continuum template provided below for each instance.

1	2	3	4	5
Never	Seldom	Occasionally	Frequently	Continually

Task roles. Individuals differ in the extent to which they engage in behaviour that contributes to group problem-solving activities. Activities associated with the completion of tasks include initiating ideas, requesting further information or facts, seeking clarification of group tasks, clarifying task-related issues, evaluating suggestions of others, or (re)focusing a group on the task at hand. Circle the number on the continuum that best describes the frequency of this behaviour.

Relational roles. Individuals differ in the extent to which they devote effort to building or maintaining relationships within a group. *Group-development activities*, as they are sometimes termed, may consist of verbal and nonverbal displays that provide a supportive climate for the group members and help to solidify the group's feelings of participation. Behaviours that lead to these outcomes include efforts to harmonise or mediate arguments or conflicts between group members, comments offered relative to the group's dynamics, indications of a willingness to compromise one's own position for the sake of group consensus, displays of interest (nods of agreement, eye contact, general attending behaviours), and other supportive behaviours.

Individualistic roles. Some individuals operate in groups in a highly individualistic manner and, as a consequence, may serve to block the group's efforts at both problem-solving and relationship-building. Behaviours of this sort include statements or actions by individuals who are highly resistant to ideas of others, or who return to issues and points of view previously discussed and acted upon or dismissed by the group. Other behaviours include attempting to call attention to oneself; displaying a highly positive image by noting achievements, qualifications, vocational and professional experience, or other factors that are designed to increase the individual's credibility; manipulating the group by asserting authority through flattery, sarcasm, and interrupting; actively avoiding and resisting participation; remaining insulated from the group when the individual feels they are not successful in directing the group in a particular direction, and so on.

Behavioural Observation Guide F: Conversation Management

Instructions: People vary in their skill at managing their own and others' level of participation in conversations. Particularly with regard to taking turns in discussion and initiating and terminating interaction based on the needs of others, some individuals display great skill, while others do not. For each participant, indicate on the 1 to 5 continuum which pattern was most characteristic during the period of observation.

Description

1. *Low skill.* The individual appears to be unconcerned with taking turns in discussion. They may dominate or refuse to interact at all, may be unresponsive to or unaware of other's needs for involvement and time sharing, may initiate and terminate discussion without regard for the wishes of other individuals, may continue to talk long after obvious displays of disinterest and boredom by others, or may terminate discussion – or generally withhold information – when there is clear interest expressed by others for continuing the exchange.
2. *Moderately low skill.* The individual appears to be minimally concerned with taking turns in discussion. They often either dominate or are reluctant to interact, are unresponsive to other's needs for involvement and time sharing, and initiate or terminate conversations with minimal regard for others.
3. *Moderate skill.* The individual appears to be somewhat concerned with taking turns in discussion. They seldom either dominate or seem unwilling to interact, and generally show a concern for time sharing and initiating and terminating interaction in a manner that is responsive to the needs of others.
4. *Moderately high skill.* The individual appears to be quite concerned with taking turns in discussion. They seldom either dominate or fail to engage in interaction and at most times show a concern for time sharing and initiating and terminating interaction in a manner that is responsive to the needs of others.
5. *High skill.* The individual is extremely concerned with providing equal opportunity for all participants to share in contributions to discussion. In the initiation

and termination of discussion, they always indicate concern for the interests, tolerances, and orientation of others who are involved.

Rating

Circle the number that best describes the individual's behaviour.

1	2	3	4	5
Low Management				High Management

Behavioural Observation Guide G: Ambiguity Tolerance

Instructions: Some people react to new situations with greater comfort than others. In these situations, some individuals appear to be anxious, highly frustrated, or hostile towards the new situation or those who may be present (who may be identified as sources of their problems). Others encounter new situations as a challenge; they appear to function best wherever the unexpected or unpredictable occurs and quickly adapt to the demands of changing environments. On a 1 to 5 continuum, indicate the manner in which the individual observed responds to new or ambiguous situations.

Description

1. *Low tolerance.* The individual seems quite troubled by new or ambiguous situations and exhibits excessive nervousness and frustration. He or she seems slow to adapt to the situation and may express hostility towards those in authority or leadership roles. Negative feelings may also lead to verbal hostility directed towards other individuals present in the situation and especially towards those perceived to be in control.
2. *Moderately low tolerance.* The individual seems somewhat troubled by new or ambiguous situations, exhibits nervousness and frustration, is somewhat slow to adapt to the situation, and may express some hostility towards those perceived to be in control.
3. *Moderate tolerance.* The individual reacts with moderate outward nervousness and frustration to new or ambiguous situations but adapts to these environments with reasonable speed and resilience. There are no apparent personal, interpersonal, or group consequences as a result of the individual's uneasiness. Those perceived as being in leadership or authority positions may be the target of minor verbal barbs – sarcasm, joking, and mild rebukes – but there are no significant signs of hostility.
4. *Moderately high tolerance.* The individual reacts with some outward nervousness and frustration to new or ambiguous situations. They adapt to the situation quite rapidly with no personal, interpersonal, or group-directed expressions of hostility. Those in leadership and authority positions are not a target for verbal barbs or sarcasm.

5. *High tolerance.* The individual reacts with little or no outward nervousness or frustration to new or ambiguous situations. He or she adapts to the demands of the situation quickly with no noticeable personal, interpersonal, or group consequences and seems to adapt very rapidly and comfortably to new or changing environments.

Rating

Circle the number that best describes the individual's behaviour.

1	*2*	*3*	*4*	*5*
Low Tolerance				High Tolerance

Note

1 From: Ruben, B. D., De Lisi, R., & Gigliotti, R. A. (2017). *A guide for leaders in higher education: Core concepts, competencies, and tools.* Stylus, Appendix A, pp. 367–380. Adapted from Ruben, B. D. (1976). Assessing communication competency for intercultural adaptation. *Group and Organization Management, 1*(3), 34–354; and Ruben, B. D. & Kealey, D. J. (1979). Behavioural assessment of communication competency and the prediction of cross-cultural adaptation. *International Journal of Intercultural Relations, 3*(1), 15–47.

Index